CYCLICAL MOVEMENTS IN THE BALANCE OF PAYMENTS

T0300513

CYCLICAL MOVEMENTS IN THE BALANCE OF PAYMENTS

BY

TSE CHUN CHANG

PH.D. (CANTAB)

CAMBRIDGE

AT THE UNIVERSITY PRESS

1951

CAMBRIDGE UNIVERSITY PRESS
Cambridge, New York, Melbourne, Madrid, Cape Town,
Singapore, São Paulo, Delhi, Tokyo, Mexico City

Cambridge University Press
The Edinburgh Building, Cambridge CB2 8RU, UK

Published in the United States of America by Cambridge University Press, New York

www.cambridge.org
Information on this title: www.cambridge.org/9781107615229

First published 1951
First paperback edition 2011

A catalogue record for this publication is available from the British Library

ISBN 978-1-107-61522-9 Paperback

To

MY MOTHER

CONTENTS

LIST OF TABLES

PREFACE

This study presents the results of a statistical survey of the balance-of-payments data of different types of country in the period 1924–38. Its purpose is to show the pattern of cyclical behaviour particular to each type of country; and to suggest, in the light of the Keynesian theory of employment, a possible explanation for the general nature of the equilibrating process in the balance of payments.

This book is divided into three parts. Part I consists of five chapters. After Chapter I, in which an *a priori* formulation of the equilibrating process in the balance of payments in general is made, this Part is mainly devoted to the statistical investigation of the predominant factors determining the cyclical behaviour of the constituent items of the balance of payments. International comparisons of the various elasticities of imports and exports, of the price-elasticities of various commodities in the world markets and of the foreign-trade multipliers are made. In the actual calculations, the methods of partial correlation analysis are applied.

The cyclical movements in the balance of payments of different types of country are examined in Parts II and III. On the basis of the salient features of the structure of trade, the trading countries are classified into five types: (1) the highly industrialised and deficient type, (2) the highly industrialised and self-sufficient type, (3) the less-industrialised type, (4) the purely agricultural type, and (5) the mining type. For each type, a representative country is chosen.

The British balance of payments, chosen to represent those of the first type, is examined in the two chapters of Part II. In Chapter VI a detailed statistical investigation of the British demand for imports is outlined; and, in Chapter VII the cyclical pattern and the equilibrating process in the British balance of payments are fully discussed. As these two chapters were written before the rest, there are some repetitions of the arguments in Chapters I and II.

ix

PREFACE

In Part III, the U.S.A., Sweden, Australia, and Chile are chosen to represent respectively the other four types of country. Four chapters are devoted to giving brief sketches for each country; and the cyclical patterns in the balance of payments are verified by further statistical calculations. In addition, the Canadian balance of payments is studied because of its peculiar features.

This study was first suggested to me by Mrs J. Robinson; and under her supervision it has been carried out. To her I owe a deep debt of gratitude for inspiration, encouragement and advice which mark the relation between teacher and pupil. I am also deeply indebted to my former classmate, Mr C. F. Carter, from whom I have received constant help and keen criticisms. I must acknowledge the kindness of Messrs N. Kaldor and J. R. Stone in reading the whole manuscript and in giving me many valuable suggestions for improvement. To Messrs C. W. Guillebaud and P. Sraffa I am also grateful for their constant advice regarding my research work during my stay in Cambridge. Messrs D. Missen and J. Claydon, the Assistant Librarians of the Marshall Library of Economics in Cambridge, have always willingly given me assistance.

The British Council awarded me a scholarship for the period 1943–7, without which this study could never have been carried out.

Acknowledgements are due to the Editors of *The Canadian Journal of Economics and Political Science*, *Economic Journal*, *Review of Economic Studies* and *Review of Economics and Statistics* for their kind permission to reprint in this book articles which appeared first in these journals.

TSE CHUN CHANG

ST JOHN'S COLLEGE
CAMBRIDGE

PART I

SOME INTERNATIONAL COMPARISONS

CHAPTER I

EQUILIBRIUM IN THE BALANCE OF PAYMENTS

§ I

The classical approach to the problem of equilibrium in the balance of payments is fundamentally the application of the concept of static equilibrium to the theory of international trade. In this theoretical model, the international movement of merchandise is assumed to be a function of the relative price levels, as determined by the principle of comparative costs. Under the assumption of full employment both at home and abroad, the effect of international trade is to increase the average productivity of the factors of production employed in the trading countries. Therefore, as imports can contribute as much as exports to the international division of labour, it will necessarily bring a net gain to the home country.

Furthermore, the classical theory assumes equality between the value of exports and that of imports of any country.[1] Thus foreign lending and borrowing do not normally exist; and the balance of trade of any country is always balanced. In essence, the external equilibrium of a country represents a unique and static position, which reflects the difference between this country's productivity and the world's.

The 'disturbance' to this unique and static equilibrium in the balance of payments is said to be possible only because of the occurrence of disruptive events in international trading relations. According to the classical theory, the disruptive events may generally be classified into two groups. First, they may arise out of changes in the real demand and supply conditions,

---

[1] A. Marshall, *The Pure Theory of Foreign Trade*, p 1. In it, he says: 'The pure theory of foreign trade satisfied these conditions. This theory is based upon the hypothesis that two countries, say England and Germany, carry on trade with each other but only with each other. It is assumed that they are not under any obligations to make foreign payments except those arising from trade, so that *in equilibrium the exports of each country exchange for her imports.*' (Italics are mine.) This passage was first pointed out to me by Mrs Robinson.

1-2

which operate initially upon the balance of trade. However, having assumed away international cyclical fluctuations, there is no possibility of such changes in the short period, except the random changes caused by war, harvest, etc. The second group of disruptive causes consists therefore of capital movements—that is, of unilateral transfers—and these are far more important. In normal cases, the unilateral transfers do not directly and immediately induce equal but offsetting changes in the balance of trade. But, according to the classical theory, they will definitely set in motion the price-specie-flow mechanism, so that the necessary adjustment can be effected. In other words, into its static model, this adjusting mechanism is introduced in order to ensure that any 'disturbance' to the equilibrium in the balance of payments of a country is but a temporary phenomenon and is eventually 'eliminated'.

A whole series of inductive verifications has been produced to prove this proposition.[1] But, in several important cases, they have failed to obtain any conclusive verification at all. More striking and interesting is the fact that, in most cases, the adjustment has been observed to work in a smoother and less roundabout way than that expounded by the classical theory. It is sufficient to recall Taussig's conclusion in his survey of the British balance of payments before 1914, which runs as follows:

> The actual merchandise movements seem to have been adjusted to the shifting balance of payments with surprising exactness and speed. The process our theory contemplates—the initial flow of specie; the fall of prices in the lending country, rise in the borrowing country; the eventual increased movement of merchandise out of the one and into the other—all this can hardly be expected to take place smoothly and quickly....
> One thing...stands out in the British phenomenon. This is the unmistakably close connection between international payments and the movements of commodity imports and exports. All this closeness of connection...is found again in other countries also.... The re-

---

[1] For instance, F. D. Graham, 'International Trade under Depreciated Paper, the United States, 1862–1879', in the *Quarterly Journal of Economics*, 1922; J. Viner, *Canada's Balance of International Indebtedness, 1900–1913*; J. H. Williams *Argentine International Trade under Inconvertible Money, 1880–1900*; H. D. White, *The French International Account, 1880–1914*; G. Wood, *Borrowing and Business in Australia*; C. Bresciani-Turoni, *Inductive Verification of the Theory of International Payments*; and F. W. Taussig, *International Trade*.

4

corded transactions between countries show surprisingly little transfer of the only 'money' that moves from one to the other—gold. It is the goods that move, and they seem to move at once....The presumable intermediate stage of gold flow and price changes is hard to discern, and certainly is extremely short.[1]

Undoubtedly, the fatal defect of the classical theory of the mechanism of adjustment lies in its unrealistic assumptions of general world full employment and balanced trade. By these assumptions, it ignores the fundamental fact that the trade cycle is an inherent part of our economic system; and, consequently, it has failed to see that a country's income and long-term capital account change regularly in relation to the different phases of the general world trade cycle. It is therefore the purpose of this study to examine statistically the cyclical behaviour of the constituent items in the balance of payments and to explain, in the light of the Keynesian theory of employment, the general nature of its equilibrium process.

§ II

For any country in an open system, the following four fundamental relationships subsist:[2]

(1) *Trade with the outside world*

Net balance on income account

= Exports of goods and services
   − Imports of goods and services.

(2) *Income produced and earned (at factor cost)*

Net national income

= Private consumption
   + Government expenditure on goods and services
   + Private home capital formation
   + Net balance on income account.

---

[1] Taussig, op. cit. pp. 239–40 and pp. 260–1.

[2] Our procedure follows in general the definitions given in the British National Income White Paper. These definitions are, however, of universal applicability. See also Meade and Stone, *National Income and Expenditure*, passim.

(3) *Private saving (at factor cost)*

Private saving
= Net national income
+ Transfer payments
− Private consumption
− Private expenditure on public services
− Direct and indirect taxes.

(4) *Government finance*

Net budgetary surplus
= Direct and indirect taxes
+ Private expenditure on public services
− Government expenditure on goods and services
− Transfer payments.

If these equations hold, so does the following equation:

Private saving = Exports of goods and services
− Private home capital formation − Imports of goods and services.
+ Net budgetary surplus

Or, this equation may be rewritten in the form:

Private saving = Exports of goods and services
− Net total home investment − Imports of goods and services.

This is the equation of the balance of payments of a country. It shows that total private saving in the home country exceeds or falls short of net total home investment, according as its total exports are greater or less than its total imports.[1] To look at the same thing in a different way, the sum of the items on the left-hand side of this equation measures the home supply of 'foreign saving', or the home demand for foreign securities; whereas, the sum on the right gives the foreign demand for investible funds from the home country, or the supply of foreign securities to the home country. The external equilibrium of the home country therefore requires that the home purchase of foreign securities

[1] Mrs Robinson, *Essays in the Theory of Employment*, pp. 201–2.

is equal to the supply; which means that there is no change in the international cash reserves of the home country.

In the language of the balance of payments, this condition of equilibrium is reflected in an offsetting equality between the variation in the balance on income account and that of the net long-term capital movement. The variations in both are normally influenced and determined by the world trade cycle; and, therefore, the equilibrium in the balance of payments is itself a cyclical phenomenon. In other words, the equilibrium is not a unique and static position, but represents a dynamic process in the balance of payments which changes constantly in response to the different phases of the world trade cycle.

Such a dynamic process would seem to mean a definite pattern of cyclical behaviour for the balance of payments of each country. That is to say, for a particular country, a surplus on its income account is generally matched by net export of long-term capital in times of general world prosperity, and, during world depression, a deficit and net import of capital tend to go together; or, the cyclical pattern is just the reverse. It is therefore interesting to find the predominant factors which determine the cyclical pattern of the balance of payments in general, and to examine the definite pattern which is commonly associated with a particular type of country. Moreover, if the offsetting changes in the income and long-term capital accounts are not complete in any short period of time, what are the devices for meeting this temporary disequilibrium; and are they equally important for different countries or under different circumstances? In this chapter, we attempt to give some *a priori* generalisations, which will be verified statistically in the rest of the study.

§ III

Let us first examine the cyclical behaviour of the constituent items of the income account. In an open system, the level of home income and that of world income are linked together by the operation of the foreign-trade multiplier: each therefore tends to affect and determine the other. A boom within a country will inevitably exert its impulse towards expansion abroad, because an increase in home employment and income leads to an increase in the home demand for imports which will then result in an increase in the exports of other countries and hence in their incomes. Similarly, because exports are equivalent to home investment in generating income[1] any cyclical expansion or contraction originated abroad will sooner or later bring a home country into line with this general movement.[2] It is through this channel that cyclical fluctuations tend to transmit and synchronise internationally and therefore no country can keep itself completely insulated from them.

The world trade cycle starts when prosperity or depression occurs in one country or one group of countries relatively large and important in the world economy.[3] This expanding or contracting force tends to be transmitted to other countries by way of trade. The general features of the world trade cycle are there-

[1] The procedure of using the net balance on income account as the equivalence to home investment may be convenient, if the point under discussion is capital formation and its relation with home saving and consumption. In connection with the relationship between home income and the balance of payments, we should use the value of total exports, because both home investment and exports provide income and both home saving and imports absorb it. Otherwise we would appear to suggest that the importance of foreign influences is much smaller than is in fact the case. Strictly speaking, the total value of exports minus the value of imported raw materials to be embodied in exports should be used as the multiplicand, as proposed by Harrod. (Vide *The Trade Cycle*, pp. 152–4.) Nevertheless, in most cases, the proportion of imported raw materials embodied in exports is not large. Therefore, in the actual calculation, we may use the 'uncorrected' total value of exports as an approximation.

[2] An illustration of the operation of the foreign-trade multiplier in the case of a disclocation in a *single* country seems necessary in this connection. A rise or fall of exports induces corresponding changes in home income, which in turn influence the level of the home demand for imports. Consequent upon this change in home income, total receipts and total payments in the home income account will tend to *converge*; but there is no necessity that, at this new level of equilibrium, the induced changes in the two will just cancel each other out. Let us assume that there is an initial equilibrium in the income account and that home exports fall as a result of foreign competition. Home income will fall, and so will the home demand for imports. However, the shrinkage of imports will not be equal to the initial fall of exports, unless no individual in the home country reduces his saving. This condition means that the home marginal propensity to save is equal to zero. If it is not equal to zero, the fall in imports will be short of that in exports; and, consequently, the income account turns into a deficit as compared with its initial position. The reason is as follows. The fall in exports reduces home income; but the fall of income reduces home saving as well as imports. As long as the sum of saving and imports is less than the initial fall of exports, home income continues to fall, causing a continued shrinkage of saving and imports. Only when the fall of exports has been completely offset by those in saving and imports, will home income have reached its new equilibrium level. But at this new level, the imports exceed the exports by the amount of the fall in the home saving.

[3] Harrod, *International Economics*, pp. 143–4.

fore expressed in the fluctuations of the *total* value of world trade, rising in times of world prosperity and falling during world depression and recession. But, owing to the differences in their economic set-up, individual countries react differently to this world-wide movement. Some countries find their trade rising or falling at a faster rate than the world total; whereas others have the opposite experience.

Moreover, from the point of view of the world as a whole, world prosperity or depression will always result in the equality of imports and exports. For individual countries, it is not so. Some countries find that the rate of expansion or contraction of their exports is always greater than that of their imports; whereas, to others, the converse is true. In other words, during world-wide cyclical fluctuations, individual countries experience not only changes in the absolute levels of imports and exports, but also changes in the net balance of trade (or of their whole income account). Thus, in relation to the different phases of the world trade cycle, each country has its own pattern of cyclical behaviour of the balance of trade.

In general, changes in home and world incomes affect a country's import and export values through three main channels. They are the cyclical change in the relative quantities, the cyclical change in the terms of trade and the general relationship between home and world cycles. Let us discuss them more fully.

§ IV

The cyclical changes in the relative quantities of imports and exports are predominantly determined by the size of their respective income and price elasticities.

The income elasticities are fundamentally set by the composition of a country's trade. A classification of the types of the trading countries in the world may therefore be made on the basis of the predominant features of a country's imports and exports. In general, the main types are three: industrial, agricultural and mining. The industrial type may be further subdivided into (1) highly industrialised and deficient countries, (2) highly industrialised and self-sufficient countries, and (3) less industrialised countries with an admixture of home agricultural production. We can make some generalisations about the income-induced changes in the relative quantities for these types.

First, a country belonging to the highly industrialised and deficient type supplies the world with manufactured goods and imports mainly foodstuffs and agricultural raw materials. For its exports which consist mainly of capital goods and high standard of living consumers' goods, the world demand tends to have a high income elasticity. On the other hand, imported foodstuffs are necessities for which home demand remains comparatively stable as between prosperity and depression; whereas the import of raw materials fluctuates sensitively with respect to home income changes. Thus, the income elasticity of demand for imports as a whole depends upon the relative proportions of foodstuffs and raw materials. In general, the higher the proportion of the former in the total, the smaller the total income elasticity; and conversely. *A priori*, it is unlikely that the income elasticity for imports will be larger than that for exports. Therefore, in a given period, a general world-wide cyclical expansion of the economic activity of the same magnitude in this country and abroad will necessarily result in a larger change in the quantity of exports. With the terms of trade remaining unchanged, this means an export surplus in terms of value.

The second type of country is one which is characterised by an advanced stage of industrialisation combined with a high degree of self-sufficiency in foodstuffs and most of the important raw materials. Owing to its self-sufficiency, a country belonging to this type imports only consumers' luxuries and some raw materials which cannot be produced at home; and, moreover, it generally spends only a very small part of any increase in home income on imports. But because of its composition, the percentage change in the quantity of imports still tends to be elastic with respect to the percentage change in home income. On the other hand, since its exports consist mainly of capital goods and other manufactured consumers' durables, the world demand for them has also a high income elasticity. On balance, it is to be expected that the income elasticity of exports would tend to be even higher than that of imports. Thus, during a period of general world prosperity, both the quantity of exports and that of imports would increase more than proportionately to the respective changes in income; but, with an equal percentage expansion of incomes everywhere in the world, there will result a surplus of export quantity.

Thirdly, among the industrialised countries, there is a group of less industrialised ones which have an important home agricultural production. A large part of the foreign trade of this type of country consists of transactions in specialised manufactures and materials. The income elasticities for both imports and exports tend to be fairly high; but, in general, these two elasticities may not be much different. Thus, with an equal economic expansion at home and abroad, the change in the relative quantities in either direction does not tend to be large.

Fourthly, for the agricultural type of country the cyclical pattern of change in the relative quantities is to be expected to be just the opposite to that of the first two types of industrialised country. Its exports consist mainly of foodstuffs and agricultural raw materials; whereas, on the other hand, its imports are capital goods and manufactures of various kinds. With respect to income changes, the change in the quantity of the former is rather inelastic and that of the latter is very elastic. Therefore, with an equal percentage economic expansion all over the world, there will be a cyclical surplus in the quantity of imports.

Lastly, there is the mining type of country. It is quite similar to an agricultural country in regard to export concentration. But, in contrast, its exports are products of mining industries and are generally demanded by the world heavy industries. Therefore, the income elasticity tends to be very high. On the other hand, the income elasticity of imports is also very high, because of the predominance of capital goods and other manufactures in the total. Although it is rather difficult to say, purely on *a priori* grounds, which elasticity is in fact larger, yet it would seem that they may not be much different. In other words, associated with an equal percentage economic expansion or contraction all over the world, the ratio of the cyclical changes in the relative quantities may remain fairly constant.

So far we have concentrated on generalisations about the cyclical changes in the relative quantities due to the difference in the income elasticities of the imports and exports of a given country. But the net changes in the relative quantities are the combined results of cyclical changes in both income and prices.

All price indices are sensitive to the trade cycle; and, therefore, the import and export prices of a given country tend to rise and fall together with the world cycle. The influence of price changes upon the relative quantities is determined by the magnitude of the import-price elasticity and the export-price elasticity.[1] Nevertheless, this influence tends, on the whole, to be small, because of the low values of these elasticities usually found. The general reason for the low import-price elasticity is the fact that the imports of a country consist mainly of the commodities which cannot be produced or cannot be produced cheaply at home. The export-price elasticity may also tend to be low, because there exists, as in the home economy, an imperfect market. Moreover, even if the magnitude of this price elasticity is high, the cyclical change in the export prices of a country may still not induce large absolute change in its export quantities. During a period of world-wide economic fluctuations, the prices of the competitors' exports move closely with those of the home country. Given an equal amplitude of fluctuation the rise or fall of the home export prices relative to those of the competitors does not tend in general to be large. Consequently, the absolute change in the export quantity may not be large.

In general, it may be concluded that the cyclical changes in the relative trade quantities of a country are predominantly determined by the fluctuations in incomes and that the effects of the price changes are comparatively unimportant. But the net change in the balance of merchandise trade is related to *values* of imports and exports, which are the product of their respective quantities and prices. Therefore, the predominant influence of price changes lies in the determination of values rather than of quantities. In reality, the import prices and the export prices do not change at an equal rate. In other words, the terms of trade of a country may become favourable or unfavourable. It is conceivable that, in a particular case, a favourable change in the relative quantities may be completely offset by an unfavourable change in the terms of trade, thus

---

[1] It may be more convenient to discuss this problem in terms of the relative price elasticities. The ratio of import prices to the home prices may be used to obtain the import-price elasticity; whereas the ratio of export prices to the competitors' prices is used to obtain the export-price elasticity.

giving no net change in the balance of merchandise trade. In the next section we attempt to give some *a priori* generalisations regarding the cyclical changes in the terms of trade of different types of country.

§ V

All prices are subject to cyclical instability, but their amplitude of fluctuation is not similar. In general, agricultural and mineral products have larger cyclical swings of prices than manufactured commodities. As has been pointed out by Harrod, the much more violent price fluctuations in the former are *inter alia* due to the superimposition upon their secular movements of the cyclical factors. The secular shift of demand away from these products has already caused a downward movement of their prices. Nevertheless, such secular movements are halted in the upswing of the trade cycle; but, during the depression, they are further accentuated.[1] Moreover, even the cyclical factors alone would lead to larger price fluctuations of these commodities for two reasons. First, as the countries producing these commoditites are generally those with less dense population or with less developed home industries, their annual production cannot be consumed locally and has to be sold in the world market. Therefore, the prices are *inter alia* much more dependent upon the changes of world demand. Furthermore, the elasticity of supply being low, any change in the world demand during the world cycle is likely to lead to a more than proportionate change in the prices. This situation is more serious, if, owing to traditional connections, a large part of these commodities is sold in one or a few foreign markets. Secondly, because of the inelastic supply of these commodities the practice of excessive stockholding tends to further accentuate the cyclical swings of their prices. During the trade cycle, speculators generally expect prices to continue in the same direction for several years; and therefore, they tend to buy when prices are rising in the upswing and to sell in the converse case, thereby accentuating the movements on which their expectations are based.[2]

[1] Harrod, *International Economics*, pp. 51–4.

[2] In the case of price fluctuations arising from abnormal harvests, the effect of speculative buying and selling is different. For instance, when a bumper harvest

It follows that, because of the differences in the amplitude of the cyclical changes of various prices, the fluctuations of the import and export prices of a country are generally not equal. In other words, there is a favourable or an unfavourable change in the terms of trade. The direction and amplitude of this change are dependent upon the relative compositions of a country's imports and exports. As has been shown above, such cyclical changes in the terms of trade do not generally have much effect upon the quantities of imports and exports; but they directly alter the values. In this connection, it is convenient to consider the different types of country.

Broadly speaking, during a period of world prosperity, the terms of trade turn in favour of the agricultural and mining countries, and change against all the highly industrialised countries. But in the case of the less industrialised countries, the cyclical change in the terms of trade is less obvious.

The effect of a cyclical change in the terms of trade upon the net balance of merchandise trade is most important and obvious in the case of mining countries. As pointed out above, the cyclical change in its relative quantities is likely to be fairly small; but the increasing favourable terms of trade as prosperity advances necessarily lead to a larger percentage change in the value of exports, and thus to an export surplus. In the case of less industrialised countries, as the relative compositions of the different groups of commodities in their imports and exports are quite similar, the cyclical changes in their terms of trade are not large. The smallness of the cyclical changes in both relative quantities and relative prices means that these two factors are less important in determining the cyclical pattern of the balance of merchandise trade of these countries. Or, in other words, if these countries do have a definite cyclical pattern, its predominant determinants must lie somewhere else.

The favourable change in the terms of trade of the agricultural countries during prosperity tends to cancel the unfavourable change in their relative quantities; whereas, in the case of highly industrialised countries, the converse is true. Whether the unfavourable (or favourable) change in the relative

appears and tends to depress the price, a part of the supply is generally held back by the producers in the anticipation of the return of the price to its normal level. This practice will therefore have a stabilising effect upon prices.

quantities is partly cancelled, completely cancelled or more than completely cancelled by the favourable (or unfavourable) change in the relative prices, depends upon the circumstances of each case; and it is difficult, purely on *a priori* grounds, to say anything very definite.[1] But very broadly speaking, we may expect that the quantity effect tends to be greater than the terms-of-trade effect. The changes in the import and export quantities are predominantly determined by their respective income elasticities; and, for a country, the difference in the magnitude of these two elasticities may be very great. On the other hand, all price indices move together during the trade cycle; and it can hardly be expected that the percentage increases or decreases of the import and export prices of a country are in general very divergent. Therefore, in most cases, the favourable or unfavourable change in the relative quantities will probably not be completely offset by the unfavourable or favourable change in the relative prices.

§ VI

The foregoing discussion has been made under tne assumption of a synchronous cyclical expansion or contraction of an equal magnitude everywhere in the world. But this is not in fact the case; because, as a result of difference in their economic constitutions, the time and the intensity of cyclical fluctuations in the different countries are not the same. Therefore, the ratio of the changes of home economic activity to the corresponding changes in the rest of the world is the third predominant factor in determining the cyclical pattern of the balance of trade of a country.

A priori, there are many possibilities with regard to the general relationship between the home and the world cycles. The cyclical fluctuations in the home country may be particular to it, while the economic activity in the rest of the world remains unchanged. The home cycle may be synchronous, in front of,

---

[1] The cancellation is partial, complete, or more than complete, according as the ratio of the cyclical change of the quantity of imports to that of exports is larger than, equal to, or smaller than, the ratio of the cyclical change in the prices of exports to that of imports. In symbolic form this is:

$$\frac{\text{Cyclical change in import quantity}}{\text{Cyclical change in export quantity}} \gtreqless \frac{\text{Cyclical change in export prices}}{\text{Cyclical change in import prices}}.$$

or lagging behind the world cycle; and, moreover, the amplitude of fluctuation may be greater or smaller. Each of these theoretical possibilities would tend to exert a different influence upon the change in the balance of trade of a country. Nevertheless, in reality, the cyclical fluctuations in different countries tend to synchronise as a result of the operation of the foreign-trade multiplier. Moreover, when the annual data are treated, the short-period lead or lag may be ignored. Therefore, our generalisations concentrate on the influence upon the balance of trade of the unequal amplitude of economic fluctuations.

Given the various elasticities of imports and exports, the actual changes in their quantities and prices depend on the amplitude of the income changes. Thus, an unequal amplitude of economic fluctuations will be reflected in the magnitude of the net change in the balance of trade. Compared with the case of an equal amplitude, this fact would necessarily result in a relatively larger change in imports or exports, according as the home cyclical fluctuations are more or less violent than those in the rest of the world. Consequently, the absolute amount of the import or export surplus would tend to be larger. The importance of this fact may be illustrated by two examples.

First, assuming two countries alike in the structure of trade, the difference in the net changes in their balance of trade would be entirely accounted for by differences in the amplitude of fluctuation. Let us further assume that these two countries generally tend to have a large percentage increase in import value during world prosperity. For the country with a more violent home cycle relative to the world, the import surplus will tend to increase further. On the other hand, for the other country with the reverse pattern of cyclical fluctuations, its inherent tendency towards a larger import surplus would tend to be offset by the increased exports arising from more violent world fluctuations.

Secondly, the factor of an unequal amplitude of fluctuations is also important in the cases in which the cyclical changes in both relative quantities and relative prices are not great. As shown above, the less industrialised type of country is generally in such a situation. Its definite pattern of cyclical change in the balance of trade must be predominantly determined by the unequal amplitude of fluctuation.

§ VII

When the cyclical pattern of a particular country is considered, one additional factor, though less important than the previous three, should be included.

As a result of historical development, individual countries in the world have either an export surplus or an import surplus on their merchandise trade. In order to determine the net change in the absolute amount of their balance of trade, the percentage increases or decreases of the values of imports and exports due to the above-mentioned three factors should be related to the actual levels of imports and exports in the initial period. In other words, the ratio of values of imports and exports are important in determining the absolute changes.

Let us take, for illustration, a country whose cyclical change in exports is normally larger in percentage that that in imports. If this particular country habitually runs an export surplus on the balance of merchandise trade, a larger percentage cyclical increase in the value of exports would necessarily lead to a larger increase of the export surplus in absolute amount than in the case of a country with a balanced trade in the initial period. Moreover, even if the percentage increases of imports and exports are equal, this fact of a habitual export surplus can still lead to an increase in export surplus as compared with the initial position.

However, the situation is less clear-cut if this country is one which runs a habitual import surplus. During a period of prosperity, the question of whether the cyclical surplus, as determined by the changes in the relative prices and the relative quantities, will be able to lead to a decrease in the initial import surplus, would be dependent upon the ratio of the initial import value to the initial export value. Stated formally, the initial amount of import surplus will decrease, remain unchanged, or even increase, according as:

$$\frac{\text{The cyclical increase in the export value in per cent}}{\text{The cyclical increase in the import value in per cent}}$$

$$\gtreqless \frac{\text{The initial value of imports}}{\text{The initial value of exports}}.$$

Looking into the actual data of the countries for a number of years, we find that, in spite of the various absolute amounts of import and export surplus for different countries, the average ratio of import value to export value is not much above unity.[1] On the other hand, the values for the ratio expressing the cyclical percentage changes in exports and imports are, in general, much above unity. Therefore, an initially unbalanced trade will not generally change the direction of cyclical surplus or deficit.

§ VIII

The foregoing *a priori* generalisations may be briefly summarised. The changes in the balance of merchandise trade of different countries are the result of the general world economic fluctuations. Owing to the difference in the structure of trade, each type of country tends to have a distinct cyclical pattern of changes of its own. But, in determining the patterns, different factors are not equally important in individual cases. In the case of less industrialised types of country, the factor of unequal amplitude of fluctuations seems very important. As to the mining type of countries, both the cyclical change in the terms of trade and the unequal amplitude of fluctuation seem to have the predominant influences. For the other types, all the factors mentioned seem to have their places. These *a priori* formations will be statistically verified in Parts II and III.

§ IX

So far we have confined ourselves to the study of the cyclical behaviour of the trade items; but in fact all other current transactions also show cyclical sensitivity. The shipping receipts or payments are highly correlated with the volume of trade, which changes positively with world economic activity. The interest receipts or payments on long-term investments consist of two parts: dividends from equity investments and interest from fixed-interest-bearing bonds. The former tends to increase as world economic activity is in its upswing; and the latter also to increase because of the decline or disappearance of defaults.

---

[1] As a matter of fact, the most common values seem to lie within the range from 1·1 to 1·3.

Other current transactions, such as tourist expenditures and receipts, insurance, commissions, etc., are also income-sensitive. Moreover, it would be expected that these transactions tend, in general, to have fairly high income elasticities.

With regard to these receipts or payments, it is impossible to make *a priori* generalisations for different types of country. All we can say is that they tend to rise in prosperity and to fall in depression. The rise or fall, taken together with the contemporaneous change in the balance of merchandise trade, gives the net cyclical fluctuations of the income account as a whole.

§ X

Do the international long-term capital movements also exhibit any cyclical pattern of fluctuations? In general, the volume of international long-term capital movements is determined by the world trade cycle, tending to rise in times of general prosperity and to fall during depression and recession. But by its heterogeneous nature, the movements of the constituent items are not always in the same direction as those of the total. For instance, flotations of equities and direct investment in the international field are closely correlated in a positive manner with the level of world economic activity. On the other hand, the new issues of fixed-interest bonds tend to have an opposite relationship. This fact is mainly due to the cyclical behaviour of long-term interest rates, which tend to rise in times of prosperity and to fall during depression, and thereby to discourage or to encourage borrowing in the form of fixed-interest bearing bonds.[1] It follows, therefore, that the cyclical movements of the long-term capital exports and imports of individual countries are bound to be different in accordance with the percentage compositions of these items in the total. Nevertheless, subject to these complications, we are still able to give some generalisations with regard to their cyclical behaviours.

From the point of view of the world as a whole, the total volume of long-term capital exports is necessarily equal to that of imports during all phases of the trade cycle. But what are the

---

[1] Moreover, from the point of view of the investors, the bonds with fixed incomes would generally be preferred to the more risky industrial shares when business is in the downward swing.

reasons for the cyclical fluctuations of the volume? For the countries which habitually import long-term capital the volume of capital imports tends to rise and fall with the trade cycle. This is because the movements are generally the cause and the effect of the economic fluctuations. Most of the international borrowing countries are primary producers whose internal capital investment is low and whose exports therefore constitute the main determinant of their home incomes. During a period of general world prosperity, world demand for their exports increases; and, hence, their incomes. As incomes are rising, more home investment decisions will be made. Because of a lack of internal capital resources, they demand foreign long-term capital for purchasing from abroad the necessary capital equipment and for 'financing' these investment programmes. As a result, long-term capital imports tend to increase. Once the boom is under way and is being maintained, the prospect of rising profits and increasing returns will encourage them to raise still more funds abroad and will make foreign investors more willing to lend to them. Therefore, a cumulative movement of long-term capital imports into these countries should be expected in times of world prosperity. Conversely, during depression and recession, net import of long-term capital tends to decrease; and, moreover, because of the annual repayments and maturities, the long-term capital movement may even reverse itself and become a net export.

On the other hand, the cyclical changes in long-term capital exports from the habitual lending countries are closely connected with the nature or structure of the capital market of the particular country in question. Let us first consider the case of a lending country where international trade bears a high percentage to its total home economic activity. Because of the importance of international trade, the home cycles of this country generally originate abroad. Thus, during a period of general world prosperity, its national income increases as a result of the rise of world demand for its exports. At the same time, at the new level of income, both total saving and total imports are increased. As shown in the equation in § II the total saving at home exceeds or falls short of the home saving, according as there is a surplus or a deficit on the home income account. Nevertheless, the actual lending countries under this category are generally the highly industrialised countries, whose income accounts are likely to show a surplus during prosperity, thus resulting in an excess of home saving. Owing to the imperfection of the international capital market, the excessive home saving may not be automatically devoted to long-term foreign investment. But, as the prosperity in these countries is induced by the external forces, their amplitude of economic fluctuation tends to be smaller than that in the borrowing countries. The relatively more violent fluctuations in the latter would generally be reflected in a larger and faster rising of the long-term interest rates and profits, which tends to encourage the former's lending to them. The converse holds true for the case of general world depression and recession. Therefore, it may be concluded that, for this type of lending country, the long-term capital exports are likely to rise and fall together with their world economic activity.

However, if in a lending country international trade is not important, and, hence, its cycles are generally of domestic origin, its long-term capital exports would be more influenced by internal factors. Here, the amplitude of economic fluctuations is important. Let us take the actual case of the U.S.A., where the economic fluctuations generally tend to be more violent than those in the rest of the world. During a period of general prosperity, as interest rates and profits are rising faster and higher at home than abroad, the ratio of long-term capital exports to the total capital used for home investment tends to fall; and it is even conceivable that the absolute amount of capital exports would tend to fall too.

§ XI

The cyclical equilibrium in the balance of payments of a country is reached when the change in the balance on income account is matched by an equal and opposite change in the balance on long-term capital account. As both accounts are influenced by the trade cycle, and exhibit definite patterns of cyclical behaviours, such an equilibrium for a country does in fact reflect a *natural* harmony. Although it is difficult, without statistical verification, to say whether this natural harmony exists in the balance of payments of *every* country, yet our previous *a priori* generalisations do point out the presence of this harmony in certain types of country. Let us take, for instance, the case of agricultural countries. During a period of prosperity, the income accounts of these countries generally tend to show deficits; but, at the same time, they engage in long-term foreign borrowing, which tends to lead to a net import of capital. In the converse case, a surplus is matched by a net export of long-term capital.

In spite of the inherent tendency towards broad cyclical equilibrium in the balance of payments, an absolute equality between the cyclical changes in the two accounts in any period for any country would be accidental. However, a country in common with other economic entities must have an exact balance between its total payments and total receipts. In other words, the home country as a whole cannot pay out more than it receives except by drawing on its international cash reserves or by short-term foreign borrowings; and inversely for the foreign countries as a whole. To look at the same thing in another way, the sum of the payments made by the home country on all current and long-term capital transactions constitutes the 'supply of home currency'; and, similarly, the corresponding receipts of the home country under these items constitute 'the demand for home currency'. Whenever there is a temporary discrepancy between the demand and supply, gold movements and shifts of short-term capital must occur to maintain the equilibrium; otherwise, the home exchange rates would not remain stable. Acting in such a capacity they become 'balancing items', and are therefore normally of a *passive* character.[1]

§ XII

The mechanism for calling forth the balancing short-term capital movements is an automatic change of the relative level of the home rates of interest to the world rates of interest, determined by the change in the general balance of payments. If long-term capital exports from the home country just equal its surplus on income account, there would not be an excess of home saving, nor an insufficiency of home saving; and, moreover, the liquidity position of the home country *vis-à-vis* the world as a whole would remain unchanged. But an excess of

---

[1] 'Hot-money' transfers are ignored here.

net long-term capital exports over the surplus on income ac-count would lead to an insufficiency of home saving relative to home investment. If this shortage of home saving should give rise to an immediate increase of home long-term interest rates, there would be a tendency towards the re-establishment of equilibrium by decreasing the net foreign lending of the home country. Nevertheless, such an immediate rise of home long-term interest rates would not be realised immediately, because (provided that the excess lending is not too large or does not last too long) the operation of speculators in home securities would tend to maintain the prices or the long-term rates by increasing speculative stocks as pointed out by Kaldor. But home short rates tend to rise because of two reasons. First, given the supply of money in the home country at any short period of time, the excessive foreign lending leads to a shift of money from the 'industrial circulation' to the 'financial circulation', and thereby the money available for transactional purposes is decreased. Second, the liquidity of the home banking system is decreased, as a smaller proportion of the capital assets of the banks consists of cash or deposits. These two forces tend to raise the home short rates, which will induce an inflow of international short-term capital to the home country. Later, the home long rates will also be raised; in consequence, the excessive net long-term lending by the home country will be checked.

The equilibrating short-term capital movements generally play a prominent part in the adjustment of the balance of pay-ments of the more developed countries. But the less developed countries, which are not equipped with a short-term money market at home, can hardly get much assistance from it. The main balancing item which they can rely upon is their inter-national cash reserves.

CHAPTER II

INTERNATIONAL COMPARISON OF DEMAND FOR IMPORTS[1]

§ I

Demand for imports may be compared internationally by studying the following three general aspects: (1) the actual degree of economic self-sufficiency of a country; (2) the relationship between the change in the value of imports and that in the national income of a country during the trade cycle; and (3) the cyclical behaviour of the demand for imports belonging to different economic classes.

TABLE 1. *International comparison of average propensity to import*

	(1) Average propensity to import (average value for 1924–38)*	(2) Average real income *per capita* in international units (average: 1925–34)†		(1) Average propensity to import (average value for 1924–38)*	(2) Average real income *per capita* in international units (average: 1925–34)†
Denmark	41·8	286·3	Austria	18·4	240·7
Belgium	36·1	254·0	Estonia	18·3	127·1
Netherlands	35·2	340·7	Czechoslovakia	15·7	184·8
Norway	34·7	216·8	Australia	15·5	460·7
Eire	29·8	282·0	Italy	15·4	179·0
South Africa	27·0	200·0	Hungary	14·5	140·0
New Zealand	26·0	460·7	Portugal	12·0	142·2
Greece	24·0	144·0	Roumania	12·0	108·0
Switzerland	23·7	475·0	Poland	11·0	114·2
United Kingdom	23·1	477·7	Yugoslavia	10·6	101·0
Finland	22·6	131·4	India	9·6	160·0
Chile	22·0	155·1	Bulgaria	8·9	91·8
France	22·0	304·3	Lithuania	8·6	83·0
Sweden	20·4	283·7	China	5·6	25·0
Japan	20·3	353·0	U.S.A.	5·0	551·7
Germany	19·6	275·5	U.S.S.R.	2·6	119·0
Canada	18·9	524·1			

* As a rule, the average value of total retained imports for the period 1924–38 is divided by the average money income for the same period. For some countries whose income indices are not complete for the whole period, we use the average

---

[1] This chapter is a slightly improved version of my article in *Review of Economic Studies*, vol. XIII, no. 2.

The degree of economic self-sufficiency of a country is reflected in the degree of dependence of that country upon international trade. Generally speaking, the satisfactory measure for it would be the ratio to its national income of the total value of goods and services consumed within it which come from

value for the period during which the income figures are available. The data for the merchandise are obtained from the League of Nations' *International Trade Statistics* of various years. The sources of income indices are as follows:

AUSTRALIA: C. Clark and J. G. Crawford, *The National Income of Australia.*
AUSTRIA: *Statistiches Jahrbuch für das Deutsche Reich*, 1938.
BELGIUM: *Bulletin de l'Institut de recherches économiques*, February, 1938.
BULGARIA: Statistical Institute of Economic Research, 1937.
CANADA: *Official Year-book of Canada*, 1941.
CHILE: C. Clark, *Conditions of Economic Progress*, p. 36.
CHINA: P. S. Ou, 'A New Estimate of China's National Income', *Journal of Political Economy*, December 1946.
CZECHOSLOVAKIA: National Bank of Czechoslovakia, *Monatsbericht*, 1939.
DENMARK: *Statistik Aarbog*, various years.
ESTONIA: Estonia Institute for Economic Research.
FINLAND: Bank of Finland, *Monthly Bulletin*, no. 2, 1937.
FRANCE: Clark, *Conditions*, p. 99: and League of Nations' *World Economic Survey*, 1938/39.
GERMANY: *Statistiches Jahrbuch für das Deutsche Reich*, 1938.
GREECE: Clark, op. cit. p. 40.
HUNGARY: *The National Income of Hungary*, by M. Matolcsy.
INDIA: Shirras, 'India's National Income', *Revue de l'institut international de Statistique*, no. 4, 1936.
EIRE: League of Nations, op. cit, p. 84.
ITALY: Clark, op. cit. p. 38.
JAPAN: Mitsubishi Economic Research Bureau, *Monthly Circular.*
LITHUANIA: Clark, op. cit. p. 38.
NETHERLANDS: Derkersen, *A System of National Book-keeping.*
NEW ZEALAND: *Official Year-book.*
NORWAY: Norge Bank, *Monthly Report.*
POLAND: *Petit Annuaire Statistique*, 1937.
PORTUGAL: Clark, op. cit. p. 145.
ROUMANIA: *La Situation Economique de la Roumania*, Memorandum by Slavesco, 1934.
SWEDEN: Ohlin and others, *National income of Sweden*, 1880–1930; and Clark, op. cit. p. 86.
SWITZERLAND: Clark, op. cit. p. 137.
U.K.: R. Stone, *An Analysis of Market Demand.*
UNION OF SOUTH AFRICA: S. H. Frankel, 'An Analysis of the Growth of the National Income of South Africa, in the Period of Prosperity before the War'. *Journal of South African Economics*, 1944.
U.S.A.: Data for 1924–28 are estimates by Kuznets, *National Income and Capital Formation*, 1919–35; and data for 1929–38 are estimates of the Department of Commerce.
U.S.S.R.: *Monthly Review*, U.S.S.R. Trade Delegation to the U.K. (1938: Plan).
YUGOSLAVIA: *Weltwirtschaftliches Archiv*, September 1938.

† An international unit is defined by C. Clark as the amount of goods and services which one dollar would purchase in the U.S.A. over the average period 1925–34. (Clark, op. cit. p. 41.) The real incomes in international units for various countries are given by Clark on p. 40 (table), pp. 78–176 and 179. In order to get real income *per capita* for all the countries, we divide incomes by their respective figures of total population in 1930, which are obtained from League of Nations' *Statistical Year Book.*

25

abroad. In technical language, this ratio is called the average propensity to import. The more dependent upon international trade a country is, the larger the magnitude of its average propensity to import; and conversely. Therefore, an international comparison can be made by examining the relative magnitude of average propensities of all the countries in the world. Here, as an approximation, we use the data of retained merchandise imports only; and the actual figures for thirty-three countries, arranged in a descending order, are shown in Table 1. An examination of the figures in column (1) of Table 1 reveals that the absolute level of average propensity to import of the thirty-three countries differs exceedingly widely. Denmark has the highest value as she devotes more than two-fifths of her national income to buying imported goods; whereas, in the case of the U.S.S.R. the average propensity to import is as low as 2·6%. Within this range, the remaining countries, with their varying stages of economic development, are distributed rather randomly. Countries of very different stages of economic development may have the same value for their average propensity to import; which is illustrated by the case of the U.K. *vis-à-vis* Finland. On the other hand, countries of similar economic set-up, such as Australia and New Zealand, may have different average propensities to import. *Prima facie*, this fact would suggest that the factors determining the level of average propensity of different countries in the world are so different and so various, that it is impossible to disentangle them in a simplified way and thus to draw any generalisations with regard to the distribution of the average propensities. But, in fact, it is not so, if we study the average propensities of different countries together with their respective real income *per capita*. For this purpose, we relate the figures in column (1) with those in column (2), as shown in Fig. 1.

Such 'horizontal' comparison between the average propensities of the thirty-three countries in roughly the same period reveals two very striking facts. First, the fundamental factor seems to be the real income *per capita* of a country, with which the average propensities are closely positively correlated. Secondly, it can be noted from the diagram that the average propensities of the thirty-three countries fall into three main groups: and the patterns of distribution within the first two groups are quite similar to each other. These facts, however, need explanation.

As to the first fact, it can be seen that the wealthier countries tend to import more while the poorer countries import less. In other words, there is a straightforward connection between the progress of economic development and larger imports. The rise of real income *per capita* in a country improves its fundamental capacity to produce and maintain a high level of economic activity and, hence, a high standard of living. This is equivalent to saying that, if a country has a higher real income *per capita* compared with others, it becomes able to buy more imports, paying for them by increased exports.

Look at the same thing from the point of view of the international division of labour. The poorer countries are generally primary producers. Since they do not produce manufactured goods at home, they usually obtain them by the export of primary produce. But, as a result of general low average productivity and over-population in such countries, the 'exportable' surplus of primary produce over the amount which is required to feed the domestic population is also small. Therefore, their ability to buy foreign goods, or the average propensity to import, is bound to be small. Nevertheless, in some agricultural countries where the land is less densely populated and hence the average productivity of labour is generally high, there is a high margin of 'exportable' surplus of domestic primary production which can be used in exchange for a larger volume of manufactured imports. This fact is reflected in the relatively high values of average propensity to import of these countries. New Zealand, Canada and Australia may be chosen to compare with the south-eastern European countries.

On the whole, the industrialised countries tend to have a higher average propensity to import than the agricultural countries. The interchange of commodities among industrialised countries is not simply based upon the notion of international division of labour as postulated by the classical economist. Rather it is based upon the international division of specialised skill.[1] Apart from exchanging manufactured goods for food-

[1] H. Frankel, 'Industrialisation of Agricultural Countries and the Possibilities of a New International Division of Labour', in *The Economic Journal*, June–September, 1943.

stuffs and raw materials, highly industrialised countries import and export the same kind of manufactured goods. This fact seems mainly due to difference in qualities. For instance, the U.K. produces electrical machinery and so does Germany; but they still exchange with each other, because the electrical machines they produce respectively are of different grades and therefore suitable for different purposes. Another interesting

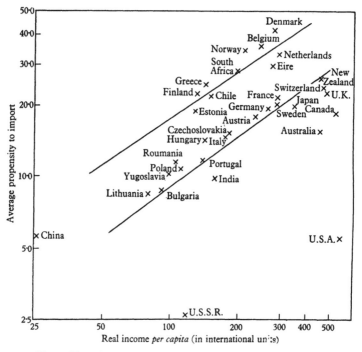

Fig. 1. The relation between average propensity to import and real income *per capita*

example is furnished by the British data of camera imports and exports. The U.K. produces and exports cameras of lower qualities suitable for certain foreign markets; on the other hand, she imports high-quality cameras to meet her home demand. Thus, when real income *per capita* in the industrialised countries increases, they will increase their demand for imports not only of the goods which cannot be produced at home but also of the goods which have broadly similar substitutes at home. Moreover, the more deficient in natural produce an industrialised country is, the higher its average propensity tends to be as compared with those of the countries belonging to the same group. For instance, the U.K. tends to have a higher average propensity to import than the U.S.A., because she is very deficient in foodstuffs and raw materials.

Furthermore, our argument that the magnitude of the average propensity to import is predominantly determined by the level of real income *per capita* in the country concerned can also be proved by examining trade and income figures over a period of years. In other words, we would expect the same result from inter-temporal comparison.[1] In general, when a country is in the process of economic development, its home income and its international trade will rise together. This is not only because in some cases the country has to rely upon foreign sources for essential raw materials for internal economic expansion, but mainly because it must import capital equipment and buy manufactured goods to meet the rising standard of living of its people.

But the fact that the countries fall into three groups has not yet been explained. The groups lie one above the other, as shown in Fig. 1. In group I, there are ten countries whose average propensity to import varies from 18 to 42%. In group II, there are twenty-one countries with an average propensity to import from 6 to 26%, the mean of which is, however, below 20%. The U.S.S.R. and the U.S.A. form an odd group III. These two are countries on the scale of a continent, which can provide raw materials and develop division of labour within themselves. This fact of high degree of self-sufficiency accounts for the very low average propensities of both countries. In the case of the U.S.S.R., this is also partly explained by state control.

When groups I and II are compared, their similarities are twofold. First, within each group, there are countries of varying stages of economic development. However, the relatively poorer agricultural countries stand always in the lower left-hand position, while the rich agricultural and industrial countries occupy the top right position. Secondly, when two straight lines

[1] For 'vertical' comparison for one country at succeeding date, see E. Staley, *World Economic Development*, ch. VIII.

TABLE 2. *Degree of specialisation of thirty-one countries*

Country	Specialised exports[1] (Average value 1927-9)	Degree of specialisation, as reflected in	
		(a) Exports: % of specialised exports in total exports	(b) Home production: % of specialised output in total output
Chile	Nitrates of soda (47·0); copper (34·5); iodine (4·0)	85·5	21·6[1,2]
New Zealand	Butter and cheese (37·4); wool (28·4); meat (18·2)	84·0	27·4[3]
Finland	Timber (62·4); paper (10·9); wood pulp (10·0)	83·3	24·2[4]
Canada	Wheat flour (39·8); wood and paper (23·3); minerals (12·7)	75·8	42·5[5]
Denmark	Dairy produce (38·5); bacon (31·2); cattle (5·3)	75·0	27·6[6]
South Africa	Gold (40·0); wool (21·0); diamonds (13·0)	74·0	25·5[7]
Norway	Fish (25·9); timber (25·5); minerals (21·3)	72·7	—
Japan	Silk, yarn and tissue (45·6); cotton, yarn and tissue (20·9); apparel (6·2)	72·7	—
Greece	Tobacco (54·0); currants (14·0); olives (4·0)	72·0	—
Eire	Cattle (36·4); dairy produce (24·4); beer (10·6)	71·4	41·8[8]
Australia	Wool (44·6); wheat and flour (19·6); hides and skins (6·7)	70·9	17·9[9]
Estonia	Butter (30·1); wood and paper (20·0); cotton, yarn and tissue (11·9)	62·0	21·8[10]
Sweden	Wood and paper (44·1); iron ore (9·4); iron and steel manufactures (7·1)	60·6	20·0[11]
Roumania	Petroleum and benzine (31·5); barley (14·7); timber (14·3)	60·5	—
Belgium	Minerals (22·3); iron and steel manufactures (16·1); textiles (14·1); machinery and vehicles (7·1)	59·6	—
Netherlands	Horticultural produce (18·1); dairy produce (18·0); machinery (11·9); textiles (10·5)	58·5	—
Italy	Textiles (37·8); fruits (12·0); stone (4·7)	54·5	—
Poland	Wood (20·1); coal (14·1); cattle (10·1); minerals (10·0)	54·3	—
Yugoslavia	Timber (23·0); maize (19·3); cattle (11·1)	53·4	—
Switzerland	Textiles (24·4); machinery (14·4); watches (11·1)	53·4	—
Austria	Textiles (24·6); wood and paper (21·3); machinery (7·1)	53·0	—
U.K.	Textiles (28·3); machinery and vehicles (15·3); iron and steel manufactures (9·3)	52·9	30·1[12]
Portugal	Wine (30·7); tinned fish (17·8); cork sheets (4·2)	52·7	—

Bulgaria	Tobacco (32·9); eggs (12·0); maize (6·2)	51·1	17·6[13]
Lithuania	Wood (26·0); cattle (14·0); dairy produce (11·0)	51·0	—
Hungary	Wheat (28·5); cattle (14·6); dairy produce (7·9)	51·0	16·9[14]
France	Textiles (30·2); machinery and vehicles (11·2); iron and steel manufactures (5·3)	46·7	—
Czechoslovakia	Textiles (32·9); iron and steel manufactures (7·1); glass (6·7)	46·7	—
Germany	Iron and steel manufactures (16·6); machinery and vehicles (15·0); chemicals (13·2)	44·8	—
India	Raw cotton (19·5); raw jute (9·3); tea (8·1)	36·9	2·0[15]
China	Silk (15·5); soy beans (11·8); tung oil (4·0)	31·3	—

[1] In context, 'textiles' denote the products of cotton, silk and woollen industries. 'Iron and steel manufactures' do not include machinery and vehicles. The figure in parentheses denotes the percentage of that particular export in the total exports.
[2] Ratio of gross value of production of butter and cheese, wool and meat to that of total production. (Official Year-book of New Zealand.)
[3] Percentage of forestry income in national income. (Bank of Finland, *Monthly Bulletin*, No. 2, 1937.)
[4] Ratio of gross value of production of wheat and flour, wood and paper and minerals to that of total production. (Canadian Year-book.)
[5] Ratio of alimentary production to total production. (*Statistisk Aarbog.*)
[6] Ratio of gross value of production of wool and mining industries to that of total production. (Official Year-book of Union of South Africa.)
[7] Ratio of gross value of production of fish, minerals, and timber and paper to that of total production (*Statistisk Arbok for Norge.*)
[8] Ratio of net value of production of food and drink industries to that of total output. (Irish *Census of Production.*)
[9] Ratio of gross value of production of wool, wheat and flour, hides and skins to that of total production. (Official Year-book of Australia.)
[10] Ratio of gross value of production of paper and plant, butter and milk to that of total production. (Estonian Economic Year-book.)
[11] Ratio of gross value of production of timber, paper and minerals to that of total production. (*Statistisk Årsbok för Sverige.*)
[12] Ratio of net value of production of textile, iron and steel and engineering industries to that of total production. (Bowley, *National Income.*)
[13] Ratio of gross value of production of tobacco and dairy produce to that of total production. (Publication of the Statistical Institute for Economic Research, State University of Sofia.)
[14] Ratio of gross value of sales of animals, grains and dairy produce to national income. (Matolcsy, op. cit.)
[15] Ratio of gross value of production of tea, cotton and jute to that of total production. (Shirras, op. cit.)

are drawn to pass near the points in the two groups, their slopes tend to be nearly the same. These similarities may lead us to the conclusion that the rate of growth of average propensity to import, as determined by the rate of growth of real income *per capita*, is about the same in the two groups. But, why do these countries fall into two groups? Or, what are the factors which, in addition to real income *per capita*, may also influence the magnitude of average propensities of different countries?

The reason would seem to lie in the relatively higher degree of specialisation of the countries belonging to group I. The exports of these countries may concentrate on certain agricultural or mining staples, or may be confined to manufactures of certain narrow categories; and the value of home production of these specialised exports bears a very high proportion to their respective national incomes. The fact of high specialisation makes these countries very dependent upon foreign sources for other goods to meet their home needs. Therefore, given the real income *per capita*, the more specialised a country, the higher its average propensity to import; and conversely. In other words, there is a positive correlation between the average propensities to import and the degrees of specialisation. If this be the explanation, the phenomenon of separate groups should disappear when the average propensities of different countries are plotted against their respective degrees of specialisation.

It is difficult to find a precise measure for degrees of specialisation of different countries. One useful method is to calculate and to compare their ratios of the value of specialised output to national income or total output. Because of lack of data, this is possible only for a limited number of countries. If, however, we assume that the relative composition of a country's exports generally reflects the pattern of its home production, the 'degree of specialisation' may be used as an approximation. In Table 2, an index of 'degree of export specialisation' is therefore compiled by taking each country's first three items or categories of exports (in terms of value) as its specialised products, and by calculating its ratio to the value of total exports. This index is arbitrary and crude; nevertheless, it is able to give us some indication of the relative degrees of specialisation of different countries.

When the average propensities of different countries are plotted against their respective degrees of export specialisation as shown in Fig. 2, the phenomenon of separate groups disappears. All the countries tend to cluster along a straight line with a positive slope; and the correlation is fairly high. This is in conformity with our expectation. The higher the degree of specialisation, the larger the value of the average propensity to import; and conversely. For the purpose of comparison, Fig. 3

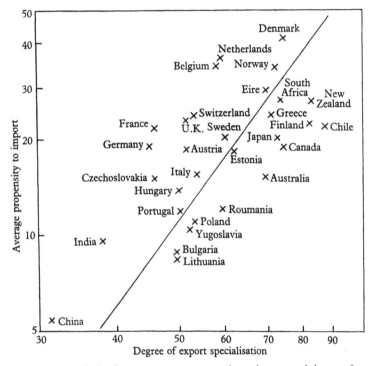

Fig. 2. The relation between average propensity to import and degree of export specialisation

is drawn by correlating the average propensities with the degrees of specialisation in home production. The result is broadly the same, but the correlation is improved. This is due to the fact that the ratio of specialised output to total output generally provides a better measurement of a country's degree of specialisation than the ratio of specialised exports to total exports.

As compared with Fig. 1, the relative position of different countries in Fig. 2 has not materially changed. Denmark,

Belgium, Netherlands, Norway and Eire still stand in the right top corner, while China is still at the opposite end. Moreover, when the countries with the same degree of specialisation are compared, those which have higher average propensities to import are generally the richer countries, and conversely. This fact is complementary with that revealed in Fig. 1. There, the average propensies of the more specialised countries tend to be higher than those of less specialised countries with the same real income *per capita*.

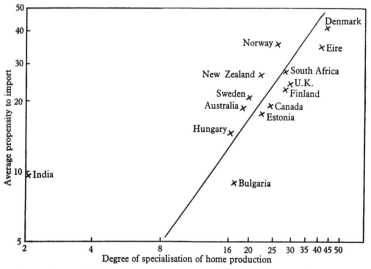

Fig. 3. The relation between average propensity to import and degree of specialisation of home production

In conclusion, the two fundamental factors, which determine the economic self-sufficiency of different countries in the world, are the level of real income *per capita* and the degree of specialisation of home production in exports. The U.S.A. and the U.S.S.R. are the exceptions, to which the factor of geography seems to be more important.

§ II

The international comparison of average propensities to import, though interesting by itself, becomes less important when we come to study the variations of the balance of payments of different types of country in relation to the trade cycle. From the point of view of the international trade cycle, what is more relevant is the change in the value of imports consequent upon a simultaneous change in national income. The relationship between the value of total imports and that of total national income depicts the result of historical development; whereas, the relationship between the changes in imports and those in national income tells the cyclical behaviour of demand for imports of a country during a short period of time.

The relationship between changes in imports and national income can be expressed in two ways. If we set out the change in imports that typically results from a unit change in income, the relationship being measured is the marginal propensity to import of a country. Whereas, if we correlate proportional changes in imports and in income, we are measuring the income-elasticity of demand for imports.[1] In this section, we shall attempt to make an international comparison of the marginal propensity to import.

The imports of a country can be divided into three broad groups: (1) goods mainly purchased by consumers for the purpose of immediate or 'deferred' consumption; (2) goods mainly entering into the production of consumers' goods; and (3) mainly producers' goods.[2] The relationship between the change

---

[1] With ordinary arithmetic scales, plot the crude figures of total imports (as Y) against the national income (as X). We get a series of points on a scatter diagram, one for each year; and, because the relationship between Y and X is very roughly linear, we can fit a line $Y = a + bX$ to these points. 'b' is the marginal propensity to import, dY/dX, and is a constant for all values of X. The average propensity to import at income X is the proportion of that income spent on imports, or $a/X + b$. If 'a' is positive, the average propensity exceeds the marginal propensity, but is a declining function of income. If 'a' is negative, the average propensity is less than the marginal propensity and is an increasing function of income. If 'a' is zero, the two propensities coincide. For the relationship of imports to national income investigated here, 'b' is positive; but negative values of 'b' must exist in the case of inferior goods the demand for which rises with falling income. If the scatter diagram is plotted with logarithmic scales, the regression coefficient of imports on income denotes the income elasticity of demand for imports. But a simpler way is to estimate the mean elasticity, $e = \dfrac{dY}{dX} \dfrac{X}{Y}$, from the equation $Y = a + bX$ (See H. Schultz, *The Theory and Measurement of Demand*, pp. 190–2.)

[2] However, in general practice, and especially in official publications, the imports of a country are divided into three general groups: foodstuffs, raw materials and semi-manufactures, and manufactured goods. This classification is too arbitrary. Our present classification, though not free from arbitrariness, tends to reflect better the economic behaviour of a society.

3-2

in national income and the change in expenditure on any one of these groups is obvious and direct. With regard to (1) and (2), that the change in the consumption expenditure is related positively to the change in national income is an established fact;[1] and, in an open system, a part of any increase in consumption expenditure is necessarily devoted to imported goods. Therefore, so far as these are concerned, the marginal propensity to import is the application of the concept of the marginal propensity to consume to the field of international trade.

Moreover, the demand for imported producers' goods is directly determined by the fluctuations of basic economic conditions at home, which are in turn reflected in the changes of national income. Since this group of goods is generally investment goods, the 'aggregate' marginal propensity to import measures the changes in expenditure not only on imported consumers' goods but also on imported investment goods.

In general, the change in national income does not equally affect the expenditures on these groups of goods. For instance, with a given change in national income, the consumption expenditure changes less than investment expenditure: and, moreover, among the consumption expenditure, the demand for immediate consumption goods changes less than that for 'deferred' consumption goods. Therefore, the magnitude of the marginal propensity to import of a country is, *inter alia*, very much dependent upon the relative composition of its imports, which is in turn determined by the type of economic set-up of that country. In accordance with the main characteristics of the economic set-up, we may roughly divide the countries in the world into two groups: agricultural and industrial. The imports of the countries in the former group tend to have a relatively higher proportion of investment goods and 'deferred' consumption goods; while, in the case of the countries in the latter group, imports consist less of these goods but more of goods for immediate consumption and raw materials for making consumption goods. Looking at this fact broadly, we would expect that the marginal propensity to import of agricultural countries

[1] R. and W. M. Stone, 'Marginal Propensity to Consume and the Measurement of the Multiplier', *Review of Economic Studies*, October 1938.

tends to be larger than that of industrial countries. The result of our statistical calculations is shown in Table 3.

TABLE 3. *International comparison of marginal propensities to import*[1]

Countries	Marginal propensity to import
A. Industrial group:	
U.S.A.	0·07
Germany	0·24
Switzerland[2]	0·29
U.K.	0·29
France	0·31
Japan	0·33
Sweden	0·34
Czechoslovakia[3]	0·40
B. Agricultural group:	
Canada	0·30
Australia	0·35
Finland[4]	0·43
South Africa[5]	0·43
New Zealand	0·46
Norway	0·47
Roumania[6]	0·48
Hungary[7]	0·52
Bulgaria[8]	0·53
Denmark	0·54
Eire[9]	0·70
Austria[10]	0·72
Estonia[11]	0·73

[1] Unless otherwise stated, the years included in our calculation are 1924–38. In order to isolate the cyclical behaviour of demand for imports, the trend is eliminated from both series.

[2] 1929–34.
[3] 1929–37.
[4] 1929–36.
[5] 1922/3–1938/9.
[6] 1929–33.
[7] 1924/5–1937/8.
[8] 1929–35.
[9] 1931–5.
[10] 1929–35.
[11] 1929–36.

It must be noted that, in some cases, the period covered is rather short and the income indices used are, in the strict sense, not very reliable; and, therefore, the results may fail to be precise. However, this defect will not invalidate our attempt to discuss the general relationship among the marginal propensities of different countries in the world. With regard to the results given out in Table 3, three observations may be made.

First, the results come out in conformity with our expectation that the magnitude of the marginal propensity to import of a country is, to a very large extent, dependent upon the composition of its import trade, which is in turn determined by its general economic structure. Therefore, comparing the industrial countries as a whole with the agricultural countries as a whole, we find that the marginal propensity to import of the former tends to be lower than that of the latter.

Secondly, with the exception of the U.S.A., the marginal propensities of the industrial countries cluster closely along the value of 0·3. The U.S.A. stands by her own with a marginal propensity to import well below 0·1. This is no doubt due to her natural self-sufficiency in foodstuffs and most of the important raw materials for her home industries. In contrast, the marginal propensities of agricultural countries vary greatly; and the mean value for the group lies probably in the range from 0·45 to 0·5.

Lastly, within each group, there is also a regular distribution of the marginal propensities. Of the industrial group, the countries, which are less industrialised than the rest and consequently import relatively more investment goods, tend to have higher marginal propensities. Similar regularity is present also in the case of the agricultural group. At the top of the group are generally the countries whose home manufacturing industries are relatively more developed and which consequently tend to have lower marginal propensities; whereas, the countries with least developed manufacturing industries at home stand generally at the bottom of the group.

§ III

The foregoing analysis gives the crude marginal propensity to import of a country, which shows the change in the value of imports associated, on the average over a period of years, with a unit change in its national income. The international comparison of such crude values provides only an imperfect guide to the understanding of the cyclical behaviour of demand for imports of different countries during a period of world-wide economic expansion or contraction.

First, this is because the marginal propensity to import calculated in terms of money does not take into consideration the effect of cyclical changes in the 'terms of trade'. The difference in the magnitude of cyclical changes in the import and home prices tends either to overestimate or to underestimate the marginal propensity of a country. For instance, for a country whose import prices relative to home prices tend to rise more in times of general world prosperity and to fall more during world depression and recession, the marginal propensity to import is likely to be relatively overestimated in the above calculation; whereas, on the other hand, for a country with the opposite pattern of cyclical changes in the relative prices, it is likely to be underestimated. Therefore, the import series and the income series should be deflated by their respective price indices. Or, in other words, we should study the relationship of their cyclical changes in real terms.

Moreover, the magnitude of the change in real imports associated with a change in real income may be better judged by relating them to their respective absolute levels in the initial period of equilibrium. When the proportionate changes of these two variables are correlated, we get the income elasticity of demand for the imports of a country.

Secondly, in addition to income, there are other factors which are equally important in determining the cyclical change of imports. The quantity of imports of a country changes also with changes in price levels during the cyclical fluctuations; or, in other words, we have to calculate the price elasticities of demand for imports. (1) There is the change in the level of import prices. However, the notion of import prices is not a simple one. From the point of view of home consumers, the cost of buying imported commodities is not the price quoted by foreign sellers, but the quoted price c.i.f. plus import duties. Any change in tariff is equivalent to an increase or a decrease of import price. Therefore, when we discuss the price elasticity of demand for imports, we have to correct the absolute level of import prices by the change in tariff. (2) There are price substitutions of home-produced goods for imports. Any increase in the prices of similar home-produced goods would generally induce an increase in the quantity of imports; and conversely. Moreover, the substitution of home-produced goods for imports can still be conceived to take place even if there are no similar substitutes at home. In this case, the substitution is through the competition between imports and home-produced goods for the purchasing powers in the hands of home consumers.

Lastly, some countries are dependent upon imported raw materials for making exports. Therefore, the change in the quantity of imports is also determined by the change in the quantity of exports. Accordingly, we have a further elasticity, i.e. the export elasticity of demand for imports.

§ IV

The foregoing discussion reveals that the cyclical change in the quantity of imports of a country is determined by four elasticities: (1) the income elasticity of demand for imports; (2) the price elasticity of demand for imports (with tariff corrected); (3) the price elasticity of substitution of home-produced goods for imports; and (4) in some cases, the export elasticity of demand for imports. We can use partial correlation analysis to get all these elasticities.

For the total imports of a country, the tariff changes may be corrected in the following way. The Customs revenue is first reduced to an index number with the base year similar to those of import quantity and price indices. This index is then divided throughout by the quantity index of the same period. The resultant ratios representing the tariff changes are added to the price index for the corresponding years; therefore we get the import prices including tariff for a country.[1] This procedure is only an approximation; but it is thought that it would be sufficient for our present purpose.

In general, we use a wholesale price index or cost of living index to represent the prices of home-produced substitutes. Moreover, in order to simplify our statistical calculations, we divided the corrected import prices of a country by its home prices to get relative prices; and, consequently, the elasticity means a relative price elasticity of demand for imports.

Let $\log x_1$ = quantity of imports;
$\qquad \log x_2$ = real income or home employment;
$\qquad \log x_3$ = relative prices;
$\qquad \log x_4$ = quantity of exports.

Then, the partial correlation equation, with the trend of all these series eliminated, is of the form:

$$\log x_1 = b_{12.34} \log x_2 - b_{13.24} \log x_3 + b_{14.23} \log x_4.$$

[1] That is $\qquad\qquad$ Price + $\dfrac{\text{Customs revenue}}{\text{Quantity}}$.

Here, $b_{12.34}$, $-b_{13.24}$, and $b_{14.23}$ give respectively the income elasticity, the relative price elasticity and export elasticity of demand for imports of a country. The square of the multiple correlation coefficient will then give the percentage of the sample variance of the quantity of imports which can be explained by the variations of these three factors.

One point should be borne in mind. Our estimates of elasticities are made by the usual regression analysis, which assumes the whole error-variation concentrated in the dependent variable. Theoretically, the estimates are therefore not the best estimates of the true structural relationships existing in the data.[1] However, the error is probably not large; but the method is simpler.

The results of our calculations of the various elasticities of imports for different types of country are given in Table 4.[2] Moreover, for the sake of comparison, the elasticities of demand for imports of the world as a whole (i.e. the sum of imports of all countries) are also calculated.

The countries chosen for each type are confined to the cases in which all the series involved in our statistical calculations are available for the period under study: but, it is expected that, in general, they would form representative samples of their respective types. Therefore, any generalisations based upon them would seem justified.

With regard to the magnitude of the income elasticity of demand for imports of different types of country, the results are in conformity with our *a priori* expectation. For the industrial countries as a group, the income elasticity though greater than unity does not tend to be very high; and, moreover, it is well below that for the agricultural countries as a group (or mining countries as a group). It is interesting to compare the income elasticity for these groups with the income elasticity calculated for the world as a whole. In our calculation, the world's income elasticity of demand for imports is given as $+1\cdot50$, which means that the cyclical fluctuations in the quantity of total world

[1] Cf. G. Tintner, 'Some Applications of Multivariate Analysis to Economic Data', *Journal of American Statistical Association*, December 1946.

[2] To classify the different countries into some rigid types is not free from arbitrariness. Some countries belong to a kind of mixed economy. Canada is a good example. However, our classification based upon the main economic features of different countries is useful for the present purpose.

TABLE 4. *The international comparison of various elasticities of demand for imports*[1]

Countries	Multiple correlation coefficient	Income- or employment-elasticity[2]	Relative-price-elasticity	Export-elasticity
I. World as a whole[3]	0·89	1·50	−0·56	—
II. Industrial countries:				
A. Highly industrialised and self-sufficient type:				
U.S.A.	0·92	1·27	−0·97	—
B. Highly industrialised and deficient type:				
U.K.	0·94	1·10	−0·28	0·25
Germany	0·82	1·20	−0·37	0·40
C. Relatively less industrialised type:				
Italy	0·64	0·94	−0·27	—
Switzerland	0·85	1·32	−0·26	0·13
Japan	0·84	1·35	−0·47	0·49
France	0·83	1·46	−0·32	—
Sweden	0·85	1·74	−0·37	—
Czechoslovakia	0·84	2·39	−0·23	—
III. Agricultural countries:				
Norway	0·83	1·70	−0·86	—
Canada	0·98	1·75	−1·34	—
Denmark	0·85	2·28	−0·63	—
New Zealand	0·89	2·56	−0·34	—
Australia	0·98	2·80	−0·67	—
Finland	0·94	2·90	−0·25	—
Estonia	0·90	3·02	−0·34	—
Yugoslavia	0·94	3·04	−0·85	—
Latvia	0·97	4·16	−0·48	—
Hungary	0·73	5·36	−0·54	—
IV. Mining countries:				
South Africa	0·85	2·30	−0·64	—
Chile	0·87	3·25	−0·32	—

[1] The period covered in our calculation is in general from 1924 to 1938. The quantity and price indices for individual countries are obtained from *Review of World Trade*, 1938. The indices for home prices (either wholesale or cost-of-living index) are obtained from the Statistical Year-books of various years.

[2] When the income index for a country is not available for a sufficiently long period, we use index of home employment, which can be obtained from the *International Labour Review*. The countries in this case are: Italy, Switzerland, Czechoslovakia, Finland, Estonia, Yugoslavia, and Latvia. The period covered is generally from 1929 to 1938. But in the case of U.K. we also use the index of home employment.

[3] The index of real world income is compiled as follows. Estimates for the money national income for fourteen countries in the period 1924–38, from sources as shown in footnote to Table I, are deflated by the cost-of-living indices of the respective countries. Colin Clark (in *Conditions*, p. 56) has given the average percentages of real income of various countries in the world total for the period from 1925 to 1934. For our present purpose of compiling an index of world real income, these percentages are modified and used as weights. The modification is made because it seems reasonable to use the index of a country to represent also the countries whose internal economic activities are closely connected with it. For

imports tend, on the average over the period under investigation, to be 1·5 times more violent than those in the world real income. The value, 1·5, stands just between the average values for the industrial group and that for the agricultural group (or mining group). This is equivalent to saying that, given a uniform economic expansion or contraction all over the world, the quantity of imports of the industrial countries tends to fluctuate less than that of the world average; and, that of the agricultural countries tends to fluctuate more. This fact, however, can be easily explained. As the imports of the industrial countries consist of a smaller percentage of capital equipment and other manufactured goods than the total world imports, the former should remain more stable than the latter during the trade cycle; and the converse is true for the cases of agricultural countries. Moreover, this comparison, *inter alia*, points out another feature of cyclical movements of world trade. It is the inherent tendency of the distribution of world trade to shift during the trade cycle. It would seem that, as the quantity of total world trade is rising during world prosperity, the total imports into agricultural countries will be rising faster than those into the industrial countries; and that, in times of world slump and recession, the former will be falling faster than the latter. On *a priori* grounds, we would expect opposite cyclical shifts on the side of exports of different types of country. These two facts taken together provide a very important clue to the cyclical pattern of change in the balance of merchandise trade of different types of country in the world.

Furthermore, it seems that the difference in the size of the income elasticity of different countries in the same broad group also reflects the relative composition of the imports of that particular country. We have to divide the industrial countries into three sub-types. So far as their respective compositions of imports are concerned, the highly industrialised and self-

instance, we use British index to represent India and other British colonies: American index to represent Latin-American countries; Hungarian index to represent south-eastern European countries. The fourteen countries included and their respective weights are as follows: Australia, 10; Canada, 8; Denmark, 5; France, 15; Germany, 20; Hungary, 20; Japan, 10; Netherlands, 6; New Zealand 6; Norway, 5; South Africa, 5; Sweden, 5; the U.K., 30; and the U.S.A., 75. Estimates for Germany covering 1924 and for New Zealand covering 1924 and 1925 are extrapolated on the basis of the aggregate for other countries. Estimates for Australia and New Zealand are converted from a fiscal year to an approximate calendar year basis by averaging successive pairs of fiscal-year figures.

sufficient type of country tends to import mainly those raw materials which have no substitutes at home. The figure given shows that the U.S.A., though having a very low marginal propensity to import, still has an elastic demand for imports. The imports into the highly industrialised and deficient type of country consist not only of raw materials but also of foodstuffs: and, consequently, the income elasticity for them would tend to be relatively low among the industrial group. This is confirmed by the cases of the U.K. and Germany. For the less industrialised type of country whose imports consist of a fairly high percentage of manufactured goods and capital equipment, the income elasticity would necessarily be the highest of the group. Switzerland, Japan, France and Sweden support our argument. Moreover, some industrial countries are dependent upon imported raw materials for making domestic exports. Therefore, we find that, in these cases, there is correlation between the fluctuations in the quantity of imports and those in the quantity of exports. But, in general, the export elasticity is well below unity.

For the countries in the agricultural group, the income elasticity, in most cases, tends to be over two. The differences among them broadly reflect the various stages of development of manufacturing industries in these countries, and, hence, the relative composition of their imported manufactures.

Now let us turn to discuss the size of the price elasticity for different types of countries. It seems that the difference in their magnitudes is random; and no generalisations can therefore be made on them. But, with the exception of Canada, all the elasticities tend to be less than unity. This, however, may be explained by the fact that, as imports are generally the goods which cannot be produced at home, these fluctuations would tend to be inelastic with respect to the fluctuations in the prices. Moreover, in most cases the partial correlation coefficient between import quantity and price is not high. This is partly due to the defect of using either wholesale or cost-of-living index to represent the prices of home-produced substitutes;[1] and,

---

[1] Even if the substitution between imports and home-produced goods is regarded as a competition for the purchasing powers of the home consumers, the correlation coefficient may not be expected to be high, because such substitution is rather remote and insensitive.

more particularly, it is due to the fact that the cyclical fluctuations in the quantity of imports are predominantly determined by the changes in income.

§ V

The elasticities given in Table 4 concern each individual country's demand for *total* imports. It has been found that they generally reflect the predominance of a certain group of commodities in the total imports, which is in turn determined by the economic set-up of the country in question. In this way, our calculations fail to reflect the difference in a country's demand for different groups of commodities. If, for instance, a country importing mainly foodstuffs tends to have a less elastic income-demand for imports than a country importing mainly manufactured goods, do we also expect that a single country's income elasticity of demand for imported foodstuffs is smaller than that for manufactured goods? Or, in other words, do 'horizontal' comparison and 'vertical' comparison tend to give more or less the same conclusions? Our expectation that this will be so is confirmed by the results of further calculations, which are given in Table 5.

The American and the British data yield parallel results. The income elasticity of demand for foodstuffs tends to be less than unity. This is in accordance with the fact that consumption expenditure on food, though closely related to income, changes less than in proportion to income. For price elasticity, the U.K. has a low value. This is natural because she is deficient in foodstuffs and is therefore bound to buy abroad. The presence of home-produced substitutes will not have much influence upon the magnitude of this price elasticity, as their total quantity is small in relation to total home consumption. The U.S.A., which is self-sufficient in staple foodstuffs, tends to import some crude and manufactured foodstuffs which in general are not produced at home. An examination of the trade statistics reveals that the main items in these broad groups are tea, cocoa, coffee, and alcoholic drinks. Consequently, the American price elasticity of demand for imported foodstuffs tends also to be low.

Both countries import some raw materials which in general have no home-produced substitutes; and, therefore, their

TABLE 5. *Comparison of British and American demand for imports of different groups of commodities*

E_i = income or employment elasticity.
E_p = relative-price elasticity.
E_e = export elasticity.
R = multiple correlation coefficient.

Commodity groups	American			British			
	R	E_i	E_p	R	E_i	E_p	E_e
1. Total imports	0·92	1·27	−0·97[1]	0·94[7]	1·10	−0·28	0·25
2. Crude foodstuffs	0·75	0·23	−0·43[2]	0·86	0·55	−0·31	—
3. Manufactured foodstuffs	0·93	0·94	−0·10[3]				
4. Crude materials	0·81	1·02	−0·39[4]	0·85[8]	1·12	−0·24	0·32
5. Semi-manufactures	0·93	1·43	−0·43[5]				
6. Finished manufactures	0·86	1·39	−1·01[6]	0·98	1·44	−1·12	—

[1] From Table IV.
[2] Home price is represented by the index of wholesale prices of farm products.
[3] Home price is represented by the index of wholesale prices of food.
[4] Home price is represented by the index of wholesale prices of raw materials.
[5] Home price is represented by the index of wholesale prices of semi-manufactures.
[6] Home price is represented by the index of wholesale prices of finished products.
[7] Revised figures for those given in Chapter VI. See also my note, 'The British Demand for Imports: A Reply', in the *Economic Journal*, December 1946.
[8] Revised figures for those given in Chapter VI.

demands are inelastic with respect to changes in their respective import prices. But, as expected, the raw materials show elastic changes with respect to home income changes. Moreover, as the U.K. is dependent upon imported raw materials for making home exports, the change in the former is also correlated with the change in the latter.

Since manufactured goods consist mainly of 'deferred' consumers' goods and capital equipment, the demand for them is elastic with respect to changes in income. Moreover, the demand for this broad group of imports is also elastic with respect to changes in relative prices, because both the U.K. and U.S.A. are industrial countries and have home-produced goods substituting for the imports.

CHAPTER III

WORLD DEMAND FOR EXPORTS[1]

THE INTERNATIONAL COMPARISON OF
INCOME ELASTICITIES

§ I

Analogous to our former treatment of demand for imports, the variations in the quantity of exports of a country may also be correlated with, and explained by, changes in several predominant determinants. In general, the determinants are changes in the level of world real income, changes in the export prices of that exporting country and changes in the prices of substitutes supplied by the competitors in the world market. Accordingly, with the trend of all the series eliminated, the partial correlation equation is of the form:

$$\log z_1 = c_{12.34} \log z_2 - c_{13.24} \log z_3 + c_{14.23} \log z_4,$$

where z_1, z_2, z_3 and z_4 are respectively the quantity of exports of a particular country in question, the world real income, its export prices and the export prices of its competitors in the world market. Hence, the regression coefficients indicate the respective elasticities required. And, as before, the square of the multiple correlation coefficient gives the percentage of the sample variance of the quantity of exports which can be accounted for by the variations in all these determinants.

Here, as in the case of imports, we encounter the difficulty of finding the appropriate index to represent the prices of substitutes. Moreover, this problem is further complicated by the following three factors: (1) the variations in exchange rates; (2) similar goods supplied by different countries do not always compete in the same world market; and (3) the problem of correcting for the tariff changes imposed upon the exports of a particular country. However, for our present purpose, we adopt a method of approximation. As far as possible, we try to

[1] A part of Chapter III and Chapter IV has been published in *Review of Economics and Statistics*, May 1948.

48

compile an index of the prices of substitutes for a country whose exports are mainly belonging to a certain economic class. This index is obtained by taking a weighted average of the indices of export prices of a number of countries whose exports are broadly in the same economic class as the exports from the country under consideration. The weights are given in accordance with the relative shares of the countries in total world export trade; and the separate indices are reduced in terms of the currency of the particular country by the average exchange rates of the year. For instance, in the case of the U.K., an index of prices of substitutes in the world market is compiled by taking a weighted average of the export prices, in terms of sterling, of four principal industrial competitors—U.S.A., France, Germany and Japan.

Moreover, partly because of the fact that exports from a country are, in some cases, so different from exports from other countries, and partly because of the amount of work which is necessarily involved in the compilation of indices for individual countries, we are further compelled to use in some cases an even more general method. Here, we regard the competition among countries in the world market as taking place not in the form of substituting each other's similar exports, but in the form of getting a larger share of total world exports by price cutting. Accordingly, we use the index of prices of total world exports *in gold* as a representative index.

As before, in order to simplify our calculations, we divide home export prices by prices of substitutes in the same unit of currency; and consequently, the price elasticity of world demand for home exports is a relative price elasticity. The effect of tariff policy can be traced in .the trade statistics for a single country, but cannot be estimated for exports as a whole; it is therefore ignored in our calculation.

The index for the world real income has been compiled as shown in Table 4, n. [3]. As this index includes the world as a whole, we have to eliminate a country's index from this aggregate index when we come to consider the world income demand for that country's exports.[1]

---

[1] But for the countries which are not included in our compilation, we use this aggregate index without correction.

§ II

The results of our statistical calculations are given in Table 6.

TABLE 6. *Elasticities of world demand for exports from individual countries*[1]

Countries	Multiple correlation coefficient	Income-elasticity	Relative-price elasticity
I. World as a whole[2]	0·89	1·50	−0·56
II. Industrial countries:			
A. Highly industrialised and self-sufficient type:			
U.S.A.	0·97	2·91	−0·43[3]
B. Highly industrialised and deficient type:			
Germany	0·84	2·00	−0·58[4]
U.K.	0·94	1·81	−0·53[5]
C. Relatively less industrialised type:			
Sweden	0·94	1·50	−0·36[6]
France	0·81	1·23	−0·77[7]
Switzerland	0·90	1·36	−0·44[8]
Japan	0·70	1·08	−0·60[9]
Italy	0·70	0·95	−0·81[10]
III. Mining and raw-material producing type:			
Chile	0·93	3·38	−0·17[11]
Canada	0·91	1·52	−0·35[12]
British Malaya	0·74	1·52	−0·18[13]
South Africa	0·80	1·17	−0·31[14]
IV. Agricultural countries:			
Estonia	0·91	0·89	−1·29[15]
Argentina	0·87	0·88	−0·46[16]
Latvia	0·81	0·84	−1·84[17]
New Zealand	0·83	0·72	−0·52[18]
Finland	0·84	0·72	−1·23[19]
Norway	0·79	0·62	−0·62[20]
Hungary	0·83	0·61	−1·10[21]
Eire	0·79	0·55	−0·65[22]
Denmark	0·80	0·35	−0·45[23]
Australia	0·92	0·22	−0·66[24]

[1] The period covered in our calculation is 1924–38.

[2] From the world point of view, total imports are necessarily equal to total exports; and therefore, the elasticities are the same as those given in Table 4.

[3] Average export prices of U.K., Germany, Japan and France, in terms of U.S. dollars.

[4] Average export prices of U.K., U.S.A., Japan and France, in terms of old U.S. dollars.

[5] Average export prices of U.S.A., France, Japan and Germany, in terms of pound sterling. The elasticities are different from those given in my former calculation. (C. F. Carter and T. C. Chang, 'A Further Note on the British Balance of Payments', in *Economica*, August 1946.) This is because here the index of relative prices is used.

An examination of the results in Table 6 reveals that the quantity of exports from industrial and mining and raw-material producing countries tends to fluctuate more violently with respect to world real income changes than that from agricultural countries. So far as the magnitude of income elasticities is concerned, the former group have a value greater than unity; whereas the latter group have a value less than unity. Moreover, if we take the income elasticity of demand for the exports of the world as a whole as a mean, the elasticities for the countries in the former group tend, in general, to lie above this mean, while those for the countries belonging to the latter group lie below it. Looking at the results broadly, we find that Table 6 depicts a situation reverse to that of Table 4. The countries whose import income elasticity is less than that of the world as a whole are those whose export income elasticity is greater than that of the world as a whole; and conversely. Or, speaking more generally, for the former cases, the import income elasticity tends to be smaller than the export income elasticity; whereas, for the latter cases, the export income elasticity tends to be smaller than the import income elasticity. This fact points out a fundamental phenomenon in the cyclical fluctuations in the balance of trade; that is, given an equal magnitude of economic expansion all over the world, the former group will experience a favourable change in relative quantities, while the latter an unfavourable change; and, given an equal magnitude of economic contraction, the converse will be true. The detailed

[6] Average export prices of U.K. and U.S.A. in terms of sterling.
[7] Average export prices of U.K., U.S.A., Japan and Germany in terms of francs.
[8] Prices of total world exports in gold.
[9] Average export prices of Germany, U.S.A., U.K. and France in terms of yens.
[10], [11] Prices of total world exports in gold.
[12] Average export prices of Australia, New Zealand and Argentina in terms of pound sterling.
[13], [14], [15] Prices of total world exports in gold.
[16] Average export prices of Australia, Canada and New Zealand in terms of pound sterling.
[17] Prices of total world exports in gold.
[18] Average export prices of Australia, Argentina and Canada n terms of pound sterling.
[19], [20], [21] Prices of total world exports in gold.
[22] Average export prices of Australia, Argentina, Canada and New Zealand in terms of pound sterling.
[23] Average export prices of Australia, Argentina, Canada and New Zealand in terms of pound sterling.
[24] Average export prices of Argentina, Canada and New Zealand in terms of pound sterling.

study for individual countries, however, will be attempted in Parts II and III.

The world demand for the exports from the industrial countries shows an elastic change with respect to world real income, except in the case of Italy. The difference in the relative magnitude of income elasticities reflects, in general, the composition of manufactured exports from these countries, which is fundamentally determined by the stages of industrialisation. For instance, it is interesting to find that, since exports from the U.S.A. consist more of investment goods and high standard of living goods than do the exports from the rest of the industrial countries, the income elasticity of world demand for them is the highest in the group.[1] Moreover, the relatively low income elasticities in the cases of Japan and Italy reflects, amongst other things, the fact that their manufactured exports are designed mainly to meet consumers' needs, such as textile goods, apparel and so forth, which tend to fluctuate less violently than investment goods during the trade cycle.

As expected, the exports from mining countries show an elastic demand with respect to changes in world real income. This is because mining products are generally used by world heavy industries. Chile provides a very good example, where more than 85% of total exports consisted, on the average of 1927–9, of nitrates of soda and copper ores. To some extent, this is also true for South Africa, because more than half of her exports in 1927–9 was gold bullion and diamonds. Moreover, the agricultural countries whose exports consist mainly of raw materials rather than foodstuffs will find elastic world income demand for their exports. For instance world income demand for British Malayan exports is elastic, because, in 1927–9, rubber and tin occupied more than 40% and 25% of total value of exports respectively. The case of Canada may also be explained by the same argument; because, besides wheat, Canada exported large quantities of timber and mineral ores.

The agricultural countries whose exports consist mainly of foodstuffs find that their exports change much less than in proportion to world real income. It is interesting to find that the income elasticities of world demand for the exports from Eire, Australia and Denmark are very low indeed.

[1] For a fuller comparison among U.S.A., U.K. and Germany, see § III.

§ III

In the rest of this chapter, we shall attempt, with the aid of the income elasticities, to compare the exports from the three great industrial countries: Germany, U.K. and U.S.A. We choose them because of their importance in total world export trade. As shown by the trade statistics, on the average of 1928–30, each was responsible for more than 10% of total world exports;[1] and, collectively, they supplied more than 35% of the total. Moreover, they were important in another aspect: one or the other of them was the chief single or the principal supplier in certain markets. For the purpose of easy comparison, we may classify the export markets of these three countries into two general groups: (1) 'exclusive' markets, and (2) 'equally-shared' markets. By the former we mean those countries which

TABLE 7. *Comparison of markets of three industrial countries* (1930)

	(1) 'Exclusive' markets[1] for		(2) 'Equally shared' markets
(a) U.S.A.	(b) U.K.	(c) Germany	
Haiti	Eire	Lithuania	Portugal
Honduras	Nigeria	Latvia	Denmark[2]
Philippines	India	Estonia	Netherlands[3]
Canada	South Africa	Finland	Sweden
Dominican Republic	New Zealand	Austria	Norway
Mexico	Australia		U.S.S.R.[4]
Nicaragua			Switzerland
Panama			Argentina
Costa Rica			Brazil
Cuba			Italy
Guatemala			France
Salvador			Spain
Venezuela			Poland
Colombia			Turkey
Ecuador			Czechoslovakia[5]
Peru			Belgium
Bolivia			
Chile			
Uruguay			

[1] The countries are arranged in the order of 'exclusiveness'.
[2] Germany supplied 35% of total imports.
[3] Germany supplied 32% of total imports.
[4] The U.K. supplied less than 10% of total imports.
[5] The U.S.A. supplied less than 10% of total imports.

[1] In 1928–30, the world principal exporters whose share in total world exports was over 2·5% were, in the order of importance, U.S.A., U.K., Germany, France, Canada, India, Japan, Netherlands, Belgium, Italy and Argentina.

draw more than 30% of their total imports from any one of these exporters; while, by the latter, we denote the markets in which each of these three exporters supplies 10–30% of its total imports. From the League of Nations' *International Trade Statistics*, we are able to compile in Table 7 for the situation in the year of 1930.

The salient features of this comparison are twofold. First, the 'exclusive' markets are, in general, determined either by geographical position, as in the cases of U.S.A. and Germany, or by historical factor, such as the British exclusive markets. Secondly, the markets in which the three industrial countries compete most keenly with each other are, in general, relatively wealthy countries. Moreover, so far as the share in the total world trade is concerned, the countries in this group are more important than the countries in the former group.

§ IV

In Table 6, the income elasticities of world demand for American, German and British exports are given as $+2 \cdot 9$, $+2 \cdot 0$ and $+1 \cdot 8$ respectively. This would mean that the cyclical fluctuations in the quantity of exports from U.S.A. were the most violent with respect to changes in world real income, those from the U.K. were the least violent, and those from Germany stood in the middle way. Thus, with equal magnitude of economic expansion all over the world, the American exports would have sustained the most favourable influence, with German exports second and British exports least; and conversely. Can this fact be accounted for by the difference in the composition of exports from these three industrial countries?

TABLE 8. *Percentage of general groups of exports in the total (including re-exports), 1929**

	(1) Live animals, food and drink	(2) Raw materials and semi- manufactures	(3) Manufactures	(4) Total
World	24·5	36·0	39·5	100·0
Germany	5·6	19·8	74·6	100·0
U.K.	6·6	16·1	77·3	100·0
U.S.A.	13·8	39·1	47·1	100·0

* League of Nations' *International Trade Statistics*, 1931.

54

To begin, let us compare the general groups of the constituent items of their exports, classified according to Brussel's definition. The comparison reveals that there is similarity of British and German exports in their very high percentage of manufactured goods. A more striking fact is that in American exports foodstuffs and raw materials and semi-manufactures are as important as manufactured goods. In the group of foodstuffs, the main commodities are unmanufactured tobacco and cereals; whereas the high percentage of the group of raw materials and semi-manufactures in total American exports is explained by her export of raw cotton and cotton linters. This broad comparison, though interesting, cannot give us the explanation of the relative competitive strength of these three industrial countries in the world market. It is therefore more important to compare the percentage composition of selected commodities in the three totals. Table 9 is compiled for this purpose.

The importance of broadly similar categories of commodities in the total exports of the three countries is different. An examination of Table 9 reveals that, in the pre-Depression years, the U.K. was highly dependent upon the products of the cotton and woollen industries, which contributed nearly one-third of total British exports. To a lesser extent, she relied also upon the exportation of coal, and iron and steel and manufactures thereof. In the case of Germany, machinery, chemical products, and iron and steel and their manufactures were her main industrial exports. In contrast, the important items in American industrial exports were vehicles (including aeroplanes and ships), machinery and petroleum. After the Depression and during the 'thirties, the relative position of the three countries was not materially changed, so far as the composition of exports is concerned. But one important trend was presented in British exports. The rise of 'new' industries at home had resulted in a steady expansion of the export of machinery, vehicles, chemical products, etc.; and, consequently, textile exports had become less important in the total.[1]

It has been established that the income elasticities for individual categories of commodities are different in accordance with their nature; and, moreover, it has also been found that the income elasticity of demand for producers' goods would

[1] This fact is treated more fully in § v.

55

TABLE 9. *Percentage composition of selected exports to the total**

Commodities	Average 1927–9			Average 1930–2			Average 1935–7		
	U.K.	U.S.A.	Germany	U.K.	U.S.A.	Germany	U.K.	U.S.A.	Germany
I. Mainly consumers' goods:									
(1) Textile manufactures, including cotton piece goods, yarns, apparel, etc.	25·0	4·0	5·7	20·7	3·9	7·2	17·1	3·4	5·1
(2) Woollen and worsted manufactures	7·0	—	2·7	6·5	—	2·3	5·4	—	3·0
(3) Pottery and glasses	1·9	—	1·9	2·1	—	3·0	1·1	—	3·0
(4) Watches and implements	—	—	1·8	—	—	2·0	—	0·8	3·1
II. Mainly producers' goods:									
(5) Vehicles	5·0	11·2	1·5	7·3	6·1	1·6	5·7	11·3	5·6
(6) Machinery: electrical goods and apparatus	1·7	2·2	4·6	2·0	3·1	5·2	3·6	3·8	5·5
other machinery	7·4	8·7	10·1	8·3	9·6	10·3	7·8	10·9	12·6
(7) Iron and steel and manufactures	9·3	5·4	14·0	8·5	4·3	14·8	9·9	9·7	16·6
(8) Non-ferrous metals and manufactures	2·2	4·6	5·4	2·0	3·5	4·3	3·8	4·2	4·7
(9) Chemical drugs, dyes and colours	3·5	1·5	10·5	4·4	3·4	10·5	4·6	3·6	12·8
(10) Fuel: coal and coke	6·1	1·9	5·8	8·5	3·5	5·9	7·0	2·0	6·2
manufactured fuel	0·5	10·0	—	0·7	11·9	—	0·8	11·7	3·3

* League of Nations' *International Trade Statistics*.

WORLD DEMAND FOR EXPORTS

normally tend to be larger than that for consumers' durables, which in turn is more elastic than that for 'immediate' consumption goods.[1] Therefore, it follows that, as a result of difference in the relative compositions, the aggregate income elasticities of world demand for the total exports are bound to have different values for the three countries under investigation. From Table 9 it can be seen that American manufactured exports consisted, in general, of a higher percentage of consumers' durables and producers' goods than for both German and British exports; and consequently, the income elasticity of world demand for it has the highest value of the three; which supports our statistical results. Moreover, as German total exports are compared with British exports, the income elasticity for the former must still be larger than that for the latter. This is because, with respect to cyclical fluctuations in world income, the demand for machinery and chemicals tends to have more violent changes than that for textile manufactures. This fact therefore explains the different values for the two elasticities given by our statistical calculations.

Our results can also be supported by the calculations made by *Der Deutsche Aussenhandel unter der Einwirkung Weltwirtschaft-Strukturwandlungen.* The table is reproduced here.

TABLE 10. *Manufactured exports of U.K., Germany, U.S.A., in* 1929: *percentage distribution into commodity groups by rate expansion**

	Percentage in commodities groups expanding in international trade (1913-29)				
	Less than 25%	26–75%	76–150%	More than 150%	Total for which data available
U.K.	2·1	40·0	33·5	4·3	79·9
Germany	2·1	25·2	55·3	4·5	87·1
U.S.A.	1·0	16·1	38·8	28·6	84·5

* The selected categories of manufactured goods under each group are as follows:
(1) Less than 25% group: laces and embroideries; and pianos.
(2) 26–75% group: cotton yarn; wearing apparel; toys; cotton cloth; and shoes.
(3) 76–150% group: steel mill products; optical and mechanical products; machines; and clay products.
(4) More than 150% group: tyres and automobiles; rayon and rayon yarn; electrical communication devices; and photographic apparatus.
This table is quoted in Staley, op. cit. pp. 150–1.

[1] See Chapter IV, § 3.

57

In a seventeen-year period from 1913 to 1929, over half of a sample covering 80% of total British exports consisted of commodities the world demand for which had increased by less than 75%; and 40% consisted of the commodities the world demand for which had risen by 76–150%; and the commodities the world demand for which had risen by more than 150% occupied only 5% in total British exports. In sharp contrast, American exports, for which the world demand had increased over 150%, amounted to one-third of the total. Germany, however, stood in the middle way. Although her position regarding the more than 150% group was nearly the same as the British, yet about two-thirds of German exports belonged to the group the world demand for which had increased from 75% to 150%. On *a priori* grounds, the commodities expanding most in the international trade would have been the commodities the world income-demand for which was most elastic during cyclical fluctuations; and conversely.[1] Therefore, these findings are in conformity with, and support, our own result.

§ V

Having shown the fundamental differences in the exports of the three countries, we shall attempt to give a brief account of their year-to-year changes during this period. For this purpose, the indices of quantity of exports of the three countries, together with the index of quantity of exports of all countries after the trend has been eliminated, are plotted in Fig. 4.

Incidentally, the comparison shows that the cyclical fluctuations in the quantity of exports of industrial countries tend to be more violent than those in the exports of all countries, increasing relatively more in times of world prosperity and falling relatively

---

[1] The commodities which had expanded most during the boom period of the 'twenties recorded the heaviest contraction in world slump. Although no similar calculations have been done for this period, American figures may be used as an illustration.

	Value of exports in 1932: % change from 1929
Total exports	− 70
Rubber and manufactures	− 80
Automobiles	− 85
Rayon and rayon yarns	− 75
Electrical machinery and apparatus	− 65

faster during world slump and recession. As has been shown above, this is attributed to the fact that the total world exports consist of a higher percentage of foodstuffs and other agricultural produce, which remain relatively stable from prosperity and depression as compared with trade in manufactured goods.

But more interesting is the relationship among the indices of the quantity of exports of our three industrial countries. The actual changes of the three indices during this period may be summarised as follows:

(1) The changes in the three indices during 1924–6 were rather irregular. This was no doubt due to the random factors affecting

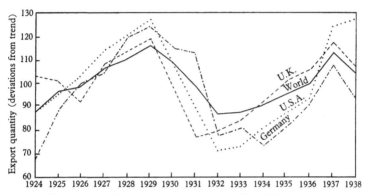

Fig. 4. Comparison of cyclical fluctuations of world, British, American and German indices of quantity of exports (1924–38)

both British and German exports. On the one hand, the over-valuation of the pound and the General Strike adversely affected the quantity of British exports; whereas, on the other hand, the low level of German exports in 1924 and 1925 was due to the after-effects of currency collapse and the disorganisation of home industrial production in the earlier years.

(2) During the prosperous years of the later 'twenties, the relationship among the three indices was what we could expect from our statistical calculations. In general, the American index showed the largest increase of the three; the British index the least.

(3) But their relative positions did not remain constant during the Great Depression. As shown in Fig. 4, in 1930–31

the British index registered the heaviest decline of the three; whereas the German index not only showed the least decline, but lay above the world total. However, in 1932, the fluctuations in the three indices followed their usual pattern.

An examination of the trade statistics reveals that the heaviest decline in the British exports was, strangely enough, attributed mainly to the enormous fall in the quantity of British textile exports.[1] In addition to the fall in world real income, there were special factors also affecting adversely the British textile exports; namely, the political disturbances and the increase of tariff on textile imports in certain main markets for British textile products, such as Chinese and Indian markets.[2] In the case of Germany, the favourable factor was the growing importance of the Russian market for German exports of machinery and other capital goods. During this period, the Russian demand showed a steady increase. As a result, the German quantity of exports did not contract as fast as those of the U.K. and the U.S.A.[3]

(4) During the recovery period of the 'thirties, the British index not only registered the earliest recovery but also lay, after 1934, above the index of world total. The fact, however, must be accounted for by three factors: (a) the earliest exchange depreciation; (b) the steady expansion of 'new' industries at home and the subsequent increase in productivity; and (c) the earlier recovery of 'exclusive' British markets.

The American index tended to lie below the index of world total during world recession and recovery. It is natural that American exports, which consist more of capital goods, tended to fall more during recession than the world total exports. But the fact of its smaller rise during the recovery period was due to slower and less complete recovery in American 'exclusive' markets. As the world regained prosperity in 1937, the American index again rose above the world index.

[1] Between 1928 and 1930, the export of textile products fell roughly from £260 mn. to £170 mn., corresponding to a reduction in quantity of about one-third; whereas the quantity of products of engineering and allied industries (including machinery, electrical goods, vehicles, etc.) remained practically stable and the fall in their values was accounted for by the fall in prices. As to total exports, the decline in quantity was about 15%.

[2] For survey of individual markets, see Y. N. Hsu, 'British Cotton Industry in Depression', ch. II. (Unpublished dissertation in Cambridge University Library.)

[3] *Review of World Trade*, 1930, pp. 27–9; and *Review*, 1931, pp. 33–5.

Throughout this period, the German index lay below the index of world total. The weak position was due to the over-valuation of the Reichmark and general discrimination against German exports by the free exchange countries.[1]

§ VI

The British case deserves special attention; and, therefore, we shall illustrate our arguments with actual trade figures.

The first favourable factor affecting British exports in the early 'thirties was the exchange depreciation. During the period from the fourth quarter of 1931 to the end of 1933, the U.K. was able to secure a larger share in the imports of many countries. But, because of the general shrinkage of world income and employment, this had only meant that the quantity of British exports had remained fairly stable. On the whole, it is difficult to assess how far this stability had been chiefly due to the fall of British export prices as a result of the depreciation of the pound. However, looking back at the history, there were factors which would make us believe that price effect of the depreciation could not have been very great. First, as shown in Table 6, the relative-price elasticity of world demand for British exports as a whole was rather low. Because the U.K. was a large seller in the world markets, any fall in her export prices would not have led to an equal proportionate increase in quantity exported. Secondly, events outside the U.K. during that time tended to diminish any favourable price effects that may have been associated with the depreciation of the pound. For instance, the fall of prices in countries remaining on gold had been accelerated; and some of Britain's industrial competitors had depreciated their currencies considerably more than the U.K.[2]

Therefore, any favourable influence on the quantity of British exports associated with the depreciation could not have been worked out, to any considerable extent, through the price effect. But the depreciation did help to maintain the stability of the quantity of British exports during this period through the 'income effect'. First of all, the depreciation of the pound had

---

[1] E. S. Ellis, *Exchange Control in Central Europe*, pp. 274–6.

[2] For instance, as against the 30% depreciation of the pound, the Japanese yen had depreciated about 50% in the same period.

brought financial relief to her debtor countries by devaluing their debts incurred in terms of pounds sterling; and this increased these countries' ability to purchase necessary manufactured goods. Moreover, the decrease of the burden of service payments had in turn lessened the pressure on agricultural debtor countries to push their produce on to the world markets, so that a further worsening of the terms of trade, and hence a further falling off of their national incomes, was avoided. This helped to maintain these countries' purchases of goods from the U.K. during a period of world-wide depression. Our argument may be supported by a comparison of the movements of the quantity indices of British total exports and of certain manufactured commodities.

TABLE 11. *Movements of quantity indices of British exports, 1929–33*

	Total exports	Manufactured textiles			Machinery
		Cotton	Wool	Silk	
1929	100	100	100	100	100
1931	62·6	56	60	69	58
1932	62·9	58	63	77	55
1933	64·4	67	72	67	48

The quantities of British manufactured textile exports showed a steady increase during this period. This increase was not attributed to the fall of prices as a result of the depreciation of the pound, because, as a matter of fact, Japanese export prices of manufactured textiles (owing to a larger percentage of depreciation) had fallen more than British export prices. In the case of the Indian market, Japan had even secured a larger share in the market expansion than the U.K.[1] Therefore, the increase of British textile exports must have been mainly due to the increase in the ability of debtor countries to purchase manufactured necessities because of external financial relief. In contrast, the quantity index of British machinery exports showed steady decline which reflected the general shrinkage in world investment activity. This, however, points out the fact that the

[1] For a large supplier in the world market, the price elasticity of world demand for its total exports tends to be generally low. But the price elasticity of substitution between similar commodities exported from the given country and exported from the competitors *in a given market* can still be greater than unity. For fuller discussion and statistical verification see Chapter IV.

world demand for such goods is mainly determined by income changes, and price changes in general cannot have much effect.

The second factor which was responsible for the increase of British competitive power in international trade during the later 'thirties was the rise of 'new' industries at home. After the Great Depression, a rapid expansion and growth took place in the field of 'new' industries, such as electrical instruments, metal manufacture, rayon textiles, chemicals, automobiles, etc. The products of such industries were generally those for which the world demand was increasing most rapidly.[1] The rise of them in the U.K. had no doubt put her in a better competitive position with the U.S.A. and Germany, as compared with the pre-Depression situation. The increase of the relative importance of the products of 'new' industries in the total British exports can be judged from the following tables.

TABLE 12. *Employment and volume of output in new industries in the U.K.**

	Employment			Volume of output		
	1924	1930	1935	1924	1930	1935
Electrical goods	100	127·5	164·5	100	121·8	181·8
Motor-cars and cycles	100	125·1	145·2	100	145·2	238·0
Aircraft	100	181·6	298·4	100	282·6	476·8
Rayon	100	173·7	203·6	100	240·0	500·0
Chemical and allied trades	100	100·1	109·0	100	100·7	149·3
Scientific instruments, etc.	100	106·3	122·7	—	—	—
All industries	—	—	—	100	103·5	117·6

* Sources: *Final Reports, Census of Production.*

TABLE 13. *The relation of exports of products of 'new' industries to total exports**

	1924	1930	1935
Total exports (£mn.)	801·0	570·8	425·8
Exports of products of 'new' industries (£mn.)	81·4	82·8	72·0
Total exports (%)	10·2	14·5	17·0

* Sources: *Census of Production,* also *Annual Statements of Trade of the U.K.*

Finally, the success of British manufactured exports in maintaining their quantity above the whole world index after 1934 was also due to the earlier recovery and prosperity recorded in the main British markets. In contrast, the American main or

[1] Vide supra, Table 10.

TABLE 14. *Economic conditions in selected countries, 1934–7 as compared with* 1929
(*percentage change from* 1929)

	(1) Physical volumes of industrial production				(2) National income				(3) Cost of living			
	1934	1935	1936	1937	1934	1935	1936	1937	1934	1935	1936	1937
I. Main and 'exclusive' British markets:												
Sweden	+10	+23	+35	+49	+2	+3	+10	+24	−9	−7	−5	−2
Denmark	+17	+25	+30	+36	+4	+10	+14	+19	−4	−1	+1	+5
Finland	+17	+25	+39	+56	−2	+3	+16	+40	−20	−19	−19	−14
South Africa[1]	+21	+44	+67	+92	+17	+28	+44	+46	−12	−12	−12	−10
New Zealand[2]	+20	+21	+29	+26	−14	−2	+16	+26	−19	−17	−14	−8
Australia[2]	[3]	[3]	[3]	[3]	−12	−1	+8	+14	−20	−19	−17	−15
II. Main and 'exclusive' American markets:												
Chile	+5	+20	+24	+32	[3]	[3]	[3]	[3]	+30	+32	+44	+62
Mexico	+2	+6	+13	+24	[3]	[3]	[3]	[3]	[3]	[3]	[3]	[3]
Canada	−14	−6	+6	+16	−40	−34	−26	−16	−22	−21	−19	−17

[1] Fiscal year ended 31 March of the following year.
[2] Fiscal year ended 30 June.
[3] Not available.

64

'exclusive' markets in the western hemisphere, which in the pre-Depression years absorbed nearly two-fifths of total American exports, showed slower and less complete recovery: and, consequently, American exports failed to maintain their position in the world total. The disparity in economic activity in the two groups of markets stands out clearly in Table 14.

In addition, most of the Latin-American countries, besides exchange depreciation, adopted direct control of trade, which was frequently so administered as to limit imports from U.S.A.

TABLE 15. *Comparison of the values of American and British exports to their respective markets*

	American exports to		British exports to	
	(1) 'Exclusive' markets*	(2) Rest of the world	(1) Empire countries	(2) Foreign countries
1929	100	100	100	100
1933	23·5	31·1	49·2	50·0
1934	33·5	43·0	57·2	51·8
1935	36·5	47·7	63·0	54·8
1936	42·4	49·5	66·8	55·3
1937	59·9	66·3	77·6	66·7

* Constructed on the basis of Table 8. Sources: *Statistical Abstract of the U.S.A.* and *Annual Statements of Trade of the U.K.*

and to favour purchases from other countries;[1] whereas, on the other hand, thanks to the Imperial Preference, the U.K. was able to increase her exports to the Empire countries. Table 15 is constructed for illustration.

[1] U.S. Department of Commerce, *The United States in the World Economy*, pp. 194–5.

CHAPTER IV

WORLD DEMAND FOR EXPORTS (*cont.*)

PRICE ELASTICITY OF SUBSTITUTION[1]

§ I

In the classical theory of international trade, it is generally assumed that the price elasticity of world demand for a single country's exports is very high so that any country, by lowering its export prices by a small fraction, would be able to attract to itself a considerable part of its competitors' market. Moreover, this is perhaps the most common view held by economists in their current discussion of the problem of exchangerates. It is therefore the purpose of this chapter to inquire whether this view can be verified by looking into the statistical data of the inter-war period.

---

[1] After this chapter had been completed, there appeared in the *Review of Economic Statistics* an interesting article discussing the same problem by Prof. J. Tinbergen. ('Some Measurements of Elasticities of Substitution', in the issue of August 1946.) The aspects of the problem he has studied are different from what are to be discussed in the present chapter (except §§ IV and VI). One of his measurements concerns 'quota elasticity'. In application, he has calculated the regression coefficient of 'the ratio of the quantum index of exports of the given country to the quantum index of world trade' on 'the ratio of that country's price index of exports to the price index of world trade'. This procedure would not seem justifiable, because the variations in the 'quantum ratio' cannot be *entirely* accounted for by those in the 'price ratio'. During the cyclical fluctuations, the variations in the 'quantum ratio' reflect also the influence of changes in world income demand. Because the relative composition of a given country's exports is different from that of the exports of all countries, there is bound to be a shift in the distribution of quantity of exports between different countries as a result of the world income change. Moreover, this shift would still take place, even if the prices all over the world remain unchanged. Take the example of an agricultural country. During a period of world economic expansion, its index of export quantity tends to rise less than the world index. As a matter of fact, this is not only due to the more violent rise of its price index relative to the world index, but also to the unfavourable cyclical shift against agricultural countries in the distribution of quantity of world exports in boom. (Vide supra, Chapter III, § II.) Some impression of the order of magnitude of the bias in Tinbergen's elasticities can be found from the League of Nations' index numbers for the quantum and prices of foodstuffs, raw materials and manufactured goods. Tinbergen's correlations are, on the whole, rather poor and his results are, it would seem, almost completely determined by the relative fall of

The results of our statistical calculations, as shown in Table 6, do not seem to confirm this view. The price elasticity of world demand for a single country's *total* exports tends in general to be less than unity. It is only in unimportant cases of very small agricultural countries such as Estonia, Latvia, etc., that we find that the changes in their export quantities are elastic with respect to the changes in their respective export prices. However, on *a priori* grounds, the fact of low price elasticity of world demand may be explained by three reasons. First, analogous to the prevailing state of affairs in the internal markets, competition in the international markets is imperfect, owing to traditional trading connections, the ignorance of home consumers about world supply conditions, special preference to the exports of a particular country, etc. Secondly, the total exports of one country can never be perfect substitutes for those of another country in the world market, even if as a whole they belong to the same economic class. A rise in Danish export prices may decrease the world demand for Danish butter and bacon and induce increasing purchases of Argentine meat instead; but it is unlikely that such substitution between not exactly similar goods can be very intensive. Moreover, the less homogeneous the exports of two countries are, the less intensive the substitution between them in the world market. For instance, if export

the various indices from 1929 to the depression low. Taking for the latter the average of the years 1933 and 1937, we find the following index numbers:

	(1929 = 100) Quantum	Price
Foodstuffs	88·5	46
Raw materials	98	44·5
Manufactured goods	74	53·5
Total trade	86	47·5

From these figures follow these quasi-elasticities of substitution for the trade of all countries exporting each of these three types of commodities:

Countries exporting foodstuffs: $\dfrac{47\cdot5}{86} \times \dfrac{2\cdot5}{-1\cdot5} = -0\cdot9$

Countries exporting raw materials: $\dfrac{47\cdot5}{86} \times \dfrac{12}{-3} = -2\cdot2$

Countries exporting manufactured good: $\dfrac{47\cdot5}{86} \times \dfrac{-12\cdot5}{6} = -1\cdot1.$

Thus Tinbergen's elasticities would appear to be at least of the order of -1 too large.

prices of an agricultural country rise, the substitution of exports of an industrial country will be very limited. Thirdly, the size of the share in the total world exports of a particular country also influences the value of the price elasticity of world demand for its exports. Comparing a larger country in the world trade with a smaller one with exports of broadly the same character, we may expect the elasticity for the larger country to be lower. It is likely that the value will tend to be less than unity. The reason is analogous to the comparison of the market of a single firm with that of an industry. Moreover, even for a smaller country, if its exports are concentrated in a given market and are the main source of supply in it, the value of the price elasticity cannot be expected to be large.

§ II

So far we have been trying to find (1) the 'aggregate' price elasticity of world demand for *total* exports of a single country, and (2) the proportionate change in the *absolute* quantity of exports of a country associated with a proportionate change in the relative level of home export prices to competitors' export prices. Now, let us look at the same problem again from another angle. It may be interesting to calculate the value of the price elasticity of substitution between two commodities or two groups of commodities in the world market, as supplied by two different countries. In the simplest case of two commodities or two groups of commodities, the price elasticity of substitution is defined as the ratio of the proportionate change in relative quantities of exports to the proportionate change in relative prices of exports. We may put this concept into symbols. Let q_1 and q_2 be the quantities demanded, and p_1 and p_2 be the corresponding prices; then[1]

Price elasticity of substitution

$$= \frac{d\,(q_1/q_2)}{q_1/q_2} \div \frac{d\,(p_1/p_2)}{p_1/p_2} = \frac{d\,(q_1/q_2)}{d\,(p_1/p_2)} \times \frac{p_1/p_2}{q_1/q_2}.$$

To get a numerical value for the price elasticity of substi-

---

[1] J. R. Hicks and R. G. D. Allen, 'A Reconsideration of the Theory of Value', *Economica*, May 1935; also R. G. D. Allen, in *Mathematical Analysis for Economists*.

tution in the simple case of two homogeneous commodities a simple regression equation of the form:

$$\log (q_1/q_2) = -a \log (p_1/p_2)$$

is used.[1] The regression coefficient is the required elasticity. But in the case of two groups of commodities of broadly similar character, the change in the ratio of relative quantities reflects also the difference between the income elasticities of demand for them; therefore, we have to eliminate this effect. Accordingly, the regression equation becomes:

$$\log (q_1/q_2) = -a \log (p_1/p_2) + b \log I,$$

where I is the real income in a given market.

In the following, we shall inquire into the price substitution (1) between exports of a broadly similar character of two countries in the world market; (2) between completely homogeneous exports of two countries in the world market; (3) between completely homogeneous exports of two countries in a given market; and (4) between imports and similar home-produced goods in the home market.

§ III

The first illustration of the elasticity of substitution is provided by considering the case in which two countries compete in the world market with goods belonging to the same economic class. Here, as distinct from the case of homogeneous goods, the substitution is remote and imperfect. However, it takes place in the form of competition for purchasing power in the world market. For instance, a rise in the prices of American refrigerators may drive away world demand in favour of buying, say, more British wireless sets. If Canadian cheese becomes dearer, world demand may shift to Danish butter or Irish meat.

For the purpose of illustration, we choose (1) the exports from two industrial countries, and (2) the exports from two agricultural countries. For the former, we compare the price-substitution between British and American exports and British and Swedish exports, as shown in Fig. 5 A and B.[2] For the latter,

---

[1] Trends of the series are eliminated.

[2] Prices are reduced in terms of sterling; and the income effect has been eliminated. The series are deviations from their respective trends.

the substitutions between Argentina, Australia, Denmark, Eire and New Zealand are studied and shown in C, D, E and F.[1] From the diagram, it can be seen that, although the correlation is generally low, there are traces of negative correlation between the proportionate changes in the relative quantities and prices for the period as a whole. The elasticities for the individual cases have been calculated as follows.

TABLE 16. *Elasticity of substitution of total exports from two countries**

		Elasticity
I. Manufactured goods:		
	A. U.K./U.S.A.†	−0·30
	B. Sweden/U.K.	−0·87
II. Agricultural produce:		
	C. Eire/Australia	−0·33
	D. Denmark/Australia	−0·42
	E. New Zealand/Australia	−0·25
	F. Argentina/Australia	−0·76

Industrial countries		Agricultural countries	
U.S.A.	15·4 %	Argentina	3·0 %
U.K.	10·8	Australia	2·2
Sweden	1·4	Denmark	1·3
		New Zealand	0·8
		Eire	0·7

* The share of each country's exports in world total (average value, 1927-9).
† For U.S.A. the indices of semi-manufactures and manufactured goods only are used.

Owing to the limited number of cases we have treated, it would seem dangerous to draw any definite conclusions based upon these statistical results. But, in general, the low price elasticity of substitution may be explained by two facts. First, in reality, the total exports of two countries, even if they are more or less of the same character, do not provide perfect substitutes for each other in the world market; and, therefore, their substitution should not be intensive with respect to price changes. Secondly, 'world market' is an ambiguous notion. As a matter of fact, each country has its own 'exclusive' markets; and exports of similar goods of other countries do not compete with home exports everywhere in the world. Conse-

[1] For all these countries, export prices in gold are used. Trends of all these series are eliminated.

quently, when the total exports of two countries are considered, the change in their relative prices may not bring about a large change in their relative quantities. Therefore, in order to get a clearer picture of the price elasticity of substitution, we should consider homogeneous exports from two countries and also their competition in a common specified market.

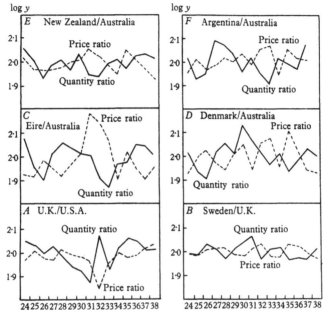

Fig. 5. Comparison of price elasticities of substitution between two groups of commodities in the world market

§ IV

We now consider price substitution in the *world* market between homogeneous staple commodities exported from any two countries. Here, we choose wool, butter and cheese.

Australia, New Zealand, and South Africa are the world's most important wool exporters; therefore, we study the price substitution for their export quantities. For butter, we choose New Zealand and Denmark; and, for cheese, Canada and New Zealand. With trend eliminated, the indices of quantity ratio are compared with their respective indices of price ratio in

TABLE 17. *Elasticity of substitution between staple exports of two countries in the world market*

	Correlation coefficient	Elasticity
I. *Wool**		
South Africa/New Zealand	−0·60	−1·30
South Africa/Australia	−0·78	−1·10
Australia/New Zealand	−0·73	−0·69
II. *Butter†*		
New Zealand/Denmark	−0·67	−1·35
III. *Cheese‡*		
Canada/New Zealand	−0·59	−1·32

* *Wool.* Export quantities of these countries are taken from their respective Official Year-books. New Zealand Year-book provides also the index of export price of wool. For South Africa, the index of export price is compiled by weighting the export prices (pence per lb.) of various years by the actual export quantity in 1930. For Australia, we use the average market price per lb. of greasy and scoured wool and the export quantity of 1929/30 as weight.

† *Butter.* Export quantities of these countries are taken from their respective Year-books. The prices are average annual wholesale price per lb. in Denmark and New Zealand, as given in *Agricultural Statistics* of various years.

‡ *Cheese.* For New Zealand, average wholesale price per lb. of full-cream cheese in New Zealand is used. For Canada, we use export price.

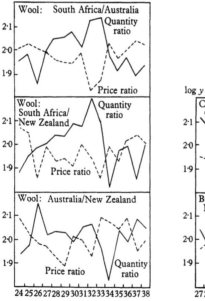
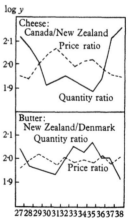

Fig. 6. Comparison of price elasticities of substitution of staple goods in the world market

Fig. 6. A fairly high degree of negative correlation between the variations in quantity ratio and those in price ratio is present in each case. Any change in the relative prices of homogeneous staple exports of two countries therefore leads to substitution between them in the world market. The numerical values of the price elasticities of substitution are given in Table 17.

As compared with the results in Table 16, the correlation coefficients are much improved. This is what is expected, because the demand tends in general to react more sensitively to variation in the prices of homogeneous goods exported by different countries, than to variation in the prices of broadly similar goods. Moreover, the price elasticity of substitution is generally greater than unity; but, contrary to the generally accepted view, it is not very high. In the case in which the two suppliers are nearly equally important in the world market, the elasticity should tend to be low. This is illustrated by the wool exports from New Zealand and Australia.[1]

§ V

It is also possible to calculate the price elasticity of substitution between homogeneous staple exports of two countries in a *given* market. The results of calculations are given in Table 18.

When homogeneous and standardised commodities compete in a given market and there is no special trade discrimination against either of them, the price elasticity of substitution between them tends to be very high; and so is the correlation coefficient. Moreover, in the case of a particular commodity, the difference in the size of the elasticities would seem to suggest that the relative size of different suppliers in the given market is important. The smaller the supplier in a given market, the larger the price substitution for its competitors' similar exports; and conversely. For instance, in the case of butter, the average ratio of the amount supplied by Denmark and that by New Zealand in the British market for the whole period is approximately equal to one; whereas the Dutch supply amounts only to about 15% of either. We find, therefore, that the price substitution of Dutch

---

[1] For the period under investigation, the average ratio of the amount of wool exported from New Zealand to that from Australia is about 75%. (See *Official Year-book of Australia* and *Official Year-book of New Zealand*, various years.)

TABLE 18. *Elasticity of substitution between homogeneous staple exports of two countries in a given market*

	Correlation coefficient	Elasticity
A. IN THE BRITISH MARKET:		
I. Butter[1]:		
Denmark/New Zealand	−0·73	−2·84
Netherlands/Denmark	−0·69	−4·11
Netherlands/New Zealand	−0·71	−4·67
II. Wheat[2]:		
Argentina/Canada	−0·87	−5·04
Australia/Canada	−0·83	−4·18
Argentina/Australia	−0·82	−5·80
Uruguay/Canada	−0·74	−6·30
III. Raw Cotton (except linters)[3]:		
Brazil/U.S.A.	−0·80	−1·71
Egypt/U.S.A.	−0·73	−1·45
B. IN THE INDIAN MARKET:		
I. Cotton Piece Goods[4, 5]:		
Japan/U.K.	−0·81	−1·94
C. IN THE CHINESE MARKET:		
I. Cotton Piece Goods[6, 7]:		
Japan/U.K.	−0·87	−2·31

[1] The quantities imported into the U.K. from the countries under investigation are obtained from the *Annual Statement of Trade of the United Kingdom* of various years. The prices are calculated by dividing the imported value in a given year by the respective quantity.

[2] *Annual Statement.* The prices are unit values of imports.

[3] Quantities are obtained from the *Annual Statements*. The prices are obtained from Agricultural Statistics of various years.

[4] Quantities and unit values are obtained from the *Annual Trade Returns of India* of various years.

[5] Because British cotton piece goods are generally of higher quality than Japanese cotton piece goods, the income elasticities of Indian demand for them are different. Therefore, we have to eliminate the change in the relative quantities caused by income change. For our purpose we use the index of quantity of total imports as the best available representative of real income in India.

[6] The indices of quantity and price are obtained from the Chinese *Customs' Report* of various years.

[7] The index of quantity of total imports is used as the best available representative of real income in China.

butter for both Danish and New Zealand butter is much more intensive than the price substitution between the latter two supplies. Moreover, it is also interesting to find that the price substitution between Danish and New Zealand butter in a given market is more intense[1] than that in the world market, as shown in Table 17.

[1] That is, a higher regression coefficient.

In the case of wheat, as Uruguay supplies only about 3% of what Canada supplies in the British market, the price substitution between Canadian and Uruguayan exporters is accordingly very high.

As Brazil and Egypt supply, on the average of the period, respectively 20 and 27% of the cotton imported into the U.K. by the U.S.A., therefore the price elasticity of substitution between Brazilian and American cotton or between Egyptian and American cotton tends to be larger than unity. But the absolute values are relatively low. This may be explained by the fact that products of different countries are not equally suitable for various industrial uses.

When unequal income demand for British and Japanese cotton piece goods in a given market has been eliminated statistically, we find that the change in the relative prices will induce a more than proportionate change in relative quantities. This is illustrated by the Indian and Chinese demands.

§ VI

When there are home-produced goods similar to the imports, the price elasticity of substitution will tend to be high. This is illustrated by the British demand for cotton manufactures, for motor-cars, and for iron and steel manufactures.

TABLE 19. *Elasticity of substitution between British imports and home-produced goods*

British imports/British home-produced goods:	Correlation coefficient	Elasticity
1. Cotton yarns and manufactures*	−0·79	−3·54
2. Motor-cars†	−0·70	−2·62
3. Iron and steel manufactures‡	−0·64	−1·50

* The import prices have been corrected for tariff changes. The indices of home output and home prices are taken from Mr Hsu's unpublished dissertation. Because imported cotton manufactures are generally low-quality goods, we have eliminated the different income effects on the relative quantities.

† For 1929–38 only. The index for home output is obtained from Society of Motor Manufacturers and Traders, 'The Motor Industry of Great Britain': and 1938 figures from 'Commercial History and Review of 1938', *Economist*, 12 February 1939. The index includes private cars, taxis, commercial vehicles and omnibuses. The price index relates to private cars only.

‡ The indices relating to home production are obtained from Mr Tew's unpublished dissertation (in Cambridge University Library).

§ VII

Two conclusions may be drawn from the foregoing discussion.

(1) Between the total exports of broadly similar goods of two countries, the price substitution in the world market is in general less than elastic: and, statistically, it is not possible to obtain a good linear relation between the logarithms. The main reason seems to be the imperfect substitution between the total exports of any two countries.

(2) When the cases of homogeneous and standardised commodities competing in the world market are studied, the correlation coefficients are much improved: and the elasticities tend to be larger than unity. Moreover, the price substitutions are very intensive for homogeneous commodities competing in a given market. In general, the differences in the elasticities of different suppliers seem to reflect the relative size of a particular supplier in the given market.

§ VIII

From our statistical measurement of the price elasticities of home and foreign demand, we are now able to see the effect of exchange depreciation upon the balance of trade of the home country.

It is a well-known proposition that the effect of exchange depreciation upon the balance of trade tends to be neutral when the sum of the price elasticities of home and foreign demand is equal to unity.[1] In other words, the value unity for the sum of the elasticities is the critical value for the effect of exchange depreciation.[2]

[1] J. Robinson, op. cit. pp. 142–3; also A. P. Lerner, *The Economics of Control*, pp. 378–9.

[2] Strictly speaking, this proposition is true only in the simplest case where trade is balanced in the first instance and the elasticities of home and of foreign supply are both infinite. This critical value would be affected if these two conditions were not fulfilled. When trade is unbalanced, this critical value becomes greater or less than unity, according as the value of imports is greater or less than the value of exports. Whereas, on the other hand, the less-than-infinite supplies *slightly* reduce this critical value (except in the limiting case where both income and foreign supplies are perfectly inelastic). In reality, as the ratio of import to export value is not greatly different, the critical value would, therefore, not be much affected. In practical discussion, we may still use unity as the best approximation to the 'true' critical value.

The actual values of the sum of two elasticities for nineteen countries are as follows:

	Import price elasticity	Export price elasticity	Sum
Latvia	−0·48	−1·84−	−2·32
Canada	−1·34	−0·35	−1·69
Hungary	−0·54	−1·10−	−1·64
Estonia	−0·34	−1·29	−1·63
Finland	−0·25	−1·23	−1·48
Norway	−0·86	−0·62	−1·48
U.S.A.	−0·97	−0·43	−1·40
Australia	−0·67	−0·66	−1·33
France	−0·32	−0·77	−1·09
Denmark	−0·63	−0·45	−1·08
Italy	−0·27	−0·81	−1·08
Japan	−0·47	−0·60	−1·07
Germany	−0·37	−0·58	−0·95
South Africa	−0·64	−0·31	−0·95
New Zealand	−0·34	−0·52	−0·86
Sweden	−0·37	−0·36	−0·73
U.K.	−0·28	−0·53	−0·71
Switzerland	−0·26	−0·44	−0·70
Chile	−0·32	−0·17	−0·49

Assuming that these calculated elasticities approximate to the 'true' elasticities, some generalizations may be drawn. It can be seen that for a majority of countries the sum of the two elasticities stands not far above or below the critical value; therefore, the effect of exchange depreciation upon their balances of trade would generally tend to be very small. In some cases where the sum of the two elasticities is well below unity, exchange depreciation would even worsen the balance of trade. Those countries at the head of the table would tend to experience a favourable change in their balances of trade on account of exchange depreciation. But they are international debtors having interest payments fixed in terms of the creditors' currencies. These payments are equivalent to imports of perfectly inelastic demand, and their values rise in proportion to the fall of exchange rates. Consequently, the favourable change in the balance of trade may be cancelled by the unfavourable change in the invisible items, so that their income accounts as a whole remain unchanged or even become unfavourable.

Two further points may be made. First, as has been shown, the price elasticities of substitution between similar goods in a particular market generally tend to be high. Therefore, a country whose balance of trade becomes less favourable as a

77

result of exchange depreciation, may find its balance of trade *vis-à-vis* a particular country improved.

Secondly, the price elasticities from our calculations probably remain constant only within the range of the actual observations; beyond this they would be expected to change. A very *sharp* depreciation may not necessarily have a perverse effect upon a country's balance of trade. Indeed, a favourable result could be expected. The price elasticity of foreign demand tends to become even smaller as the result of a large decrease in the exchange rate; whereas, on the import side, the demand tends to become more elastic. In the limit where the import prices become too high, the quantity of imports may fall to zero. Therefore, at some *low* level of the exchange rate, the sum of the two elasticities rises above the critical value; and a deficit on the balance of trade can be wiped out at the expense of very unfavourable terms of trade.

CHAPTER V

FLUCTUATIONS IN EXPORTS AND NATIONAL INCOME

§ I

As has been shown in Chapter I, fluctuations in the value of the total exports of a country in an open system are equivalent to those in home investment in determining its national income. When actual data are studied, we find that it plays the crucial part in two types of economy. The first type is agricultural, where home production, being closely dependent upon local peculiarities of soil and climate, is concentrated to a very high degree on one or a few staple agricultural products. Since the level of home investment is generally low, the home national income is predominantly determined by the value of the exports of such staples. Similar to these agricultural countries are those mining countries which supply the world with a special kind of mineral products. The importance of agricultural staples or mining products in the total exports of this type of country can be gauged from the following comparison.

TABLE 20. *Percentage share of certain staple commodities in total exports of agricultural and mining countries (percentages related to 1929)* *

Countries	Commodities	Total exports (%)
Chile	Nitrate and copper	83
Egypt	Raw cotton	80
Cuba	Sugar	75
Brazil	Coffee	71
Finland	Timber	70
British Malaya	Rubber and tin	66
Greece	Tobacco	57
South Africa	Diamonds and gold	54
Argentina	Wheat and maize	47
Australia	Wool	40
Mexico	Copper, lead and zinc	40
New Zealand	Cheese and butter	37

* *International Trade Statistics*, 1930.

79

CYCLICAL MOVEMENTS IN THE BALANCE OF PAYMENTS

Demand for agricultural products is liable to cyclical shifts, because of variations in income, working stocks and speculative inventories in the industrial countries. But, as shown in Table 6, the cyclical change in the quantity of total exports of agricultural countries tends, in general, to be inelastic with respect to a cyclical change in world income. Or, in other words, the quantity of agricultural exports as a whole is cyclically more stable than the quantity of other commodities also entering into international trade. But, through another channel fluctuations in world income generally exert a severe influence upon the agricultural countries. Because of the low elasticity of supply of agricultural countries in general, a small variation in the demand tends to produce a violent change in export price. As a result, the values of agricultural exports fluctuate violently between prosperity and depression. In the case of mining countries, export quantities, as well as export prices, fluctuate violently during a world trade cycle. Therefore, the cyclical change in the export value of mining countries may even be greater than that of purely agricultural countries.

TABLE 21. *Exports, farming income and total national income in New Zealand**

	(1) Export quantity	(2) Export value	(3) Gross farming income	(4) % of gross farming income obtained from exports†	(5) Total national income
1928/29 (base)	100	100	100	63	100
1929/30	101	84	88	62	96
1930/31	106	66	68	61	86
1931/32	113	62	60	65	77
1932/33	134	67	60	66	73
1933/34	137	88	76	69	76
1934/35	122	76	72	70	86
1935/36	134	94	91	70	95
1936/37	140	115	111	70	112
1937/38	134	110	106	69	121

* All the indices are taken from Official Year-books of various years.
† The average of 1928/29–1929/30, etc.

The income of export industries in these countries usually bears a high percentage to their national income; and, moreover, it is also the income of the export industries which tends to change constantly and violently. Any cyclical change in the value of exports directly influences the income of export industries which will in turn bring the total national income into line. Their relationship may be illustrated with the case of New Zealand (Table 21), where the various data required are available.

A comparison of columns (1) and (2) reveals that the cyclical variations in the export value are more influenced by the changes in export prices than by the export quantity. When the index of the value of exports is compared with that of gross farming income, we find that there is a very high correlation between them. Not only does the direction of their fluctuations tend to agree throughout this period, but the amplitude is not much different. The closeness of the fluctuations in the two series is undoubtedly due to the high percentage of gross farming income derived from exports, as shown by the figures in column (4). For the period under investigation, the average ratio of farming income to the total national income in New Zealand reaches a level as high as two-fifths. Therefore, as a result of a change in farming income due to a change in export value, the level of total national income will also be affected. The correlation between total national income and farming income is also high; but, in some years the direction of their changes does not agree. This fact, *inter alia*, points out that the fluctuations in the export value, though playing the crucial part in determining the national income of New Zealand, is not the only factor; or, in other words, the level of home investment, though generally low, also has a bearing on the problem in question.

The second type of country, in which the fluctuation in the value of exports also plays a crucial part in determining the national income, are some industrial countries. On the one hand, analogous to the agricultural and mining countries just discussed, there are some industrial countries whose home production, owing to historical development or natural environment, is concentrated in certain specified manufactures designed for exports; and whose national incomes are therefore very sensitive to the cyclical change in exports. Belgium may be chosen as an example. On the other hand, there are industrial countries whose home production is diversified; but if the activities in the export industries bear a high percentage to the total activities of the home country, the fluctuations in exports are still very important. This is exactly the case of the U.K.

It may be useful to compare the cyclical fluctuations in export value and those in national income for different countries in a diagrammatic form. This is done in Fig. 7. A glance at the diagram reveals that their cyclical relationship is close. Moreover, in the cases of New Zealand, Canada and Australia, the troughs of the index of value of exports occurred before the troughs as shown in their respective income indices. This fact can be interpreted as meaning that the values of exports are the main determinant of the respective national incomes in these countries, and the fluctuations in them tend to lead those in national income. This is what should be expected.

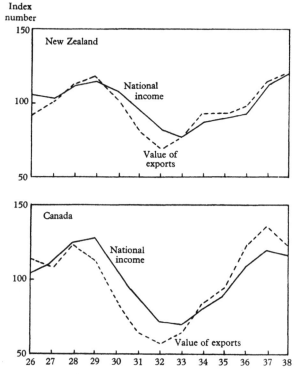

Fig. 7 a. Cyclical relationship between value of exports and national income

Moreover, the comparison also reveals that the two series do not always agree. This would suggest that the fluctuations in home investment may be used to account for the discrepancies.

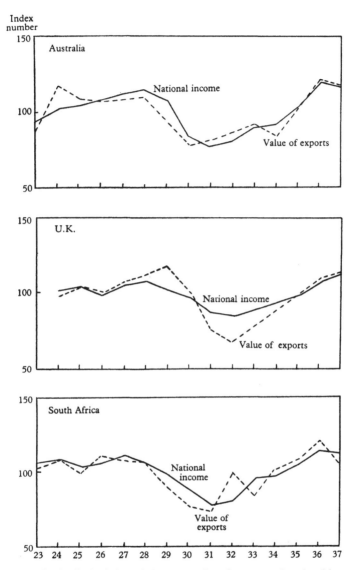

Fig. 7 *b*. Cyclical relationship between value of exports and national income

Two obvious cases can be cited. First, the British index of income tends to lie above the index of total export value in the recovery period of the 'thirties. This is clearly due to the relatively high level of home investment by the building industries. Secondly, in the case of Canada, the income index lies above the export index before 1933, whereas their relationship is just the reverse after that. This, however, may be explained by the fact that there had been very heavy industrial investments in Canada before the depression and, in the 'thirties, the Canadian industries tended to be using up this excess capacity.

The crude comparisons, though being able to suggest the relationship between exports and income, do not provide a precise measurement for it. In the following section we shall attempt to make statistical measurement of the 'foreign-trade-multiplier'.

§ II

Let us take the case of Canada in which the index of home investment is reliable.[1] In his article 'Exports and National Income in Canada',[2] Mr Munzer has estimated statistically the export multiplier for Canada for the period 1923–39. He concludes that, on the average over this period, an export of one dollar in year n was followed by a national income received of 3·8 dollars in year $n+1$. This size of export multiplier would seem too high for any country in an open system. It is especially so in the case of Canada, as she was much dependent upon import trade.

Undoubtedly, the high numerical result is due to Mr Munzer's attempt to account for the changes in Canadian national income *entirely* by the fluctuations in the value of exports. As a matter of fact, in the period under investigation, home investment was also an important factor in determining Canadian national income. Although the absolute level of home investment was much lower than that of exports, the size of the year-to-year fluctuations of the former was as great as that for the latter. This fact can be seen in Table 22.

In order to facilitate comparisons, two diagrams are shown below. In Fig. 8 national income is plotted against the value

---

[1] With some additions and slight verbal alterations, this section is taken from my article, 'A Note on Exports and Income in Canada' in the *Canadian Journal of Economics and Political Science*, May 1947.

[2] The *Canadian Journal of Economics and Political Science*, February 1945.

of exports: and in Fig. 9 national income is correlated with net home investment. The trend of these series has been eliminated. It can be seen from Fig. 8 that, in spite of a high correlation between income and exports, the deviations of the observed

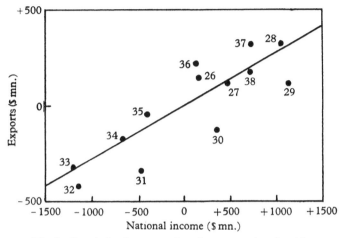

Fig. 8. Correlation between value of exports and national income
(deviations from trend)

TABLE 22. *Canadian national income value of exports and home investment (in millions of dollars)*

Year	(1) Money, national income*	(2) Value of exports, including non- monetary gold†	(3) Net home investment‡
1926	4,494	1,291·2	958
1927	4,682	1,242·6	1,094
1928	5,138	1,379·4	1,312
1929	5,149	1,189·4	1,224
1930	4,326	902·7	1,256
1931	3,498	644·7	750
1932	2,893	559·9	396
1933	2,795	611·5	145
1934	3,171	763·7	421
1935	3,381	844·0	508
1936	3,829	1,069·8	420
1937	4,342	1,142·4	818
1938	4,246	998·6	886

* Canada's *Year-book*, 1941.
† Dominion Bureau of Statistics, *The Canadian Balance of International Payments. A Study.*
‡ Excluding maintenance and repairs. Dominion-Provincial Conference on Reconstruction, *Public Expenditure and Capital Formation*, table 1 a.

values from the fitted line are not at all random. In other words, the value of exports may not have been the only factor affecting the Canadian national income during the cyclical fluctuations in the inter-war period. Our expectation is, however, confirmed, if we take into consideration the relationship between income and home investment as given in Fig. 9. A comparison reveals that, in a particular year, when the actual level of income stood

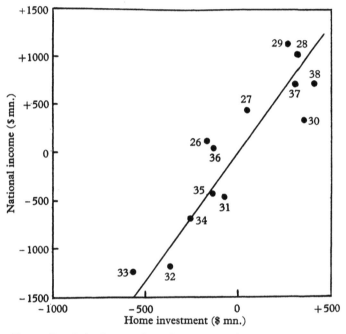

Fig. 9. Correlation between home investment and national income
(deviations from trend)

above that as indicated by the income-export equation, the volume of net home investment was larger than that as deduced from the income-investment equation. For example, in the year 1931, the actual income level was higher than the theoretical value which would have been associated with the given value of exports in that year, and lay to the right of the fitted line in Fig. 8—this is because the actual investment was larger than its corresponding theoretical value given by the line fitted in Fig. 9. The converse is also true and it may be illustrated by the case of 1926. Moreover, when a year falls on the regression line in one diagram, it also shows a coincidence on the other. The year 1934 is a good example. There are exceptions to these generalisations. But, since during the trade cycle the value of exports and home investment tend to move in the same direction, we may conclude that home investment had been also a factor in determining Canadian national income in the interwar period.

The true magnitude of the multiplier can be determined by partial correlation analysis. Let x_1 be the money national income; x_2 the value of exports, and x_3 the net home investment. Then the partial regression coefficients of x_1 on x_2 or x_3 indicate the required multiplier. The regression equation is

$$x_1 = 1 \cdot 452 \ x_2 + 1 \cdot 438 \ x_3,$$

with multiple correlation coefficient equal to 0·956. As expected, the two regression coefficients are nearly equal; and they denote that, in the period 1926–38, an increase of one dollar either in exports or in home investment was, on the average, followed by an increase in Canadian income of 1·4 dollars.

Moreover, in his article, Mr Munzer has assumed the temporal relationship between export and income in the case of Canada is one year, i.e. a change in the export in the year n will bring about a change in national income in the year $n + 1$. It is difficult to conceive of any type of country in which the multiplier effect will take such a long time to work out. Mr Munzer's assumption, therefore, seems unrealistic. The average timelag between investment (home and foreign) and income changes in the case of Canada can also be determined by statistical calculations.

In Fig. 10 national income figures are plotted against net home investment plus value of exports, with all trends eliminated. To these scatter points a regression line is fitted, as denoted by II'. Then, by treating 1926–8 as a triennium and both 1932–3 and 1937–8 as biennia, the points are joined together in chronological order. It can be seen that they form a polygon and rotate regularly around the line II' in a clockwise direction. This means that there is a time-lag between total investment and national income: and the line II' represents the approximate relation between total investments in a given period and the induced income at a later time. For instance, corresponding to the actual investment in 1935, the theoretical induced income is measured by the abscissa of the point I_c on the

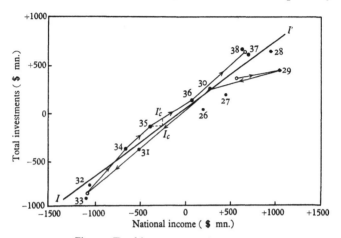

Fig. 10. Total investment and national income

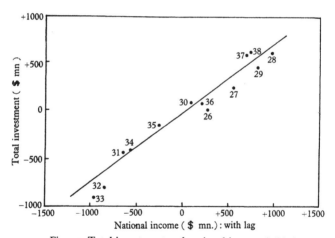

Fig. 11. Total investment and national income (with lag)

line II'. But, as given by I'_c on the polygon, the theoretical income will be realised at a date between 1935 and 1936. On the average, it appears that the time-lag is about one-quarter. Thus, in order to know the correlation between present total investment and the induced income one-quarter hence, we pair off the sum of three-quarters of income in 1926 and one-quarter of the income in 1927 with the total investment in 1926; and so on. The points are plotted in Fig. 11, and a regression line is then fitted. The deviations of the observed value from the fitted line are now relatively less than those in Fig. 10. The slope, or the multiplier, is about 1·5, which is in conformity with the former result obtained by partial correlation analysis.

TABLE 23. *Fluctuations of total investment in durable physical assets in different industries**

Year	(1) Agriculture, mines and wood operation, percentage change as compared with 1926	(2) All other industries percentage change as compared with 1926	(3) Percentage of (1) in total investment
1927	+22	+13	13·6
1928	+57	+35	14·5
1929	+49	+65	11·7
1930	+24	+45	11·1
1931	−45	+ 5	7·0
1932	−63	−41	8·3
1933	−70	−59	9·5
1934	−54	−47	11·1
1935	−37	−38	12·9
1936	−25	−27	13·0
1937	− 4	+ 6	11·7
1938	+ 1	− 4	13·7

* Dominion-Provincial Conference on Reconstruction, *Public Expenditure and Capital Formation*, tables 1 *a* and 1 *b*.

We have shown that, from the point of view of statistical analysis, both the net home investment and the value of exports should be used as determinants of the value of the Canadian multiplier. Attention should, however, be drawn to the fact that some part of Canadian home investment is *directly* dependent upon the condition of her exports. This point comes out clearly, if we look at the distribution of the investment and not just totals. As can be seen from Table 23, the variations in the physical investment in her main export industries, i.e. agriculture, mines and wood operations, generally reflect the variations in her value of exports; and, consequently its amplitude tends to be larger than that in other industries.

Comparison of figures in columns (1) and (2) reveals that their fluctuations show contrary movements in some years, and the amplitude of fluctuations is also different. This is because the physical investment in agricultural, mining and wood industries are more directly affected by the cyclical fluctuations in exports than that in other industries. For instance, in 1929, when Canadian exports began to fall, investment of durable physical assets in the former was lower than in 1928; whereas, on the other hand, investment in the latter still showed increase. As exports fell very sharply during the Great Depression, so did investment in these three industries. But investment did not fall so much in other industries; and, in 1931, it was maintained even above the 1926 level.

Because of more violent fluctuations, investment in agricultural, mining and wood industries does not bear a constant ratio to total investment during cyclical fluctuations. As shown in column (3), the ratio tended to rise in the prosperous twenties and to fall in the slump.

§ III

In contrast to agricultural countries or to some industrial countries, the value of exports bears a very low percentage to total American national income; and consequently the fluctuations in the value of exports do not play a very important part in determining the cyclical change in American income. But there are certain peculiarities concerning exports and income which deserve attention.

In Fig. 12A, the value of commodity exports is correlated with American national income, both with trend eliminated. The dots do not rotate, as in the case of Canada, consistently in a clockwise manner along the fitted theoretical line; and, moreover, as from 1934 to 1938, they tend to rotate counter-clockwise. The fact of counter-clockwise rotation would seem to mean that a reverse relationship existed between American exports and national income. That is, the value of American exports was determined by American income. For instance, corresponding to the actual level of exports in 1936 (as measured by the Y-axis), the theoretical value of American national income would have been N on the fitted line. But N was equal to the actual income N', which had already been realised some time between 1935 and 1936. *Prima facie*, this sounds absurd.

However, there were factual grounds for believing that such a reverse relationship could have happened. It is true that the world demand for American exports was determined by the level of the world income; but, as the U.S.A. is large in the world economy, the level of world income might, *inter alia*, have been determined by the supply of dollars by her to the world, that is, by her demand for imports, associated with her economic activity at home. Thus, when American business was on

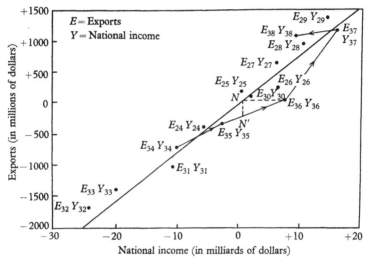

Fig. 12 A. Value of exports and national income

the upswing, her demand for imports and, hence, her supply of dollars to the world increased; and, as a result, world income was stimulated and the demand for American exports increased. The converse was true of an American business downswing. It is only in such a manner that the value of American exports may be conceived as having been determined by the American income. On this hypothesis the counter-clockwise movement, as shown in the diagram, could be supported by the fact of world-wide 'scarcity' of dollars during these years.[1] Although for the 'twenties the diagram does not show such a counter-clockwise movement, yet it may be thought that the annual data have blurred the short-period changes. Let us see

[1] U.S. Department of Commerce, *The United States in the World Economy*, passim.

whether we can support our argument by detailed statistical analysis.

For the statistical investigation, we make two hypotheses:

(1) that the American exports in the period $t + \frac{1}{2}$ is determined by the American national income in the period t; and

(2) that the value of exports in the period $t + \frac{1}{2}$, together with the value of home investment in the same period will determine the American national income in the period $t + 1$.

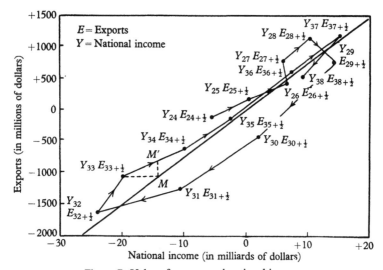

Fig. 12B. Value of exports and national income

It is interesting to find that, when the value of exports in the period $t + \frac{1}{2}$ is plotted against income in the period t, as shown in Fig. 12B, the dots after being joined chronologically tend to form a regular polygon rotating consistently clockwise round a fitted line. Moreover, the years in which the level of income was rising as compared with that in the previous year, tend to lie above the fitted line; whereas the years with falling income lie below it. By this polygon, we are able to see the determination of national income by the value of exports. The average temporal relationship between export and income may also be ascertained as before. For instance, corresponding to the actual value of exports in $1933 + \frac{1}{2}$ (measured by the Y-axis), the theoretical value of income in 1933 would have been M on the fitted line; which, however, was realised some time between 1933 and 1934 as represented by the point M'. From the polygon, it would seem that the average temporal relationship was one-half year. These findings give support to our two hypotheses. In Fig. 12C, income in the period $t+1$ (net of that as induced by the change in the home investment in the period $t+\frac{1}{2}$),[1] is

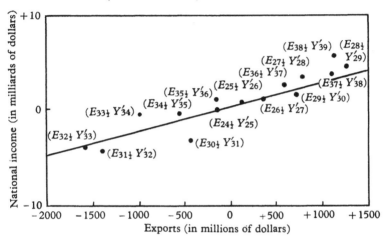

Fig. 12 C. Value of exports, home investment, and national income

plotted against the value of exports in the period $t+\frac{1}{2}$. A very close fit results and the slope of the line, or the multiplier, is about 2·8.

[1] Since home investment is also a determinant of the national income, the partial regression equation is of the form:

$$Y_{t+1} = bI_{t+\frac{1}{2}} + bE_{t+\frac{1}{2}},$$

where Y is national income, I the home investment and E the value of exports. Moreover, the above equation may be rewritten as:

$$(Y_{t+1} - bI_{t+\frac{1}{2}}) = bE_{t+\frac{1}{2}}.$$

The home investment figures are obtained from M. Ezekiel, 'Saving Consumption and Investment', *American Economic Review*, 1942.

§ IV

The same method is applied also to the cases of the U.K., Germany, Sweden, Australia, South Africa, and New Zealand.[1] The numerical values for the multiplier for various countries are given in Table 24. For the purpose of comparison the 'foreign-trade-multiplier' for Denmark, calculated by R. Stone, is also included in our table.[2]

TABLE 24. *Foreign-trade-multipliers**

Countries	Period	Total investment leading income by	Multiplier
U.S.A.	1924–38	½ year	2·8
New Zealand	1925/6–1937/8	½ year	2·5
Germany	1925–32	¼ year	1·9
Australia	1928/9–1936/7	¼ year	2·0
U.K.	1924–37	¼ year	1·5
Canada	1926–38	¼ year	1·5
Denmark	1936	—	1·5
South Africa	1923/4–1937/8	¼ year	1·4
Sweden	1923–34	¼ year	1·4

* In our calculations, budgetary surplus or deficit is included in home investment. The sources of individual countries' indices of home investments are as follows:

U.S.A.: Ezekiel, op. cit.
Germany: *Die Deutsche Volkswirtschaſt*, no. 4, 1938.
Australia: Clark and Crawford, op. cit.
U.K.: Bretherton, Burchardt and Rutherford, *Public Investment and the Trade Cycle*, p. 402.
South Africa: Frankel, op. cit.
Sweden: Lindahl, *National Income of Sweden, 1870–1930*.

Owing to the fact that the accuracies of the data used in the above calculations are different, the results should be treated as expressing only the general relationship among the 'foreign-trade-multipliers' of different countries instead of giving an exact measurement to each of them.

Since the U.S.A. is self-sufficient in natural produce and highly industrialised, and is therefore very little dependent upon import trade, her multiplier naturally has the highest value. As shown in Table 24, the multiplier is 2·8; which means that an increase of home investment or of exports of one dollar will

[1] The investment figures for New Zealand are not available. But we include in the value of exports the amount of budgetary deficits.
[2] R. and W. M. Stone, op. cit. The method for estimation is Kahn's method of leakage.

induce an increase of national income of 2·8 dollars half a year later. On the other hand, for the other countries in an open system, the values of the multipliers are surprisingly small. In general, they range from 1·4 to 2·0. The rather high value for the New Zealand multiplier is due to the fact that, owing to the lack of home investment data, we have accounted for the variations in income entirely by the variations in the value of exports and budgetary deficits.

The countries chosen in our studies, except for the U.S.A., are either industrialised deficient countries or wealthy agricultural countries. If they are regarded as good representatives of their respective types of country in the real world, we may expect that the true multipliers for other countries are probably also within this range. As to the values of multipliers for the poorer agricultural countries, it is impossible to make any guesses based upon our present results. But, on *a priori* grounds, it would be expected that, because the high marginal propensities to consume are generally offset by high marginal propensities to import in these countries, the magnitude of their multipliers cannot be large.

PART II
THE BRITISH BALANCE OF PAYMENTS

CHAPTER VI

THE BRITISH DEMAND FOR IMPORTS IN THE INTER-WAR PERIOD[1]

This chapter outlines a statistical investigation into the factors determining Britain's demand for imports during the cyclical changes of the inter-war period and the behaviour of different categories of imported commodities.

(i) THE DEMAND FOR IMPORTS AS A WHOLE

The total British demand for imports is largely determined by changes in the national income, increasing in times of business prosperity and falling with business decline. This connection is direct and obvious. Consumption is closely correlated with the level of income; and nearly half of British imports consists of foodstuffs for immediate consumption uses. Another substantial section of British import trade consists of raw materials and semi-manufactures (many of the commodities classified as manufactured goods being in fact semi-manufactures which are the raw materials of British 'finishing' industries); and the demand for this class of imports is directly determined by the fluctuations of basic economic conditions at home, which are in turn reflected in the changes of the national income.

Let Y be the money value of the total annual retained imports of commodities, as reported by the Board of Trade; and let X be the net national income at factor cost, as given by Richard Stone.[2] Then the regression equation is:

$$Y = 121 \cdot 1 + 0 \cdot 2X,$$

the unit being millions of pounds. This shows that over the period as a whole, from 1924 to 1938, each change of £1 in the national

---

[1] This chapter is an abridged and improved version of my article published in the *Economic Journal*, June 1946. Some results have been revised. Vide supra, Tables 4 and 5.

[2] Richard Stone, *The Analysis of Market Demand* (reprinted from *Journal of Royal Statistical Society*, 1945).

income of the U.K. tended to be accompanied by a change of about four shillings in the value of retained imports.[1] On the average, 23·1% of the national income has been spent on imports; this is greater than the marginal propensity to import, which is therefore a decreasing function of income. This is to be expected, as nearly half of British retained imports consists of foodstuffs, the proportionate expenditure on which should decrease as income increases.

The trends of the two time series were opposite to each other. National income showed a slightly upward trend, while the value of retained imports had a strongly downward movement owing to the violent fall in prices. The crude data therefore underestimate the marginal propensity to import, and a better result is obtained by fitting a line to the data with trend eliminated, and by considering changes in income and imports instead of total amounts. The regression of yearly changes of imports on yearly changes of income gives the equation: $Y = -37·7 + 0·283X$. When trend is eliminated by the method of least squares, the equation becomes $y = 0·295x$. These two results are close to each other; therefore we can conclude that the crude marginal propensity to import is about 0·3.

So far we have neglected changes in the terms of trade. But we can define the marginal propensity to import in real terms, the point of departure being the regression of *quantity* of imports on *real* national income. The former series is derived by multiplying an index of import quantity with the base at 1930 by the value of imports in 1930; the latter series is the figures of real national income given by Stone.[2] When trend has been eliminated the regression equation is $y = 0·136x$, which gives a marginal propensity to import of 0·136. This is much smaller than the previous result, 0·3, the difference being clearly due to the fact that import prices fluctuated much more violently than domestic prices during the period covered.

We cannot say that one of these results represents the 'true' marginal propensity to import. The minimum value is probably 0·14, while 0·14–0·3 is the range within which the marginal

---

[1] No attempt has been made to correct the value of retained imports for imports used in making exports. A rough estimate shows that the correction would be small.

[2] Stone, op. cit.

propensity to import fluctuated with changes in the terms of trade.

For the data considered so far, the correlation coefficients are not very high; but tests suggest that they are probably statistically significant.[1] In other words, the assumption of a relation between fluctuations of imports and of domestic national income can probably be established. There are two reasons for the rather low values of the correlation coefficients.

First, there have been special causes for certain unusual movements of imports. For instance, in the year 1926 the long coal strike and the General Strike compelled British industries to use foreign raw materials for making both domestic consumption goods and goods for export. The most conspicuous example was the heavy increase in the importation of coal and of iron and steel semi-manufactures, which normally came mainly from domestic resources. Consequently the quantity of imports increased at a time when the domestic income was shrinking.[2] This tendency continued into 1927; during that year there were exceptional imports of raw materials for use by the export industries in working off the contracts delayed by the previous stoppage. In 1928 this phase had passed, and it is not surprising to find that imports decreased and fell into line with movement of income. Again, the spectacular increase in imports in 1931, while domestic employment was declining, was due to heavy stock-piling of manufactured goods in anticipation of the imposition of a protective tariff.

Secondly, the yearly national income figures fail to reveal short-term fluctuations in home economic conditions, which often have an important influence on imports. Therefore, in order to study the behaviour of imports during the trade cycle, we shall relate them to the index of home employment, which is a very stable function of the national income, and is better able to reflect its short-term fluctuations. The index used is based upon the estimates of employed persons subject to insurance, excluding persons sick or on strike, published in the *Ministry of*

[1] By using Fisher's z-transformation, the correlation coefficients are statistically significant. But this test is not, of course, valid for the correlation of time series, owing to the presence of serial correlation. There is no satisfactory test which can be applied to a small number of observations of this type.

[2] Taking 1924 as base, the increase in imports of all commodities was 8·6%, that of raw materials 19·0%, and that of manufactured goods 19·3%.

Labour Gazette. It follows that henceforth we shall be calculating employment elasticity instead of income elasticity; the employment elasticity being defined as the ratio of the proportionate change in the quantity of imports to the proportionate change in home employment, when the import price remains constant.

The regression equation for quantity of imports and home employment, trend being eliminated, is $y = 0.685x$, with correlation coefficient equal to $+0.54$; which means that one point change in the index of home employment tended on the average to be accompanied by about 0.7 point change in the quantity of imports. This regression coefficient is a crude one, since other factors influencing the behaviour of imports have been ignored. But it enables us to make an approximate investigation into another interesting problem—namely, the temporal relationship between imports and home employment. On *a priori* grounds, one would expect fluctuations in employment to lead those in quantity of imports. Is this expectation confirmed, and what is the length of the lead? We find the correlation between the two variables when one is shifted forwards or backwards a certain number of months; the time-difference is then given by the largest of the correlation coefficients found. In this case we make a rough approximation by using quarterly figures of employment. Thus, in order to calculate our correlation coefficient when employment leads by one quarter, we pair off the average employment from the fourth quarter of 1923 to the third quarter of 1924 with the imports for 1935; and so on.[1] The results obtained are as follows:

	Correlation coefficient
Employment leading by two quarters	0.60
Employment leading by one quarter	0.64
No lead	0.54
Employment lagging by one quarter	0.50

It appears that fluctuations of employment lead those of quantity of imports by between one and two quarters.

We must now discuss further the employment elasticity (or income elasticity) of the demand for imports during the trade

---

[1] Both the monthly figures and the quarterly figures of quantity of imports published in the *Board of Trade Journal* are not complete for all the years under investigation; therefore we have to use the yearly figures. The quarterly figures of home employment can be found in the *Ministry of Labour Gazette*.

cycle; inquiring in particular whether the import price level, which has so far been neglected, is an equally important determinant of quantity of imports. We want to know the size of its effect, and whether the employment elasticity will be different if import price is taken into consideration.

TABLE 25. *Indices of quantity of imports, import prices, and home employment (with trend eliminated)*

Year	(1) Tota retained quantity	(2) Home employment	(3) Import price	
			(a) Average value	(b) Average value corrected for tariffs
1924	95·5	103·3	108	105·6
1925	100·0	102·9	103	103·9
1926	104·3	95·9	100	98·2
1927	105·4	104·6	99	99·2
1928	99·2	103·3	105	105·8
1929	103·4	104·1	107	105·1
1930	102·4	98·6	100	93·9
1931	104·5	93·7	85	83·4
1932	90·5	91·9	83	91·2
1933	91·7	94·0	84	94·3
1934	95·8	95·4	90	96·8
1935	96·0	98·5	96	100·4
1936	101·9	102·5	102	102·9
1937	107·8	106·6	120	110·0
1938	102·0	104·9	117	108·0

If we plot quantity of imports and employment logarithmically, as shown in Fig. 13, we obtain as the equation of the fitted line:

$$\log y = 0.81 + 0.595 \log x,$$

with correlation coefficient equal to $+0.56$. This means that the crude elasticity of demand for imports is 0.595—fairly inelastic. If the correlation coefficient had been high—that is, if the deviations of the observed values from the fitted line had been small—we should have deduced that changes in import price and other disturbing causes had had little effect, and could be disregarded. But the actual value of the correlation coefficient is low enough to suggest that, even after allowing for the random changes in 1926 and other years, home employment may not have been the only factor affecting the quantity of imports. We observe that in the years after the return to gold, when import prices were low relative to domestic prices, the observed values

lie above the fitted line in Fig. 13. After 1932, when the pound
sterling had depreciated, the observed values lie below the
fitted line. It is therefore reasonable to suppose that the variations in import prices are the disturbing factor.

The relationship between the quantity of imports and the
import price is not a simple one. First, the cost of buying
imported goods (from the point of view of the domestic con-

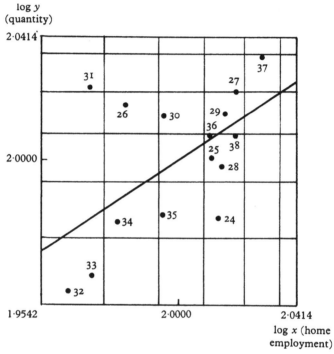

Fig. 13. Showing the correlation between the quantity of
imports and home employment

sumer) is not the price quoted by the foreign sellers, but the
quoted price c.i.f. plus import duties. The Board of Trade index
of import prices does not make allowance for changes in tariffs.
When we come to consider the behaviour of separate categories
of imported goods, we shall have to make elaborate corrections
for tariffs; but for our present purpose it will be sufficient to add
to the annual values of imports the Customs revenue for the
appropriate year. We then reduce these figures to an index of

import value including tariff, on the base 1930; dividing by the index of quantity on base 1930, we obtain an index of import price with import duties added.

Secondly, it would seem *a priori* that at a given level of home employment the quantity of imports would vary inversely, not with the absolute level of import prices, but with the relative level of import and domestic prices. For domestic products compete with imports for the purchasing power in the hands of consumers. Hence, taking the Ministry of Labour's cost-of-living index as the best representative of domestic prices,[1] we derive the 'relative import price level after allowance for duties', as shown in column (3), (b) of Table 25, by dividing the index of absolute import prices by the cost-of-living index.

Actually, over the period 1924–38 there has been a linear correlation of magnitude of 0·955 between British import price level (corrected for tariff) and the British cost-of-living index; the amplitude of the fluctuations of the import price being, however, much greater. Within narrow limits a particular level of import price has been associated with a particular level of domestic price, both being no doubt influenced by the common factor, British home employment. It follows that if a particular absolute import price level is associated with a given level of employment, so also is a particular relative import price level.

But of course in the inter-war period there were many instances where changes in the conditions of supply of British imports—that is, in the absolute import price level—were related to the level of British home employment. Thus the correlation between quantity of imports and corrected relative import price is positive, +0·24. This would seem to mean that the price elasticity of British demand for imports is positive; which sounds absurd, for in theory the elasticity of the demand for a commodity with respect to its own price must be negative except in the case where it is an 'inferior' commodity and the income effect outweighs the substitution effect. This phenome-

---

[1] The reason for not using the wholesale price index is that, besides its defect of inadequate weighting of manufactured goods, it includes the prices of the same goods in intermediate productive process—e.g. raw cotton and cotton yarn. The cost-of-living index, which includes items entering into final consumption, is therefore considered to be a better theoretical measurement of the movements of domestic prices. Besides, the wholesale price index of the Board of Trade consists of prices of many imported goods. Cf. J. M. Keynes, *A Treatise on Money*, vol. I, ch. IV.

non of positive correlation can be explained by the fact that, as the U.K. was the chief importer of certain important world exports, the world export prices (or the British import prices) were bound to move in the same direction as British domestic

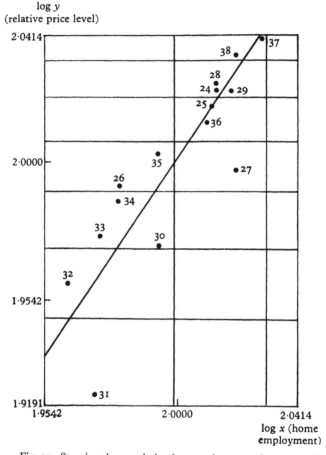

Fig. 14. Snowing the correlation between home employment and corrected import price level

employment. When employment was high, the quantity of imports was high, and therefore import prices tended to rise; and *vice versa*. This effect would be strengthened by the tendency of British employment to move with world employment. Therefore our regression equation of quantity on price represents, not the demand function with respect to price, but the foreigners' supply function for British imports. In order to get a clear idea of the influence of price on quantity, we must separate statistically the effect of employment changes on the import prices. The close association of import price with domestic employment is illustrated in Fig. 14.

The regression equation is

$$\log y = -0.6081 + 1.3036 \log x,$$

with $r = +0.86$. It is interesting to note that this diagram shows a variation opposite to that in Fig. 13. By careful comparison, we can see that in the years in which the import price was high in relation to domestic employment, the quantity of imports was low in relation to employment; and the converse is also true.

The fact that the slope of the regression line is 1.3 means that prices fluctuated more violently than domestic employment. During the years of depression the suppliers of British imports suffered not only from a shrinkage of the quantity exported to the U.K., but also from a fall in the unit value of imports.

From the results illustrated in Figs. 13 and 14, we can now calculate the price elasticity after allowing for the influence of changes in home employment on both the quantity and the price. We do this by correlating the deviations from the quantity-employment function (shown in Fig 13) with the deviations from the price-employment function of Fig 14. The result is shown in Fig. 15 and the correlation is negative.

The regression equation is

$$\log y = +3.1745 - 0.5873 \log x,$$

with $r = -0.56$. The correlation coefficient represents, in statistical language, the 'partial correlation' between quantity and price. The negative correlation apparently reveals that, besides being directly sensitive to changes in domestic employment, the quantity of British imports also varies inversely with changes in price. The price elasticity, -0.59, indicates a 'moderate inelasticity', which may be explained by the inelastic demand for the foodstuffs which form nearly half of British imports.

Proceeding by the same method, the partial correlation between quantity of imports and home employment, keeping price constant, is $+0.70$, which is larger, and therefore shows a better fit, than the crude simple correlation coefficient, $+0.56$, for the data of Fig. 13.

We can now combine our results to form a demand function for British imports. Let x_1 be the quantity imported; x_2 the home employment; and x_3 the corrected relative price. Then the

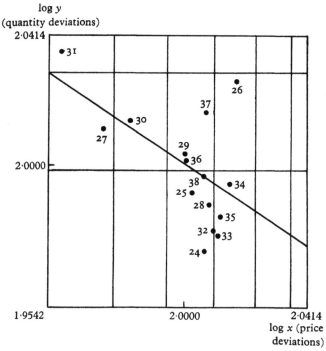

Fig. 15. Showing the correlation between the quantity deviations and price deviations

regression coefficients of $\log x_1$ on $\log x_2$ and $\log x_3$ will indicate respectively the employment and price elasticity of British demand for imports. The regression equation is

$$\log x_1 = +0.4207 + 1.4297 \log x_2 - 0.6405 \log x_3.$$

The multiple correlation between quantity of imports (as dependent variable) and home employment and corrected relative price (as independent variables) is of the magnitude of

0·75, showing that in the period considered the variables of employment and price explain 56% of the variance in quantity of imports.

As pointed out in the above, 1926 and 1931 were two exceptional years during which the changes in the import quantity were affected mainly by some abnormal events. Excluding these two years from our calculation, we get the following equation:

$$\log x_1 = +0\cdot4301 + 1\cdot414 \log x_2 - 0\cdot46 \log x_3,$$

with multiple correlation coefficient equal to 0·85. The elasticities are slightly different, but the correlation coefficient is much improved.

Two conclusions may be drawn from the equation. First, the employment elasticity, at $+1\cdot4$, though fairly high, is not much different from other industrial countries. Secondly, the price elasticity is 'moderately inelastic'; and therefore any deliberate attempt on the part of suppliers to decrease their prices will not increase proportionately the quantity they export to the U.K. On the contrary, as the experience of the depression proves, such an attempt will make their balance of trade with the U.K. still worse.[1]

(ii) THE VARYING NATURE OF THE
DEMAND FOR IMPORTS

Over the trade cycle there has been a close association of total quantity of imports with home employment and with corrected relative price; but, nevertheless, individual categories of imported commodities have manifested a variety of behaviour patterns, reflecting different types of domestic demand for imports. For instance, the behaviour of imported producers' goods differs considerably from that of consumers' goods; imports of finished products vary differently from those of raw materials and semi-manufactures; fluctuations in imports of

---

[1] This applies only to those suppliers whose exports consist mainly of 'low-price elasticity' agricultural products and whose exports to the U.K. are a very high proportion of their total exports. The situation is, of course, different in the case of those suppliers whose exports are mainly manufactured goods of high-price elasticity (see § III below). But since the former case predominates in the British import trade, our argument is *generally* true.

consumers' luxuries are different from those of essentials, and so on.

Those various patterns of change will be further complicated by fluctuations of inventories or stocks. Inventories tend to fluctuate with the trade cycle and to amplify the cycle. The reason for this is the entrepreneurs' need to carry several months' stocks in the normal process of productions; so that increasing consumers' expenditure makes entrepreneurs add to their stocks in order to preserve their normal inventory ratio. Moreover, sometimes the element of speculation comes in to amplify the cyclical fluctuations.

In the case of the U.K., many categories of raw materials and semi-manufactures are imported both for home consumption uses and for making exports. If the latter demand predominates over the former, then the quantity imported is determined, not so much by the general economic conditions at home, as by the exports of the corresponding category of manufactured goods. The import of raw cotton is a typical example.

This section also uses partial correlation analysis, but it involves a more elaborate technique. The basic data are the Board of Trade indices of quantity and average value for retained imports, which are given for five groups of commodities, of which we shall neglect two, 'Animals, Not for Food', and 'Parcel Post'. The index numbers are given for the years 1928–9 on base 1924; for 1924 and 1931–6 on base 1930; and for 1936–8 on base 1935. H. W. Macrosty has given the figures for 1925–7 on base 1924.[1] We can therefore link all these together to give a continuous series on base 1930.

A more elaborate method is required for the tariff corrections. We must give separate considerations to specific duties, *ad valorem* duties, and Imperial Preference. The method adopted is to obtain from the *Board of Trade Journal* all the duty changes in the period, ignoring the effect during fractions of a year; then to work out the average duty on the category for the year 1924, using as weights the value of the items imported in 1930; and finally to correct this from year to year as the duties were altered (i.e. by adding or subtracting each change in duty multiplied by the proportion which the value of the item to

[1] H. W. Macrosty, 'The Oversea Trade of the United Kingdom, 1924–31', *Journal of Royal Statistical Society*, 1932.

which the change applied bore to the total value of that category imported in 1930). In the case of specific duties, the duty was reduced to a percentage of the value per unit in 1930 of the item to which it applied, and the average specific duty was compiled as a separate series. This is therefore added to the average value instead of being multiplied into it.[1]

Let A_b = the average *ad valorem* duty on commodities imported from British countries,

A_f = the average *ad valorem* duty on commodities imported from non-British countries,

S_b = the average specific duty on commodities imported from British countries,

S_f = the average specific duty on commodities imported from non-British countries,

I_b = the total value of imports in the category under consideration from British countries,

I_f = the same total for imports from non-British countries,

P = the Board of Trade index number of average value,

P_t = the index of average value corrected for tariffs.

Then,

$$P_t = P \frac{I_b(A_b + 100) + I_f(A_f + 100)}{100\,(I_b + I_f)} + \frac{I_b S_b + I_f S_f}{I_b + I_f}.$$

The final result is the 'average internal value of retained imports'.

Let x_1 = log (quantity of imports),

x_2 = log (home employment),

x_3 = log (import price corrected for tariffs)

x_4 = log (price of similar home-produced goods).

If we take the quantities for a particular category of imports, we obtain a demand function for that category:

$$x_1 = a + bx_2 - cx_3 + dx_4.$$

The regression coefficients $+b$ and $-c$ are approximations to the employment elasticity and price elasticity of demand for

[1] The late P. R. Marrack has discussed the problem in great detail in an unpublished article; and this formula is his. He has made the corrections for several series for the years 1928–38, and also graphic representations showing the correlation between quantity, price and employment (without elimination of the trends).

imports. In contrast to the analysis applied to total imports, this conclusion is correct only under certain assumptions. These assumptions are: (1) that the quantity of imports is very large or very small compared with the home supply, or (2) that the home supply is very elastic to home price and is not much affected by general changes in home employment. If these assumptions are not fulfilled (or, in other words, if changes in x_2 and x_3 react on x_4), we require to know both demand and supply functions for home-produced goods used as substitutes for the category of imports in question.

We now turn to the actual data. The three Board of Trade groups which we are considering are: (a) Food, drink and tobacco; (b) Raw materials and articles mainly unmanu-factured; and (c) Articles wholly or mainly manufactured. This classification is not without defects, for in the third group many articles are in reality semi-manufactures imported for the final process of production in this country. But, even so, the employ-ment and price elasticities of these general groups will be interesting and useful.

(a) *Food, drink and tobacco.* The import price index is corrected for tariff changes, and then expressed in terms of the relative price level (as we have done before for the total imports)—i.e. it is divided by the Ministry of Labour's cost-of-living index.

The simple correlation between quantity of food imports and home employment is negative, -0.54. At first sight this is absurd, since the commodities of this group cannot in general be 'inferior goods'. But the data show that the price moves in the same direction as home employment, so that the phenome-non can be accounted for in either of two ways: first, if the quantity is very inelastic with respect to employment, but very elastic with respect to price; secondly, if the quantity is inelastic with respect both to price and to employment, but prices have fluctuated so greatly that they outweighed the influence of employment. We can choose between these explanations only after using partial correlation analysis.

The partial correlation coefficients are as follows:

Quantity on employment, with price constant $+0.55$

Quantity on price, with employment constant -0.80

Employment on price, with quantity constant $+0.91$

The partial regression equation is

$$\log x_1 = 1 \cdot 5268 + 0 \cdot 55 \log x_2 - 0 \cdot 314 \log x_3,$$

where x_1, x_2 and x_3 are quantity, employment and price respectively. The multiple correlation coefficient is $0 \cdot 86$.

As would be expected, the demand is inelastic with respect both to employment ($+0 \cdot 55$) and price ($-0 \cdot 314$), so we must choose the second explanation for the apparent anomaly mentioned above. The multiple correlation coefficient means that 75 % of the fluctuations in the quantity can be explained by means of the variables of employment and relative price.

By the same method we obtain $+3 \cdot 7$ for the partial regression of relative price on employment, quantity being kept constant. In other words, 1 % change in home employment was on the average accompanied by a $3 \cdot 7$ % change in relative price level. Thus while the 1 % increase in employment increased the quantity of imports by $0 \cdot 55$ %, the simultaneous increase in relative price (associated with increase of employment) decreased the quantity by $3 \cdot 7 \times 0 \cdot 314$, or $1 \cdot 16$ %. Thus there was a net decrease in imports of foodstuffs.

(b) *Raw materials and articles mainly unmanufactured.* After correction for tariff, the absolute import price level is divided by the Board of Trade index of average wholesale prices of basic and intermediate industrial materials,[1] thus giving a relative price level. The regression equation is

$$\log x_1 = 0 \cdot 1167 + 1 \cdot 4912 \log x_2 - 0 \cdot 551 \log x_3,$$

with a multiple correlation coefficient equal to $0 \cdot 746$.

(c) *Articles wholly or mainly manufactured.* The import price level corrected for tariff is divided by the index of wholesale prices of manufactured goods. The regression equation is

$$\log x_1 = 1 \cdot 3942 + 1 \cdot 4420 \log x_2 - 1 \cdot 12 \log x_3.$$

The demand for imports in this category is seen to be elastic with respect to variations in price; doubtless because most of the imported manufactures can be produced at home. The multiple correlation coefficient is $0 \cdot 975$, which means that only 5 % of the fluctuations in quantity of imports cannot be explained as connected with variations of employment and prices.

---

[1] This index suffers from the defect that it consists of prices of many imported raw materials. We use it as deflator because of no better alternative.

TABLE 26. *Elasticities for certain particular categories of imported commodities* *

	R	E_e	E_i	E_h
I. *Goods mainly purchased by consumers:*				
(1) For immediate consumption:				
Meat (Id)	0·85	0·12	−0·48	+0·72
Animals, living, for food (Ic)	0·76	0·29	−0·38	—
Dairy produce (Ie)†	0·89	0·43	−0·34	+0·17
Fresh fruits and vegetables (If)†	0·87	0·56	−0·47	+0·35
Grain and flour (Ia)	0·94	0·84	−0·59	+0·24
Tobacco (Ii)‡	0·89	0·98	−0·45	—
Feeding-stuffs for animals (Ib)	0·70	2·00	−0·13	—
(2) For 'deferred' consumption:				
Other textile goods (IIIl)	0·87	1·30	−1·70	—
Apparel (IIIm)	0·75	1·29	−1·80	—
Wood and timber manufactures (IIIh)	0·83	1·70	−1·80	—
Cotton yarn and manufactures (IIIi)	0·91	2·02	−4·69	+3·82
Cutlery, hardware, etc. (IIIc)	0·80	2·30	−1·10	—
Pottery, glassware, etc. (IIIb)	0·85	3·10	−5·90	—
Woollen manufactures (IIIj)	0·81	3·60	−5·40	—
Silk manufactures (IIIk)	0·78	4·70	−1·12	—
II. *Goods mainly entering into the production of consumers' goods:*				
Paper-making materials (IIl)	0·87	0·72	−0·10	—
Wool and woollen rags (IIg)	0·74	0·89	−0·47	—
Other textile materials (IIi)	0·90	1·01	−0·21	—
Hides and skins, undressed (IIk)	0·76	1·05	−0·43	—
Raw cotton and cotton waste (IIf)	0·66	1·37	−0·25	—
Raw silk (IIh)	0·75	4·10	−0·46	—
III. *Goods mainly entering into production in general: producers' goods:*				
Oil-seeds and nuts, etc. (IIj)	0·86	0·90	−0·72	—
Oils, fats and resins, manufactured (IIIp)	0·64	0·91	−0·72	—
Wood and timber (IIe)	0·60	2·13	−0·41	—
Electric goods and apparatus (IIIf)	0·88	3·10	−5·90	—
Non-metalliferous mining and quarry products (except coal) (IIb)	0·96	3·10	−1·31	—
Machinery (IIIg)	0·95	3·16	−2·10	—
Non-ferrous metals and manufactures (IIId)	0·69	3·40	−4·50	—
Non-ferrous metalliferous ores and scrap (IId)	0·86	4·14	−0·31	—
Iron and steel manufactures (IIIc)	0·72	5·10	−1·15	—
Vehicles (IIIs)	0·84	6·45	−1·10	—
Iron ore and scrap (IIc)	0·94	9·45	−1·91	+1·27

* The number in parentheses indicates the category number in the Board of Trade's classification. The rest of the categories have not been dealt with. The sources of the price of home-produced substitute are:

(1) *Meat.* Compiled by taking weighted average of the prices of mutton, beef, lamb and pork, as published in *Agricultural Statistics*.

(2) *Dairy produce.* Compiled by taking weighted average of the prices of milk, cheese and butter, as published in *Agricultural Statistics*.

(3) *Fresh fruit and vegetables.* The price series of 'Fruit, vegetables and glasshouse produce' has been published in *Agricultural Statistics* for the years 1927–38.

(4) *Grain and flour.* For 1927–38 the price series of 'cereal and farm crops' as published in *Agricultural Statistics* is used, for 1924–6 the prices of wheat, oats and barley are used.

(d) *Elasticities for certain particular categories of imported commodities.* Table 26 shows the elasticities of demand for certain imported commodities with respect to employment (E_e) and absolute import price (E_i); and in several cases with respect to home price of substitute (E_h). The multiple correlation coefficient (R) for each category is also listed. It is interesting to note that on the whole the elasticities of the particular categories conform to those of the group to which they belong. For foodstuffs, E_e and E_i are both less than 1; raw materials have E_e greater than 1, but E_i less than 1; manufactures have both elasticities greater than 1.

Some imports are mainly purchased by consumers for the purpose of immediate or 'deferred' consumption; others are used for the production of consumption goods; while some imports are mainly producers' goods. Table 26 is therefore divided into these three classes.[1]

The square of the multiple correlation coefficient indicates the percentage of fluctuations in quantity of imports which can be accounted for by a linear relationship with the variations of employment and import prices (and in several cases also of the home prices of substitutes). In our present study, the significance of the correlation is different for individual categories of commodities. But in general we may say that the changes in home employment and import prices are important factors in determining the behaviour of individual commodities.

With the exception of 'feeding-stuffs for animals', all categories in the group of 'immediate consumers' goods' are rather insensitive to employment changes. This is in accordance with the fact that consumption, though closely related to income,

[1] This classification is arbitrary; but it reflects the economic behaviour of a society better than the classification given by the Board of Trade.

---

(5) *Cotton yarn and manufactures.* Obtained from the unpublished dissertation of Mr Y. N. Hsu.

(6) *Iron ore and scrap.* The index of the home price of scrap can be obtained from Mr Tew (also unpublished dissertation). The average value of iron ore per ton can be computed from the statistics of total weight produced and of total value, published in *Statistics of the Iron and Steel Industries,* 1937, then it has been reduced to an index number on base 1930. The figure for 1938 is based upon estimation. Finally, the two indices have been given the same relative weights as ore and scrap have in the import index, to combine into a single index. This is the method used by Marrack.

† For 1928–38 only.

‡ The index of quantity has been corrected for changes in stocks.

changes less than in proportion to income. The price elasticities are low, because the U.K. is not self-sufficient in foodstuffs, and is therefore bound to buy abroad. The presence of home-produced substitutes does not alter the situation, as their total quantity is small in relation to the total home consumption.

The 'deferred consumers' goods' show an elastic demand with respect to changes in employment. The employment elasticity of silk manufactures is very high, because they are generally luxuries. The demand in this group is elastic with respect to changes in import price because there are home-produced goods competing with the imports.

Most of the raw materials in the group II show an elastic demand with respect to changes in employment; but all of them are inelastic to changes in import price because they cannot be produced at home.

The demand for 'producers' goods' is very elastic with respect to changes in employment. This reflects the fact that employment in the heavy industries fluctuates much more than employment in general. Where there are substitutes produced at home, the demand is also elastic with respect to changes in import price.

Moreover, if a considerable part of certain raw materials is used for making exports, then the volume of British exports of those particular manufactured goods is also an important factor in determining demand for imports. Raw cotton and wool are two typical examples. Let E_x be 'export-elasticity'; our results are as follows:

TABLE 27. *Elasticities for Raw Cotton and Wool*

	R	E_e	E_i	E_x
Raw cotton and cotton waste:				
(1) As shown in Table 26	0·66	1·37	−0·25	—
(2) Including volume of exports of cotton manufactures as a variable	0·91	0·65	−0·31	+0·83
Wool and woollen rags:				
(1) As shown in Table 26	0·74	0·89	−0·47	—
(2) Including volume of exports of woollen manufactures as a variable	0·87	0·32	−0·39	+0·65

(iii) SUMMARY

The findings discussed above may be summarised as follows:

(1) The total British demand for imports is largely determined by changes in home employment; and the level of relative import price is also important. The demand with respect to the changes in employment is elastic; but inelastic with respect to changes in price.

(2) The marginal propensity to import of the U.K., which fluctuates with changes in terms of trade, probably lies within the limits of 0·14 to 0·3.

(3) Individual categories of imported commodities manifest a variety of behaviour patterns, reflecting the different types of domestic demand for imports. In most cases changes in general home employment and in import price are still important factors. On the whole, the employment and price elasticities of particular categories conform to those of the group to which they belong: foodstuffs have both elasticities less than unity; manufactures have both greater than unity; for the raw materials, employment elasticity is greater than unity and price elasticity is less than unity. But in some cases changes in stocks, prices of home-produced substitutes and volume of British exports of particular manufactures are also important.

CHAPTER VII

THE BRITISH BALANCE OF PAYMENTS[1]

For the type of highly industrialised and 'deficient' country, we choose the U.K. as an example. Apart from the short-term capital and gold movements in the 'thirties, the principal items in the British balance of payments, which show constant changes to an important degree, are the balance on income account and the net movements of long-term capital. Furthermore, their patterns of fluctuation tend to exhibit definite relationship with the world trade cycle. The explanation therefore seems to lie in the fact that the fluctuations of general world economic activity *normally* affect these two in roughly equal and opposite manner. Consequently, the balance of payments is temporarily out of equilibrium when the cyclical fluctuations of these two fail to offset each other completely; and then the function of the induced gold and short-term capital movements and of the adjusting mechanism is only to handle this relatively small maladjustment. Our attention should therefore be given not to balance-of-payments disequilibrium as such, but to the question why the balance on income account and not long-term capital movements are similarly influenced and determined by fluctuations in world economic activity and also to the examination of their patterns of cyclical behaviours.

(i) FACTORS DETERMINING THE CYCLICAL BEHAVIOUR OF THE CONSTITUENT ITEMS OF THE BRITISH INCOME ACCOUNT

Generally speaking, the change in the demand for imports is predominantly determined by the change in home national income; and the fluctuation in domestic exports is closely correlated with the level of world economic activity. Therefore, the

---

[1] This chapter is an improved version of my article published in the *Economic Journal*, December 1947.

balance of income acccount is *inter alia* determined by the relative incomes at home and abroad.

In the formation of an *a priori* description of the cyclical change in the balance of merchandise trade of any particular country, four additional factors have to be considered. First, the change depends upon the 'type' of international merchandise trade of the country in question; or, in other words, it depends upon the relative level of the income elasticities of the home demand for imports and the world demand for exports. Secondly, equally important in this connection are the direction and magnitude of the cyclical change in the terms of trade. Thirdly, the change also depends upon whether that country habitually runs a surplus or deficit on merchandise trade and how large the surplus or deficit is. The last factor is the general pattern of cyclical fluctuations in the home country as compared with the rest of the world.

In the case of the U.K., the general features of her economic set-up are the combination of an advanced stage of industrialisation and deficiency in natural products. The 'type' of her international merchandise trade is therefore to exchange manufactured goods for foodstuffs and raw materials with the world. For her exports which consist mainly of capital equipment and high-standard-of-living goods, world demand tends to have a high income elasticity. Whereas, on the import side, foodstuffs are necessities, for which her demand is relatively constant as between prosperity and depression. The import of raw materials, however, varies rather intensively with the level of home income. Since foodstuffs constitute a large part of total imports, imports as a whole would probably have a smaller income elasticity than the total exports. Therefore, starting from an initial equilibrium at any given time, a general world-wide cyclical expansion of economic activity, of the same magnitude at home and abroad will, *ceteris paribus*, lead to a larger change in the volume of exports. Or, in terms of value, this results in an export surplus.

But during a period of world prosperity the terms of trade tend to change against the U.K. The general reason is given by the natural tendency of more violent cyclical fluctuations in agricultural prices. More particularly, since the U.K. is relatively large in the world economy and usually the chief buyer in certain important world markets, the prices of her imports are *inter alia* sensitive to the amount she actually purchases. The change in the terms of trade is unlikely to exert much influence either on the volume of imports or on that of exports. The import volume is inelastic with respect to price changes because there are few home-produced substitutes to compete with the imports. Nor does the export volume change very much because the export prices of British industrial competitors tend to move together. But the unfavourable change in the terms of trade is important in determining the net change in the value of imports and exports. In general, it tends to cancel or even more than cancel the favourable change in relative volumes.

Furthermore, as a result of historical development, the British balance of merchandise trade normally shows an import surplus, the value of exports being, on the average, two-thirds of that of imports. Therefore, even when, during a period of general world prosperity, the unfavourable change in the relative prices cancels the favourable change in the relative volumes so that there is an equal percentage increase in the values of imports and exports as compared with the initial period, the amount of import surplus would tend to increase. Moreover, if the value of imports has increased proportionately more than that of exports due to the effect of the change in the terms of trade, the import surplus would become still larger.

Also important are the temporal relationship and the amplitude of fluctuations of the British cycle with the world cycle in general. With regard to this, there are various theoretical possibilities. But, in the actual case of the U.K., whose internal economy is highly dependent upon the export trade, her cycle generally tends to lag behind, and to fluctuate less violently than the world cycle. This fact would therefore mitigate the above-mentioned tendency for the deficit to increase in times of world prosperity.

To sum up, so far as the balance of merchandise trade is concerned, the U.K. is more likely to experience an increased deficit in prosperity. But, against this, the change in her net receipts from abroad (i.e. her invisible exports) is very elastic with respect to the change in the world economic activity. The shipping income and commission receipts are very closely correlated with the volume of world trade which increases as a result of world prosperity. The receipts from oversea investments generally consists of two parts: dividends from equity investments and incomes from fixed-interest bonds. The former will increase very considerably when the world activity is on the upswing, while the latter will also rise because of the disappearance of defaults. As a whole, the increase of these receipts may be expected to more than offset the increase of the deficit on the balance of merchandise trade. Therefore, we may conclude that the income account of British balance of payments tends to show alternate net surplus and deficit in relation to general world prosperity and depression. This *a priori* conclusion, however, needs statistical verification.

We use partial correlation analysis to show the various elasticities and the degree of correlation existing between the constituent items of the income account and their respective determinants; and the results of the calculations are as follows.

(1) *The British demand for imports.* The main determinants of British demand for imports are home national income and the level of import prices relative to the prices of home-produced substitutes for imports. Taking home employment as representative of home national income, with which it is very highly correlated, and taking the cost-of-living index as the best representative available of the prices of home-produced substitutes, we obtain, after the elimination of the trends,

$$\log \text{(Quantity of imports)} = + 1 \cdot 414 \log \text{(Home employment)}$$
$$- 0 \cdot 46 \log \left(\frac{\text{Import prices with tariff corrected}}{\text{Cost-of-living index}} \right),$$

with multiple correlation coefficient equal to $0 \cdot 85$.[1]

(2) *The world demand for British exports.* By a similar reasoning, the world demand for British merchandise exports is predominantly determined by the level of British export prices, the prices of competing goods exported from other industrial countries,[2]

---

[1] As this chapter was actually written before the chapters in Part I, the regression coefficients used here are different from the revised figures in Table 4. But this fact does not invalidate our following conclusions.

[2] The index of competitors' prices is compiled as follows. By converting into sterling at their respective average annual rates of exchange, the export prices of France, Germany, Japan and U.S.A. are combined into an index of weighted average. The weights are given in accordance with their respective average shares in the total world exports for the period as a whole. Export prices for Germany covering 1924 are extrapolated on basis of aggregate for other countries.

and the level of world real income.[1] Equally important, however, is the factor of the purchasing countries' policy with regard to tariffs, which we have to exclude because its effect cannot be estimated for British exports as a whole. We find for the period 1924–38:

log (quantity of total exports of produce and manufactures of the U.K.)

$$= + 1 \cdot 81 \text{ log (World real income)}$$

$$- 0 \cdot 53 \text{ log} \left(\frac{\text{British export prices}}{\text{Competitors' export prices}} \right),$$

with R equal to 0·93.

(3) *Other invisible exports from the U.K.* Shipping services can be related to world real income and to freight rates by a partial regression equation:

$$\text{log (Volume of shipping services)}$$
$$= + 1 \cdot 13 \text{ log (World real income)}$$
$$- 0 \cdot 089 \text{ log (Index of freight rates)},$$

with R equal to 0·89.

Moreover, freight rates follow the equation:

$$\text{log (Freight rates)} = + 2 \cdot 85 \text{ log (Home employment)}.$$

Similarly, the money value of interest receipts and other receipts (mainly commissions and insurance) were both highly correlated with world money income. The equations are:

$$\text{log (Interest receipts)} = 1 \cdot 31 \text{ log (World money income)},$$

and

$$\text{log (Other receipts)} = 1 \cdot 80 \text{ log (World money income)},$$

with R equal to 0·91 and 0·989 respectively.[2]

From all these regression equations we are now able to derive the net change in the balance of income account as a whole

---

[1] Vide supra, Table 4, n. [3]. The index of world real income used here has been adjusted to exclude the U.K.

[2] It must be borne in mind that, in spite of the very high correlation coefficients, the regression coefficients may fail to give the precise measurement to the facts, because the figures for interest and other receipts in the British balance of payments provides, in general, a rough order of magnitude rather than anything exact.

during different phases of the trade cycle. Let us assume that the average empirical relationships for 1924–38, as given by all the regression coefficients, hold true for any single year; and then to deduce the net change associated with an equal magnitude of economic expansion, say 1%, at home and abroad.

From the equation in (1), the 1% increase in home employment is to increase the quantity of imports by 1·414%. But the increase in home employment will be accompanied by a rise of the import prices because of the dominance of the British market, and also by the rise of cost-of-living index. Associated with 1% increase in home employment, the relative price level tends to rise by 1·31%.[1] The rise of price is to decrease the quantity of imports by 1·31 × 0·46, or 0·595. The net change in the quantity is therefore +0·82%. Allowing for the rise of absolute import (excluding tariff),[2] and starting from the average import value of 1924–5 and 1927, we now deduce that a 1% increase in home employment would be associated with an increase in import value by £33·4 mn. (or 2·6%).

Similarly, the change in the export value associated with a 1% increase in world real income can be calculated from the equation in (2). The export prices are closely correlated with British home employment, the regression coefficient being +1·38%. The competitors' prices are predominantly determined by the level of world real income, the change associated with 1% increase in income being +0·50%. Substituting in the equation, the increase in the export quantity is +1·34%. Hence, starting from the average export value of 1924–1925 and 1927, and taking into account the rise of export prices, the increase in export value is £24·3 mn. (or 2·7%).

So far as the merchandise trade is concerned, the favourable change in the relative quantities is more than offset by the unfavourable change in the terms of trade; and, consequently, its deficit increases by £9·1 mn. with a 1% economic expansion

[1] The relative price level in our equation indicates the ratio of import prices including tariff to cost-of-living index. Further calculations give that an increase of 1% in British home employment was, on the average, accompanied by an increase of 2·07% in import price (including tariff) and 0·76% in cost-of-living index. Therefore, the relative price level rises by 1·31%.

[2] For the purpose of deriving the increase in import value, absolute import price excluding tariff is relevant. The regression equation for the period 1924–38 is:

log (Absolute import price without tariff) = +1·80 log (Home employment).

at home and abroad. Whereas, on the other hand, service items have net increases, which can also be deduced from equations in (3). Starting from the average value of 1924–1925 and 1927, the increases in shipping income, interest receipts, and 'other receipts' are respectively £4·5 mn., £4·9 mn., and £2·1mn. or £11·5 mn. in total.[1] Against the deficit of £9·1 mn. on the side of merchandise trade, service receipts increase by £11·5 mn. and, therefore, the net change in the balance on income account is a surplus of £2·4 mn. However, because of such a small difference between large totals some of which contain doubtful elements, the result may not be significant. Moreover, it may seem to suggest that the net change in the income account, as determined by the magnitude of various elasticities alone, remains 'neutral' to the world cyclical fluctuations. But the inherent type of British cycle, which tends to fluctuate less violently than the world cycle, will necessarily lead to a surplus on income account in times of prosperity and a deficit during depression. This can be shown by further calculations.

During the period under investigation, the average relationship between the world and the British cycles is represented by the equation

$$\log(\text{World real income}) = + 1\cdot74 \log(\text{British home employment}).$$

The fact that the more intense world cycle would increase the magnitude of the surplus during prosperity is revealed by the following comparison.

	(1) 1% increase in home employment being accompanied by 1·74% increase in world real income (£mn.)	(2) Both home employment and world real income increasing by 1% (£mn.)
Imports	− 33·4	− 33·4
Exports	+ 38·4	+ 24·3
Service items	+ 18·6	+ 11·5
Net surplus	+ 23·6	+ 2·4

[1] In (3), the interest receipts and 'other receipts' are correlated with world money income. We require therefore the average relationship between world real income and world money income, which is given by the equation:

$$\log(\text{World money income in sterling}) = + 1\cdot55 \log(\text{World real income}).$$

(ii) WORLD ECONOMIC ACTIVITY, BRITISH HOME
EMPLOYMENT AND NET LONG-TERM CAPITAL
MOVEMENTS

The salient feature of the British long-term capital movements in the inter-war period is that they show a net export of
capital during the period of general world prosperity and turn
to a net import of capital in times of slump and recession. This
pattern of cyclical behaviour must be related to the fluctuations
in the economic activity both in the borrowing countries and in
the U.K.

On the demand side, the relationship between the overseas
flotations and the level of world economic activity is positive:
borrowing tends to increase during business upswing and to fall
under slump and recession conditions. The normal overseas
borrowers in the London capital market are the economically
less-developed countries, whose internal capital investments are
generally low and whose commodity exports of natural products
therefore constitute the main determinant of their national incomes. During general world prosperity, world demand for their
exports increases; and, the elasticity of supply being low, prices
also tend to rise. In consequence, the value of exports increases;
and, by the operation of the multiplier, so do the national
incomes. When business is on the upswing, more investment
decisions are made. Because of a lack of internal capital resources, these countries have to raise more funds abroad for the
purposes of purchasing necessary capital equipment, etc., and
of 'financing' their investment programmes. As a result, long-
term capital imports tend to rise. Moreover, the relationship
between the capital imports and the internal prosperity of the
capital importing countries is an interacting one. The consequent capital imports will in turn stimulate the economic
activity in these countries by maintaining, or even improving,
the net barter terms of trade. This is because the capital imports
make it possible for them to meet the service on foreign debt
without resort to pressing their export commodities on to the
world market so as to cause adverse effects upon prices and thus
on national income. Once the boom is under way and is being
maintained, the prospect of rising profits and increasing returns
will encourage these countries to raise still more funds abroad

and will make foreign investors more willing to invest in these regions. Therefore a cumulative movement of capital imports into these countries should be expected in times of world prosperity. Conversely, during slump and recession, net import will decrease or may even reverse itself.

Now let us consider the supply side. British long-term capital exports tend to be positively correlated with cyclical fluctuations. The U.K. was a capital-exporting country from the very start and grew more and more dependent upon international trade. For these reasons, her historical cycles tended to be determined by foreign business conditions and her crises and financial booms originated mainly abroad.[1] During the inter-war period, the British cycles were generally less intense than, and lagged behind, those in her debtor countries.[2] Thus, during a period of general prosperity, the relatively higher returns abroad (in the form of interest, profits and capital gains) would tend to induce the British investors to make more foreign investment; and conversely. Moreover, at the same time, the increase in home saving would strengthen this tendency. Exports being relatively important, British national income rises considerably as a result of cyclical increase in world demand for her exports. British demand for imports also increases, but the income account as a whole shows a net surplus. At the new level of national income, total saving is increased; and it exceeds the British home investment by the amount of surplus on the income account. Since new securities in the U.K. are coming to the capital market at a rate equal to the rate of her home investment, the excess saving will be devoted to purchase of foreign securities.[3] The converse holds true for the case of world depression and recession.

Now let us turn to the actual data. In Table 28 the index of economic activity of borrowing countries is compared with new overseas flotations in London and the net movements of British

[1] For the historical description of the cycles in the nineteenth century, see J. Schumpeter, *Business Cycles*, ch. VII.

[2] The regression equation on p. 124 shows that, during the inter-war period, the world cyclical fluctuations tended, on the average, to be 1·74 times more intense than the British ones. See also the comparison made in Table 29. Moreover, if we may regard that wholesale price index can approximately reflect the short-period changes in income, a careful comparison reveals that the quarterly movements of these indices in British debtor countries tended to lead those in the U.K.

[3] J. Robinson, op. cit. pp. 201–2.

long-term capital. The index of economic activity had an upward trend. Whereas, on the other hand, the value of total overseas issues showed a sharp decline; the average figures for the 'thirties being only one-fourth of the average pre-Depression level. This was partly due to the British government's intervention against foreign landing. But the main reason seemed to lie in the world economic instability and uncertainty in the 'thirties, which made long-term foreign investment unappetising to the British public. Furthermore, this latter factor was also responsible for the increased repatriation of British capital from abroad, as shown in column (3).

When the year-to-year fluctuations of economic activity and overseas issues are compared, the positive correlation is high and significant. Nevertheless, there were exceptions attributed to special events in a particular year. For instance, the relatively high figure for overseas issues in 1924 was the result of the flotations of League of Nations' loans guaranteed by the British Government.[1] The contradictory movement of the two series in 1925 was due to the ban on foreign lending consequent upon the U.K.'s return to gold. Again, in 1929, although the economic activity in the borrowing countries was shrinking, the sharp decline in the amount of overseas issues was mainly due to the high interest rates ruling in the world's principal capital market, which induced foreign borrowers to reduce long-term borrowings and to raise indispensable accommodation as far as possible by the arrangement of short loans. In other words, the money market was preferred to the capital market whenever possible.[2] In the next year, the amount of overseas issues rose because of the seeking of foreign accommodation by overseas governments and public bodies for meeting their internal budgetary difficulties.[3]

[1] For instance, the League of Nations' loans were £8 mn. to Hungary and £7·5 mn. to Greece. In addition, there was German Dawes Loan to the amount of £12 mn.

[2] Examination of the detailed statistics for the separate borrowers in the London capital market reveals that Canada absorbed far less than in 1928, while the aggregate of British America was £15¼ mn., as compared with £20½ mn. in the previous year. The heaviest decline was Australian borrowing, the aggregate of which was £17 mn., only about one-half the 1928 total. (Midland Bank, *Monthly Review*, January 1930).

[3] Again, in 1932, such public bodies took £25·7 mn. out of the total amount of £29·7 mn., and, in 1933, £30·3 mn. out of £37·8 mn.

TABLE 28. *World cycle and British long-term capital movements*

Year	(1) Index of economic activity* (1930 = 100)	(2) Overseas issues in London† (£mn.)	(3) Capital repayments, etc.‡ (£mn.)	(4) Net movements of British long-term capital (export, −; import, +) (£mn.)
1924	87·4	−134·2	—	−134·2
1925	91·9	− 87·8	—	− 87·8
1926	97·0	−112·4	+27·0	− 85·4
1927	104·0	−138·7	+34·0	−104·7
1928	111·6	−143·4	+30·0	−113·4
1929	110·0	− 94·3	+45·8	− 48·5
1930	100·0	−108·8	+73·9	− 34·9
1931	77·5	− 46·1	+66·8	+ 20·7
1932	86·1	− 29·2	+53·0	+ 23·8
1933	89·5	− 37·8	+71·8	+ 34·0
1934	98·0	− 43·4	+22·0	− 21·4
1935	104·5	− 20·9	+31·0	+ 10·1
1936	110·8	− 26·4	+57·0	+ 30·6
1937	121·4	− 32·1	+61·5	+ 29·4
1938	120·9	− 25·4	+39·2	+ 13·8

* The countries included are the seven most important borrowers in the London capital market: Australia, Argentina, Canada, India, Japan, New Zealand and South Africa. These countries together took, on the average, nearly 90% of new money annually raised for overseas purpose in London. For individual countries, the indices used are quantity of imports for India and Argentina, real national income for the rest.

† Figures published by Midland Bank in their *Monthly Review*.

‡ This item includes capital repayments, changes in other long-term capital investments abroad and, for two years, transactions in outstanding securities. The figures for 1924 and 1925 are not available.

The combination of the series for overseas issues with that for capital repayments, etc.[1] gives the net movements of long-term capital account as a whole. It showed net export of capital in the 'twenties; and, as expected, the largest outward movement occurred in 1928 when the world economic activity was also at its highest. However, with the coming of the depth of depression in 1931, the net movement reversed its traditional direction, becoming a net inflow. Such an inflow was maintained throughout the 'thirties except for 1934.

Now, we come to the supply side. What were the facts regarding the cyclical relationship between British long-term capital export, capital raised for home purposes, and home employment? Or, what were the patterns of their short-period

[1] In general, this inward movement tended to fall in more prosperous years. But the incompleteness of the data renders the correlation less close than could be expected.

fluctuations? As the quarterly figures for the export of long-term capital are not available, for our present purpose the quarterly figures for overseas issues must be used as the best representative figures. The indices of British home employment (A), total home issues (B) and total overseas issues (C), with trend and seasonal fluctuations removed, are compared in Fig. 16. A careful examination of the movements of the series yields three conclusions. First, new overseas issues followed a path roughly parallel to that of new home issues for the period under investigation. In contrast to the experiences of New York,[1] the new issue boom in London (e.g. in 1928 and the first half of 1929) never reached the stage at which overseas issues were at a heavy discount relatively to home issues. When home issues

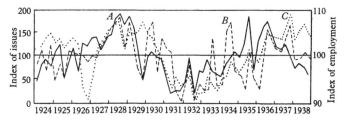

Fig. 16. Indices of home employment, home issues and overseas issues. The series of home employment has been shifted one-quarter to the right in charting

were at their maximum, the overseas issues were also at their highest level. In other words, the proportion of the overseas issues remained fairly constant over the prosperous years.[2] Secondly, as a whole, the index of overseas issues tended to fluctuate more irregularly than the index of home issues; and, moreover, there were very noticeable divergences between them in some quarters. This is generally attributed to the fact that besides the deviations between the fluctuations in British home employment and those in world employment, there had been in operation forces with a special bearing upon the volume of overseas issues, such as the ban on foreign lendings, etc. Thirdly, the apparent relationship between the overseas issues and British home employment was of a positive character: overseas issues tended to increase in times of home business upswing and

[1] U.S. Department of Commerce, *The United States in the World Economy*, pp. 92–3.
[2] For instance, the proportions in 1926, 1927, 1928 and 1929 were 44·4, 44·1, 39·5 and 37·3% respectively. Midland Bank, *Monthly Review*, January 1930.

to fall or to increase less rapidly under recession conditions in this country. The explanation seems to lie in the fact of the importance of external influences upon the British home cycles.

That the export of British long-term capital, or the overseas issues, was highly correlated with the level of employment in the borrowing countries and in the U.K. can also be established by statistical verification. Let x_1, x_2 and x_3 be respectively the index of overseas issues, the borrowers' economic activity and the British home employment. The partial regression equation, with trends of all the series eliminated, is

$$\log x_1 = -4\cdot24 + 1\cdot88 \log x_2 + 1\cdot22 \log x_3.$$

The result is in conformity with our expectations. The regression coefficients indicate that overseas issues tended to be positively associated, during cyclical fluctuations, both with overseas economic activity and with British home employment. In aggregate, with 1 % expansion of economic activity at home and abroad, the overseas issues would increase by more than 3 %. The multiple correlation coefficient is 0·77. Taking into consideration the fact that there were many random factors which also affected the behaviour of overseas issues in this period, our result is satisfactory.

Moreover, the index of total overseas issues is a heterogeneous aggregate comprising both the issues taken by public bodies and those taken by industrial undertakings. That the amount taken by the latter tended to have a closer relationship with cyclical variations in employment can be judged from Table 29. With trend eliminated, the correlation between the index of overseas issues for *industrial undertakings* (z_1), borrowers' economic activity (z_2) and British home employment (z_3), is given by the partial regression equation[1]

$$\log z_1 = +1\cdot75 \log z_2 + 1\cdot18 \log z_3.$$

The value for the multiple correlation coefficient is equal to 0·93, which, as expected, is much higher than that in the case of total overseas issues.

---

[1] Since 1932 and 1933 were two exceptional years during which an official embargo on foreign lending was imposed, we exclude them in calculation.

TABLE 29. *Constituents of total overseas issues (£ mn.)*

Year	Issues for public bodies	Issues for industrial undertakings
1924	100·2	34·0
1925	33·8	54·0
1926	56·0	56·4
1927	76·8	61·8
1928	71·9	71·5
1929	34·5	59·5
1930	68·6	40·2
1931	30·8	15·2
1932	25·7	3·5
1933	30·3	7·5
1934	11·0	32·5
1935	3·4	17·4
1936	0·9	25·5
1937	12·6	19·5
1938	10·1	15·3

(iii) EQUILIBRIUM IN THE BRITISH BALANCE OF PAYMENTS

In Fig. 17 a comparison between the curve for the balance of income account (*A*) and the curve for the net movement of long-term capital (*B*) is made for the inter-war period. It

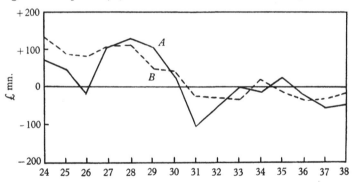

Fig. 17. Comparison between income account and capital account (£ mn.)
Export of capital is indicated by +, import by −

reveals that the two totals tended to offset each other and their approximation was close. This is what should be expected, because, as has been shown, the common underlying force determining the net changes of these two accounts was the level of general world employment, with which British home employment tended to move closely. Moreover, the annual level to which the two approximate, shows the equilibrium position of the British balance of payments at different phases of the trade cycle. In times of general world prosperity, e.g., in the 'twenties, surplus on income account was coupled with net export of long-term capital.[1] Alternately, in years of general world depression and recession, deficit on income account and net import of capital went together.

But, in spite of the natural harmony in the broad cyclical equilibrium, the annual figures for these two series did not always agree. In some years, the net export of capital was in excess of the surplus on income account; whereas, in others, the reverse was true. Nevertheless, a country just like any economic entity must have an exact balance between payments made to foreigners and payments received from them. In other words, for the U.K. as a whole, she cannot pay out more than she receives except by drawing on her cash reserves or by short-term borrowings. Whenever there is temporary discrepancy between them, gold movements and shifts of short-term capital must occur to maintain the equilibrium. Acting in such a capacity, they become 'balancing items', and are therefore normally of *passive* character. But, in the actual case of the U.K., which one of the two 'balancing items' played a more important role, and did they change automatically as a result of any temporary disequilibrium?

Fig. 18 gives the curves for the net receipts and payments of the U.K. resulting from current and long-term capital transactions (A),[2] for the net gold movement (B),[3] for the change in the recorded short-term capital movement (C),[4] and for the

---

[1] During the period 1936–8, in spite of the rising world real income and consequent increase in British visible and invisible exports, the U.K. had deficit on income account. This is accounted for by a special factor, the British rearmament programme, which caused heavy imports of raw materials. Taking 1930 as basis, the quantities of total retained imports in 1936, 1937 and 1938 were 105, 112 and 107 respectively; whereas the index for raw materials imported gave 125, 137 and 121.

[2] This curve is derived from Fig. 17. The excess of net long-term capital exports over the surplus on income account results in net payments by the U.K.: whereas the converse gives rise to net receipts.

[3] Export of gold means receipts and import payments.

[4] The data for the short-term capital movements for the U.K. are incomplete. Our series, beginning from 1928, are based upon various estimates, the sources of which are given in the Appendix. But, for 1924–7, there were no annual data whatsoever available.

recorded short-term capital including residue item (D).[1] During the period, when the U.K. was on gold, the annual gold flow was low relatively to the amount of net receipts or net payments. In addition, the directions of change were rather random. Net receipts were accompanied by net gold inflow or by net gold outflow; and, similarly, for net payments. There-fore, it seems that it must have been the shifts of short-term

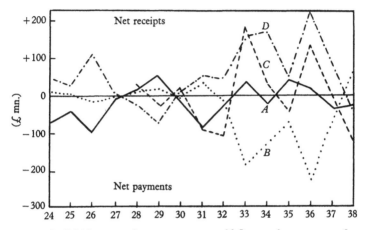

Fig. 18. British net receipts or payments, gold flows and movements of short-term capital ($£$ mn.)

capital which played the predominant role of the 'balancing item' in the British balance of payments. During 1924–7, there were net payments. Though no annual data were avail-able, it has been estimated that there were net inward move-ments of short-term capital during these years.[2] In 1928, in

---

[1] The residue item represents net omissions and errors from the estimates of other items of the balance of payments. There are no *a priori* grounds for distributing it among the other items. But, by its nature this item would seem more closely akin to short-term capital than to any other items. Curve D therefore indicates the sum of the recorded short-term capital and the residue item. Comparison between curves C and D reveals that, for the period 1928–38, their divergence is not very great, except for 1931 and 1932. Moreover, as the vertical difference between these two curves measures the magnitude of the residue item in the corresponding year, it seems that the residue item is generally of the same sign as that of the recorded short-term capital.

[2] There were two estimates regarding the magnitude of short-term capital imports during 1924–7. T. Gregory, in *The First Year of the Gold Standard*, p. 77, estimated that, from 1924 to the first half of 1926, the net inflow of short-term

spite of net receipts, the recorded short-capital movement showed net inflow. But the reverse relationship between curve *A* and curve *C* in 1929 and 1930 is in conformity with our expectation. *Prima facie*, this evidence would seem to give support to our argument. But, by itself, it is not strong and conclusive because of the incompleteness of the data. For our argument to be established, we have therefore to find out whether any mechanism was operating during this period to call forth such equilibrating short-term capital movements. In the next section, this will be dealt with.

As shown in Fig. 18 in the 'thirties, the fluctuations of short-term capital movements corresponded closely inversely to the gold flows. The changes in the two curves did not reflect the current state of the general balance of payments; and, in fact, they were the concomitant result of the abnormal shifts of funds among international financial centres.

(iv) MECHANISM OF CHANGE OF RELATIVE INTEREST RATES

The mechanism by which the 'balancing' short-term capital can be called forth, is the automatic change of the relative level of the home short rate to the world short rate, as determined by the variation in the general balance of payments.

In an open system, the rate of total saving in the home country exceeds or falls short of the rate of home investment according as the balance of income account is surplus or deficit. Normally, a part of the increase in the wealth of individuals in the home country, represented by home saving, will be used to make loans abroad. If the net long-term capital export from the home country is just equal to the surplus on income account, then the home country's rate of 'foreign saving' is equal to that of 'foreign investment' and the rate of home saving is also equal to that of home investment. These two equalities give the external equilibrium of the home country in an open system. But, if the net export of long-term capital is in excess of the surplus on income account, the rate of home saving tends to fall

capital amounted to about £130 mn. The estimate for 1925–7 by Keynes was an inflow of £150 mn. ('The British Balance of Trade, 1925–27', in *Economic Journal*, December 1927).

short of the rate of home investment which is represented by the rate of offering new home securities. The shortage of home saving may not lead to an immediate fall in the prices of securities, or a rise of home long-term rate of interest. This is because (provided that the excess of foreign lending is not too large) the operation of speculators in the securities market would tend to maintain the prices by increasing their speculative stocks under such circumstances.[1] However, there would be a tendency for home short-term rate of interest to rise. At home, the money which, with an equality between surplus on income account and long-term capital export, would have passed from one section of traders to another, now passes into the hands of foreign financiers because of the excess in lending. This part of money may be held in liquid form awaiting transfer or may be invested in home money market. But, in either case, there is a shift of money from the 'industrial circulation' to the 'financial circulation'.[2] Moreover, at the same time, for the home banking system as a whole, the liquidity has been decreased. Less liquidity is reflected in that a smaller proportion of capital assets consists of deposits or cash at banks and a larger proportion of remunerative assets.[3] These situations would tend to lead to a rise of home short-term interest rates relative to those of the world, which consequently induces inflow of short-term capital.

During the period 1924–30, when the international economic relations were more or less normal, the shifts of short funds among world financial centres were predominantly of an equilibrating character and sensitive to changes in interest differentials. Therefore, by the mechanism of change of relative interest rate, the U.K. had been able to get the necessary accommodation. Moreover, the effectiveness of such mechanism was greatly strengthened by the historically unique position of the London market. First of all, the London money market was sensitive to the movements in the bank rate. In addition, there was a high wall of short and semi-liquid claims upon foreign debtors which normally sheltered the London

[1] N. Kaldor, 'Speculation and Economic Stability', in *Review of Economic Studies*, October 1939.
[2] B. P. Whale, 'The Short-term Capital Movements', in *Economica*, February 1939.
[3] R. F. Harrod, *International Economics*, pp. 136–7.

market; because such claims, as shown by experience, responded to the slightest change of short rate more promptly and sensitively than the balance owned by foreigners.

TABLE 30. *The change of relative interest rate*

Year	Net receipts (+) or net payments (−) (£mn.)	Relative rate of interest*
1924	−62·1	1·07
1925	−41·5	1·19
1926	−99·0	1·29
1927	− 4·7	1·23
1928	+ 9·9	0·93
1929	+57·3	1·26
1930	− 7·4	1·16
1931	−83·7	2·40
1932	−29·1	1·52
1933	+32·6	0·50
1934	−28·9	0·60
1935	+36·7	0·24
1936	+10·8	0·31
1937	−37·4	0·41
1938	−30·9	0·54

* Ratio of home rate to the average world rate.

London's three-month bill rate is chosen to represent the home short rates; and an average of short rates in New York, Paris, Amsterdam and Zurich is taken to stand for the world short rates.[1] The actual changes of relative short rate in relation to British net payments and net receipts are compared in Table 30. Comparison reveals that the changes in the relative short rate may have been responsible for the short-term capital movements during 1924–30. The direction of change in the relative short rate was generally in conformity with that in the British balance of payments. In the years of net payments, viz. 1924–7 and 1930, the home rate was relatively higher than the world rate. On the other hand, when in 1928 the U.K. had net receipts, the relative interest rate fell below one. In 1929, in spite of the increase in net receipts, the home rate was raised to stop the attraction of funds to Wall Street. But when the amplitude of fluctuations is compared, the correlation is less close than can be expected. Is it possible that the yearly figures fail to give the short period

[1] The rates used are New York's ninety-days bank acceptance rate, Paris's commercial paper rate, Amsterdam's rate for private discount and Zurich's three-months bill rate.

correlation between the fluctuations of relative interest rate and those of the balance of payments?

In Fig. 19 we use quarterly figures of value of overseas issues (A) to represent the quarterly figures of net receipts or net payments, with which the quarterly movements of relative interest rate (B) are compared. These two series moved very closely together from 1924 to the second quarter of 1929. In a particular year, the absolute level of the relative interest rate was determined by the state of net receipts or net payments in the general balance of payments in that year, as shown in Table 30. But the short period movements of the relative interest rate followed a path closely parallel to that of overseas issues. The high positive correlation gives strong support to our argument.

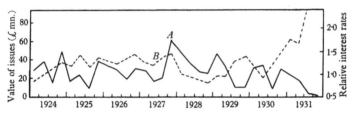

Fig. 19. Short-period correlation between the value of overseas issues and relative interest rate

However, the movement of these two series became divergent from the third quarter of 1929 to the time of the abandonment of the gold standard.

In the 'thirties, the absolute levels of interest rate in different countries were arbitrarily determined to serve the internal aims of the economic policies. In the case of the U.K., as a result of cheap money policy, her short rates tended, after 1933, to stand below the average world level; or the relative interest rate became less than unity. However, its year-to-year changes, as shown in Table 30, seemed still to reflect the current state of British balance of payments. When, in a year, net receipts were decreasing or changing into net payments, the relative interest rate tended to rise; and conversely. But it can hardly be expected that such changes would have influenced the shifts of short funds into and out of London, which, as a matter of fact, were primarily motivated by other considerations, such as safety, etc.

In this connection, a few words must be said about the

balances held as monetary and banking reserves by the sterling-area countries in London. Such sterling balances, which since the Great Depression constituted the excess of London's short liabilities over its short assets (apart from the short liabilities due to flight of capital from foreign countries), came generally from two sources. It represented the funds realised from the sale by Empire countries of current and dishoarded gold in the London bullion market, and also the balances arising out of trade with the U.K. Thus, when the U.K. paid out more to the sterling-area countries than she received from them, the sterling balances would tend to increase; and, in the converse case, to decrease. In this manner, the changes in sterling balances may have played some part of 'balancing item' to the British balance of payments. But, on the whole, the evidence is not conclusive.[1]

(v) GOLD MOVEMENT

Broadly speaking, the behaviour of gold during the inter-war period did not reflect the current state of disequilibrium in the general balance of payments of the U.K.; nor did it conform to any particular cyclical pattern applying to the period as a whole. In fact, British gold movements responded to the operation of special forces which affected the world real demand for, and supply of, gold. This was a natural result of the fact that, owing to her traditional economic and financial connections with South Africa and other gold-producing countries in the Empire, the U.K. occupied a unique position as a main distri-

---

[1] The following comparison is made on the basis of the facts given in the annual reports of Bank for International Settlements.

Year	British balance of payments	Changes in the sterling balances in London
1932	Net payments	Increase[1]
1933	Net receipts	Increase[2]
1934	Net payments	Increase[3]
1935	Net receipts	Decrease[4]
1936	Net receipts	Increase[4]
1937	Net payments	Increase[4]
1938	Net payments	Decrease[4]

[1] *Third Annual Report*, p. 8; and *Sixth Annual Report*, pp. 38–9.
[2] *Third Annual Report*, p. 8.
[3] *Fourth Annual Report*, pp. 28–9.
[4] *Fifth Annual Report*, p. 33; and *Ninth Annual Report*, pp. 82–3.

butor of gold to other parts of the world.[1] As shown in the table facing p. 144, the annual figures for the gross gold inflows and outflows were therefore much bigger than those for the net movements. As compared with the pre-1914 years, the types of London's gold transactions in the 'twenties were not changed. Gold was still exported to the East to satisfy the demand for hoarding there; also to the whole world for meeting industrial needs. It remained the source through which many Central Banks replenished their monetary reserves. The net exports to Germany, France, Netherlands, Spain and other parts of the Continent came largely under this category.

As a result of these heterogenous and varying influences determining the movements of gold, the net figures for the gold movements would not necessarily reflect the prevailing state of disequilibrium in the balance-of-payments position of the U.K. in the 'twenties. To be a 'balancing item', the net gold import should have tended to decrease (or to be replaced by a net gold export), or export should have tended to increase, when the British balance of payments showed a net payment; and conversely. In fact, only in three out of the eight years from 1924 to 1931 (i.e. 1924, 1925 and 1931) did the net movement of gold function as a 'balancing item' to offset the excess of payments arising out of the total trade, service and investment transactions of the U.K. with the rest of the world. But, it may be asked in this connection whether, during this period, the net gold movement might have been an *active* factor in the British balance of payments as expounded in the classical theory?

According to the classical theory, the first prerequisite of an adjustment sequence from long-term capital export to a balance on income account is the international redistribution of purchasing power, which is normally effected by the transfer of gold. That is to say, for a lending country, net gold import will tend to decrease (or net gold export to increase) in the years of increasing net long-term capital export; and conversely.[2] The

---

[1] T. Gregory, 'The Causes of Gold Movements into and out of Great Britain, 1925–1929', in *Selected Documents on the Distribution of Gold*, published by the League of Nations.

[2] According to the classical theory, the purchasing power may be transferred mainly through the short-term capital movements. For a lending country, increase in long-term capital export will tend to be followed by increased net inflow of short-term capital, or by a decrease in net outflow; and conversely. Whether such a

actual statistics of the U.K. indicate that, in five out of eight years in this period (i.e. 1924–5, 1927–8 and 1930), net capital export and gold outflow were positively related with each other. *Prima facie*, this would seem to give support to the classical theory. But this coincidence may have been entirely *accidental*, if the net gold movement did not bring about corresponding changes in the British internal economy.[1]

Fig. 20 therefore, compares the quarterly movements of the net gold flow (*A*), gold reserves in Bank of England (*B*), the cash basis of the whole country (*C*), the total supply of money (*D*), the total advances and investments of the commercial banks (*E*) and the Metropolitan, Country and Provincial Clearings (*F*), in the period of the gold standard.[2] Because London was the world bullion market, the gold inflows and outflows could have had influence upon the internal economy under the gold standard if they had induced corresponding changes in the gold reserves of the Bank of England. A careful comparison between curves *A* and *B* reveals that the quarterly fluctuations in the net gold flow and those in the reserves tended to move closely together. The outflow of gold from the U.K. was associated with a fall in the gold reserves of the Bank, but the former generally tended to lead the latter by one-quarter; and, conversely, the gold reserves increased one-quarter after the gold flowed into this country. As to the amplitude of fluctuations, gold reserves tended to rise and fall less than the net gold movements. But, the influence of gold movements upon the internal supply of money would depend upon two factors: (1) the Bank's decisions to change the cash basis of the whole country in relation to its

sequence had actually taken place in the U.K. cannot be tested without a record of monthly or quarterly movements. But, so far as the annual figures are concerned the short-term capital movements showed little correlation with long-term capital exports.

[1] However, the adjustment sequence in the classical theory is a 'multilateral' one, and it is likely that, in a specific situation, the major part of the adjustment may occur in the borrowing countries.

[2] Curve *B* indicates the total of coin and bullion in the Issue Department. Curve *C* is the sum of liabilities and notes in the Banking Department. Curve *D* consists of the aggregate of notes in circulation, silver coins, total deposits at commercial banks, Public Deposits and Other Accounts in the Banking Department. Curve *E* is the sum of advances and investments of the London Clearing banks. Curve *F* represents the series of Metropolitan, Country and Provincial Clearings, taken from the *Special Memorandum*, No. 46, of the London and Cambridge Economic Service.

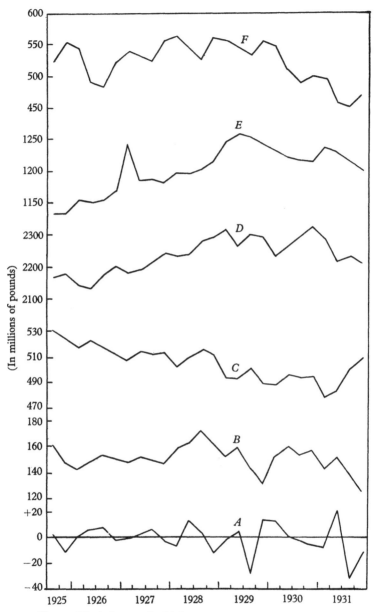

Fig. 20. The influence of gold flow upon British internal economy

141

gold reserves, and (2) the commercial banks' policy regarding their cash ratios.

When curve C is studied against curve B, it would seem that up to 1929 the Bank's policy regarding the cash basis had been to prevent inflows of gold from making themselves felt but to allow outflows to have their effects. For instance, there was an inflow of gold in the second and third quarter of 1926; and the gold reserve in the Bank had risen by £8 mn. as compared with the first quarter of the year. The rise in gold reserve was, how-ever, not reflected in the change in total cash basis, which, as a matter of fact, fell by £1 mn. The gold inflow during the first quarters of 1928 was again offset. But, in the third quarter of 1929, an outflow of gold was accompanied by an increase in the cash basis, which was due to the Bank's taking up vast quantities of government securities on its own account. When gold re-turned in 1930, it was offset and there was no permanent in-crease in the cash basis. Moreover, during the critical period of 1931, the Bank again increased the cash basis in spite of an abnormal outflow of gold.

The total supply of money and credit was also influenced by the commercial banks' cash-ratio policy. As shown by curve D, the total supply of money was steadily rising throughout the period as a result of a slight reduction of the cash ratios of the commercial banks. Its quarterly fluctuations showed no signi-ficant correlation with those of the net gold movement.

However, the net gold movement may have affected the liquidity of the commercial banks and thereby their willingness to lend to home industries even though there was no correlated fluctuation in the total supply of money. That is, the net gold inflow would be followed by an increase in the commercial banks' advances and investments; and the net gold outflow by a decrease. But a comparison of curves A and E reveals that their relation was not very close. Therefore, it seemed to suggest that the fluctuations in advances and investments had been predominantly determined by something else.

Curve F gives the series of Metropolitan, Country and Provincial Clearings, which shows the quarterly money pay-ments arising out of the current activity of creating and con-suming income.[1] Its quarterly movements showed no signi-

---

[1] We use this series to represent the short-term fluctuations of national income.

ficant correlation with either of these series. This negative result, *inter alia*, points out the fact that the level of income was determined by much more complex factors than the net gold movement and the supply of money.

But could there have been an adjustment process which operated through the changes in relative prices? Since net gold movements had relatively little effect upon the short-period fluctuations in the total supply of money and the level of income, it is very unlikely that they could have significantly determined the changes in the home price level and the terms of trade. The changes in the price levels in the U.K. during this period are given in Table 31. In general, increasing capital exports tended to be accompanied by a rise in the ratio of import to export price (i.e. in the net barter terms of trade), while the cost-of-living index tended to fall relative to both; and decreasing capital exports were associated with the opposite pattern of price changes. The fact is in line with the classical theory and seems to suggest that there was an adjustment process operating through relative price changes. But, as a matter of fact, the correlation is spurious. The fluctuations in all these series were influenced and determined by the changes in the level of British home employment, or, more generally, by the changes in world economic activity. Thus, during world prosperity, British long-term capital exports tended to increase and so did the import price, export price and cost of living. Moreover, the difference in the magnitude of the fluctuations must also be explained in terms of their relative sensitivity with respect to income changes. Empirically, with 1% increase in British home employment, import price increased, on the average, by 1·80%, export price by 1·38% and cost-of-living index by 0·76%.

TABLE 31. *Changes in the price levels (trends eliminated)*

Year	Import price	Export price	Net barter terms of trade	Cost-of-living index	Net movement of long-term capital (£mn.)
1924	106·1	103·3	102·7	100·8	− 134·2
1925	106·6	106·1	100·5	102·1	− 87·8
1926	101·2	102·5	98·7	101·4	− 85·4
1927	100·6	99·3	101·3	99·7	− 104·7
1928	105·5	101·7	103·7	100·0	− 113·4
1929	107·9	101·8	106·0	101·4	− 45·8
1930	98·6	100·0	98·6	102·8	− 34·9
1931	83·4	91·9	90·8	100·0	+ 20·7

In short, we can conclude that there was no trace of the operation of the mechanism of adjustment envisaged by the classical theory, and that the positive correlation between gold flow and long-term capital export, which we have observed for the U.K. in several years during 1924–31, was, therefore, purely accidental.

The role of gold changed when the U.K. went off gold. The huge and persistent inflow of gold was determined, both in aggregate and in detail, by the concurrent movement of short-term capital into this country. In fact, they both reflected the changes in the preferences of foreigners as to the particular form and place in which they desired to hold their assets in face of general world economic uncertainty. The close agreement between the cumulative changes of these two series can be seen from Table 32.

TABLE 32. *Cumulative changes of gold and*
short-term capital (£ mn.)

Year	Net gold inflow	Short-term capital import (including residue item)
1932	17·9	47·0
1933	209·3	205·8
1934	343·1	368·5
1935	413·2	401·8
1936	640·9	618·7
1937	720·5	725·7
1938	657·8	693·9

In contrast, the amount of British net receipts or net payments during this period was comparatively small. Since there was no conclusive evidence regarding equilibrating short-term capital movements, they must have been balanced by the corresponding changes in gold.

THE BALANCE OF PAYMENTS OF

(in millions

	1924	1925	1926	1927	1928	
I. INCOME ACCOUNT						
A. Merchandise trade:						
Imports	− 1,277·4	− 1,320·7	− 1,241·4	− 1,218·4	− 1,195·6	−
Exports	+ 941·0	+ 927·4	+ 778·6	+ 852·1	+ 845·9	+
Balance	− 336·4	− 393·3	− 462·8	− 366·3	− 350·7	+
B. Other net receipts:						
Government receipts from abroad	− 25·0	− 11·0	+ 4·0	− 1·0	+ 15·0	+
Shipping income	+ 140·0	+ 124·0	+ 120·0	+ 140·0	+ 130·0	+
Interest and dividends	+ 220·0	+ 250·0	+ 250·0	+ 250·0	+ 250·0	−
Short interest and commissions	+ 60·0	+ 60·0	+ 60·0	+ 63·0	+ 65·0	+
Receipts from other services	+ 15·0	+ 15·0	+ 15·0	+ 15·0	+ 15·0	+
Silver	− 1·5	+ 1·6	+ 0·2	0	− 1·0	−
Balance	+ 408·5	+ 439·6	+ 449·2	+ 467·0	+ 474·0	−
Net balance of income account	+ 72·1	+ 46·3	− 13·6	+ 100·7	+ 123·3	−
II. GOLD MOVEMENTS						
Imports	− 35·8	− 41·5	− 38·5	− 32·4	− 47·8	−
Exports	+ 49·4	+ 49·7	+ 27·1	+ 29·1	+ 60·5	+
Net gold movements	+ 13·6	+ 8·2	− 11·4	− 3·3	+ 12·7	+
III. CAPITAL ACCOUNT						
A. Long-term capital movements:						
New overseas issues [2]	− 134·2	− 87·8	− 112·4	− 138·7	− 143·4	−
Capital repayments [3]	—	—	+ 27·0	+ 34·0	+ 30·0	+
Other long-term investments overseas [4]	—	—	—	—	—	
Balance	− 134·2	− 87·8	− 85·4	− 104·7	− 113·4	−
B. Short-term capital movements:						
Changes in British assets abroad [6]	—	—	—	—	—	
Changes in British assets at home [7]	—	—	—	—	+ 23·2	−
Balance	—	—	—	—	+ 23·2	−
Net balance of capital account	− 134·2	− 87·8	− 85·4	− 104·7	− 90·2	−
IV. RESIDUE ITEMS	+ 48·5	+ 33·3	+ 110·4	+ 7·3	− 45·8	−

[1] In this Table the notation '—' means data not available.

[2] These figures are those compiled by the Midland Bank, which exclude (a) the amount subscribed by foreigners, and (b) conversion operations. The commissions paid to the British firms for the service of issuing are deducted.

[3] These are the estimates made by Sir Robert Kindersley. They represent the sinking funds and amortisation receipts of British investors from foreign borrowers. The repayments in 1924 and 1925 are unknown.

[4] Sir Robert Kindersley has also given estimates for the amount of long-term capital which British have lent overseas on long-term which is not represented by securities quoted on London Stock Exchange. They represent mainly foreign securities, especially American, and also mortgages and other kinds of investments. In the Table the changes from year to year are shown.

[5] They include net sales of long-term outstanding securities which have not been included in [4]. According to Sir Robert Kindersley's estimates the net sale by the British nationals in 1930 amounted to £35 mn. and in 1931 to £30 mn.

of pounds)

1929	1930	1931	1932	1933	1934	1935	1936	1937	1938
1,220·8	− 1,044·0	−861·3	− 703·1	− 675·9	− 732·3	− 756·9	−848·9	− 1,029·1	− 920·3
839·1	+ 657·6	+454·5	+416·0	+416·5	+447·4	+481·2	+501·1	+ 596·8	+532·4
381·7	− 386·4	− 406·8	− 287·1	− 259·4	− 284·9	− 275·7	− 347·8	− 432·3	− 387·9
24·0	+ 19·0	+ 14·0	− 24·0	− 2·0	+ 7·0	− 2·0	− 3·0	− 4·0	− 13·0
130·0	+ 105·0	+ 80·0	+ 70·0	+ 65·0	+ 70·0	+ 70·0	+ 85·0	+ 130·0	+100·0
250·0	+ 220·0	+170·0	+150·0	+160·0	+170·0	+180·0	+200·0	+ 210·0	+200·0
65·0	+ 55·0	+ 30·0	+ 25·0	+ 30·0	+ 30·0	− 30·0	+ 35·0	+ 40·0	+ 35·0
15·0	+ 15·0	+ 10·0	+ 15·0	+ 10·0	+ 10·0	+ 10·0	+ 10·0	+ 10·0	+ 10·0
0·8	− 0·1	− 1·6	− 1·8	− 5·0	− 9·6	+ 14·4	+ 1·0	− 10·5	+ 11·2
484·8	+ 413·9	+302·4	+234·2	+258·0	+277·4	+302·4	+328·9	+ 375·5	+343·2
103·1	+ 27·5	− 104·4	− 52·9	− 1·4	− 7·5	+ 26·7	− 19·8	− 56·8	− 44·7
62·4	− 86·7	− 98·3	− 152·3	− 251·7	− 262·5	− 244·1	− 314·3	− 295·1	− 239·6
77·6	+ 81·8	+132·9	+134·4	+ 60·3	+128·7	+174·0	+ 86·6	+ 215·5	+302·3
15·2	− 4·9	+ 34·6	− 17·9	− 191·4	− 133·8	− 70·1	− 227·7	− 79·6	+ 62·7
94·3	− 108·8	− 46·1	− 29·2	− 37·8	− 43·4	− 20·9	− 26·4	− 32·1	− 25·4
48·5	+ 38·9	+ 26·8	+ 48·0	+ 66·8	+ 42·0	+ 81·0	+107·0	+ 61·5	+ 39·2
−	+ 35·0[5]	+ 40·0[5]	+ 5·0	+ 5·0	− 20·0	− 50·0	− 50·0	0	0
45·8	− 34·9	+ 20·7	+ 23·8	+ 34·0	− 21·4	+ 10·1	+ 30·6	+ 29·4	+ 13·8
−	+ 17·8	− 7·6	− 42·2	+ 44·3	+ 11·2	− 64·1	− 1·0	− 12·7	− 37·4
27·2	− 1·3	− 91·0	− 58·0	+135·0	+ 15·0	+ 10·0	+130·0	+ 25·0	− 100·0
27·2	+ 16·5	− 98·6	− 100·2	+179·3	+ 26·2	− 54·1	+129·0	− 12·3	− 137·4
73·0	+ 18·4	− 77·9	− 76·4	− 213·3	+ 4·8	− 44·0	+159·6	+ 41·7	− 123·6
45·3	− 4·2	+147·7	+147·2	− 20·5	+136·5	+ 87·4	+ 87·9	+ 94·7	+105·6

[6] These figures are derived from the figures published in *Federal Reserve Bulletin*. In the United States, banks and bankers performing foreign banking operations make weekly reports covering not only the reporting bank's own short liabilities to foreigners, but also short obligations held for foreign account which represent claims on institutions, firms and individuals in U.S.A. In addition, figures of foreign assets and liabilities with respect to each country are provided. In the Table the changes from year to year are shown, after conversion at the average pound-dollar exchange rate of the December of the year

[7] For 1928–31 the figures consist of foreign balances held in London and London's acceptances on foreign account, as given in the *MacMillan Report*. In the Table the net year-to-year changes are shown. For the rest of the period the figures are estimates based upon the facts given by the Bank for International Settlements in its *Annual Reports*. Moreover, in the figures for 1931–3 the Treasury advances from foreign financial centres and its repayments are included.

PART III

THE BALANCE OF PAYMENTS OF DIFFERENT TYPES OF COUNTRY

CHAPTER VIII

THE AMERICAN BALANCE OF PAYMENTS[1]

The U.S.A. is the only country in the world which is highly industrialised and self-sufficient in most natural products. In American official estimates, the income account includes the items: 'Government Aid and Settlement', 'Other Government Transactions', and 'Silver Movement'. The changes in these items are arbitrary and not subject to the influence of cyclical fluctuations; and, therefore, we exclude them in our reconstruction of the American income account.

TABLE 33. *American income account (in mn. dollars)*

Year	Balance of merchandise trade	Balance of income account excluding government transactions, etc.	Balance of income account including government transactions, etc.
1924	+ 981	+ 903	+ 975
1925	+ 683	+ 620	+ 709
1926	+ 378	+ 366	+ 454
1927	+ 680	+ 624	+ 721
1928	+1037	+ 981	+1027
1929	+ 842	+ 743	+ 786
1930	+ 782	+ 620	+ 735
1931	+ 333	+ 187	+ 175
1932	+ 288	+ 153	+ 159
1933	+ 225	+ 187	+ 108
1934	+ 478	+ 447	+ 341
1935	+ 236	+ 256	− 156
1936	+ 33	− 86	− 218
1937	+ 265	+ 62	− 31
1938	+1134	+1194	+ 967

Two observations can be made. First, the U.S.A. runs a habitual surplus on merchandise trade; and, in general, the surplus tends to rise in times of world prosperity and to fall during depression. But the decline in the amount of surplus during 1935–7 was due to the much larger increase in the value of imports caused by New-Deal prosperity. Secondly, the

[1] As the American balance of payments has been described in detail in the U.S. Government document, 'The United States in the World Economy', we intend here to give only the results of our statistical calculations.

balance on income account shows the same pattern of cyclical fluctuations as the balance of merchandise trade. The divergence between the yearly figures of the last two columns in Table 33 is not large, except in 1935–7. The large deficit during these years as indicated in the last column was mainly caused by American purchases of silver from abroad. The annual payments by Americans through this channel were: 396 mn. dollars in 1935, 114 mn. dollars in 1936 and 88 mn. dollars in 1937.

These facts are supported by our results from statistical calculations. The regression equations are as follows:

1. *Merchandise trade.* Both the income elasticity of imports and that of exports tend to be larger than unity; but the absolute magnitude of the former is less than half that of the latter:

$$\log (\text{Quantity of imports}) = 1 \cdot 27 \log (\text{American real income})$$
$$- 0 \cdot 97 \log \left(\frac{\text{Import price with tariff}}{\text{Cost of living index}} \right),$$

with $R = 0 \cdot 91$;

$$\log (\text{Quantity of exports}) = 2 \cdot 917 \log (\text{World real income})$$
$$- 0 \cdot 43 \log \left(\frac{\text{American export price}}{\text{Competitors' price}} \right),$$

with $R = 0 \cdot 97$.

The terms of trade tend to change against the U.S.A. during general world prosperity, as shown in the equations:

$$\log (\text{American import price})$$
$$= 1 \cdot 375 \log (\text{American real income}),$$

with $R = 0 \cdot 91$; and

$$\log (\text{American export price}) = 0 \cdot 937 \log (\text{American real income}),$$

with $R = 0 \cdot 93$.

2. *Other current transactions.* The elasticities in connection with other current transactions are given in Table 34.

From all these elasticities, we can calculate the net change in the balance on American income account, assuming that real income expands 1 % both in America and in the outside world. But in the period under study, the economic fluctuations in the U.S.A. tended, on the average, to be more violent than those in the rest of the world. Their average relationship is given by the equation:

log (American real income) = 2·146 log (World real income).

This fact alters the amount of change in the balance on the American income account. The results are given in Table 35.

TABLE 34. *Income elasticity of current receipts or payments*

	Correlation coefficient	Elasticity with respect to	
		American money income	World money income
Interest receipts	0·84	—	+1·3970
Interest payments	0·77	+1·1319	—
Net tourist payments*	0·90	+1·2240	—
Net immigrants' remittances	0·71	+0·4143	—
Net shipping payments	0·69	+1·1450	—

* 1931 and 1932 are excluded because of the abnormal influence of world exchange depreciation.

TABLE 35. *The cyclical pattern of American income account**
(in millions of U.S. dollars)

	Economic activity expands by 1 % both in the U.S.A. and in the world	1 % world expansion associated with 2·146 % in the U.S.A.
Imports	− 81·08	− 173·27
Exports	+ 186·60	+ 195·01
Interest receipts	+ 18·88	+ 18·88
Interest payments	− 3·69	− 7·90
Net tourist payments	− 4·39	− 9·42
Net immigrants' remittances	− 1·71	− 3·67
Net shipping payments	− 0·86	− 1·84
Net change in the balance	+ 114·53	+ 17·79

* The calculated values are based upon their respective average values of 1925–6. Other equations required in our calculations are as follows:
log (Cost-of-living) = 0·668 log (American income);
log (Competitors' prices) = 1·0764 log (World real income);
log (American money income) = 1·3635 log (American real income);
and, log (World money income in U.S. dollars) = 1·75 log (World real income).

The results in Table 35 lend support to our argument that the American income account tends to show alternate cyclical surpluses and deficits in relation to world prosperity and depression. The interesting point is the importance of the difference in the amplitude of economic fluctuations. As shown above, the fact of the more violent expansion in the U.S.A.

greatly reduces the amount of surplus below that arising in the case of an equal percentage expansion all over the world. Moreover, it should be borne in mind that the impact of American fluctuations upon the world economy cannot best be judged from the pattern of cyclical changes in the balance on income account, as the total supply of dollars through American purchases of world commodities and services and her export of long-term capital shows very great cyclical variability and instability. It is, however, the change of total supply of dollars through these channels, which influences the world economic activity.

CHAPTER IX

THE SWEDISH BALANCE OF PAYMENTS

(i) GENERAL REMARKS

Sweden is chosen to represent the countries belonging to the 'less-industrialised' type. The general features of the internal economy of these countries are a fairly advanced stage of industrialisation together with a relatively high degree of self-sufficiency in foodstuffs. In the field of international trade, their exports consist mainly of specialised manufactures and raw materials which are used to exchange for those manufactures and raw materials not produced at home. By the nature of their composition, both the income elasticity of home demand for imports and the income elasticity of world demand for exports tend in general to be fairly high; but one may not expect them to be much different in absolute value. Thus, with an equal percentage economic expansion or contraction at home and abroad, the change in the relative quantities is not large. Moreover, for the same reason, the cyclical change in the relative price levels for this type of country is less obvious and less important than for other types of industrial country. Therefore, broadly speaking, the cyclical pattern of the balance of trade of these countries is not predominantly determined by the changes in relative quantities and prices.[1]

As can be seen in Table 36, the cyclical pattern of the balance of trade of six countries belonging to this type tends to be that the habitual deficit decreases in times of general world prosperity and increases during world depression. The predominant factor determining the cyclical pattern would therefore seem to be the difference in the amplitude of economic fluctuations at home and abroad. In other words, the cyclical pattern results from the fact that the amplitude of the home cycle tends, on the average, to be smaller than that of the world cycle.

[1] This is a broad statement applying to the 'typical' country of this type. But this does not mean that individual cases may not be different from the 'typical' one.

In Table 36, the balance of the merchandise trade of Sweden, Belgium, France, Czechoslovakia, the Netherlands and Switzerland has been added together.

TABLE 36. *Balance of merchandise trade of six countries (in millions of U.S. dollars at 1929 parity)* *

Year	Balance of trade	Year	Balance of trade
1924	− 466	1932	−840
1925	− 424	1933	−713
1926	− 417	1934	−491
1927	− 348	1935	−562
1928	− 519	1936	−537
1929	− 935	1937	−507
1930	− 1,053	1938	−445
1931	− 1,072		

* Compiled from League of Nations' *Statistical Year-book*, various years.

Moreover, these countries have net receipts from all other current transactions, viz. shipping services, commissions, interest and dividends, etc. In general, these items tend to have a positive correlation with the world cycle, i.e. the net receipts tend to rise in prosperity and to fall during depression. Therefore, this tendency accentuates the change in the balance of merchandise trade during a cycle. The balance on income account for Sweden, France and Czechoslovakia is available; and the sum is shown in Table 37.

TABLE 37. *Cyclical change in the balance of income account of three countries* * (in millions of U.S. dollars at 1929 parity)

Year	Balance on income account	Year	Balance on income account
1927	+609·3	1932	− 184·5
1928	+572·8	1933	− 76·4
1929	+417·4	1934	+ 8·0
1930	+279·5	1935	− 15·4
1931	− 67·8	1936	− 85·5

* Compiled from League of Nations' *Statistical Year-book*, various years.

In general, we may conclude that the cyclical pattern of the income account of the less industrialised countries tends to run an alternate surplus and deficit in relation to world prosperity and depression.

(ii) THE CYCLICAL PATTERN OF THE
SWEDISH INCOME ACCOUNT

1. *Exports.* Sweden is one of the European industrial countries in which export trade is very important to the home economy. With regard to the value of exports in proportion to the size of population, the industrial countries in Europe which can be compared with her are the U.K., Netherlands and Belgium. Moreover, Sweden is very specialised in international trade.

First, this specialisation is reflected in the quite similar pattern of the relative composition of her imports and exports. That is to say, she is specialised in the production of certain manufactures and raw materials, and exchanges them for those which cannot be produced at home with the best advantage.

TABLE 38. *Pattern of Swedish imports and exports*
(based upon 1929 *value)*

Commodity groups	Imports (%)	Exports (%)
Food and drink, including live animals	21·8	9·5
Raw materials	33·9	49·7
Manufactures	44·3	40·8

Secondly, despite the broad similar relative compositions, Swedish exports as a whole consist of a narrower range of goods than her imports. For instance, her exports of raw materials are confined to two categories of goods, i.e. iron ore and timber and timber products; whereas, on the other hand, the imported raw materials consist of coal, oil, dyestuffs, copper, etc. As to the manufactures, she produces a few high quality goods which are used to exchange for mass-produced cheaper manufactures. One interesting example in this connection is that, because of her high specialisation in steel production, she has to depend upon the outside world for steel of different grades. With regard to foodstuffs, her imports and exports of cereals are roughly balanced except for harvest fluctuations; and there is even a small excess of exports of meat and dairy produce, especially butter. But she relies upon foreign sources for fruits, coffee and tobacco. A better picture of Swedish exports can be seen in Table 39.

Thirdly, the fact of Swedish specialisation can be viewed from another angle. Swedish share in total world exports is, on the average of the inter-war period, less than 1·5%. But the role of Sweden in the world economy cannot be judged from this low percentage. As a matter of fact, she supplies the world with 40–45% of its wood pulp; and, moreover, nearly half of the iron ore entering into world trade comes from Sweden.[1]

TABLE 39. *Composition of Swedish exports*
(based upon 1929 value)

Commodity groups	%
Products of forestry and wood goods industry	19·0
Products of wood pulp and paper industry	26·0
Sub-total	45·0
Ores and other minerals	14·0
Products of metal and machine industry	22·0
Agricultural produce	10·0
Others	9·0

* Skandinaviska Kreditaktiebolaget, Quarterly Report, January 1932, p. 6.

Lastly, the ratios of her specialised exports to the corresponding total home production are high, as shown in Table 40.

TABLE 40. *Ratio of exports to total production of certain commodities (average quantity figures of 1926–30)* *

Commodities	%
Iron ore	96·0
Wood pulp	69·0
Pig iron	22·0
Steel	20·0

* Quoted in A. Montgomery, *How Sweden Overcame the Depression*, pp. 31–2.

The high percentage of raw materials and manufactures would lead us to expect that the cyclical change in the quantity of Swedish exports would be elastic with respect to world income change; whereas, on the other hand, because of its being a specialised trade, it would tend to be inelastic with respect to the change in Swedish export prices relative to her competitors'

[1] Based upon 1935 figures. League of Nations' *International Trade in Foodstuffs and Raw Materials*, 1935.

prices. Our expectations are supported by the results derived from statistical calculation.

$$\text{Log (Quantity of exports)} = 1 \cdot 498 \text{ log (World real income)}$$
$$- 0 \cdot 358 \text{ log} \left(\frac{\text{Swedish export price}}{\text{Competitors' price}} \right),$$

with $R = 0 \cdot 942$.

The Swedish export price is closely correlated with her own income; but its amplitude of cyclical change is not as great as in the case of agricultural countries as is shown by the equation,

$$\text{log (Swedish export price)} = 1 \cdot 1394 \text{ log (Swedish real income)},$$

with $R = 0 \cdot 87$.

2. *Imports.* The cyclical change in the Swedish quantity of imports can also be explained by similar factors. The average relationship for the period as a whole is given by the following equation:

$$\text{log (Quantity of imports)} = 1 \cdot 742 \text{ log (Swedish real income)}$$
$$- 0 \cdot 367 \text{ log} \left(\frac{\text{Swedish import price with tariff}}{\text{Cost of living index}} \right),$$

with $R = 0 \cdot 85$.

The import prices are correlated with the world real income, the regression equation being:

$$\text{log (Swedish import prices)} = 0 \cdot 925 \text{ log (World real income)},$$

with $R = 0 \cdot 89$.

3. *Cyclical change of the balance of merchandise trade.* From the above equations, supplemented by further calculations, we can derive the cyclical pattern of the Swedish balance of trade.[1]

Assume that real income in Sweden and in the world change simultaneously by 1%. Taking into consideration both the income elasticity and the price elasticity, the net change in the quantity of imports is an increase of 1·5309% while that in the quantity of exports is 1·5295%. Thus, the relative quantities remain unchanged during the cyclical fluctuations. However,

---

[1] The other regression equations needed in our calculations are: log (Cost of living) = 0·35 log (Swedish real income), with $R = 0 \cdot 81$ and log (Competitors' price in kronor) = 1·29 log (World real income), with $R = 0 \cdot 91$.

TABLE 41. *Cylindrical change in the balance of merchandise trade (in mn. kronor)*

	1 % increase in income in Sweden and in the world	1 % increase in Swedish income associated with 1·14% increase in the world
Exports	+36·30	+40·00
Imports	−35·94	−36·90
Net increase in the favourable balance	+ 0·36	+ 3·10

the terms of trade tend to change slightly in favour of Sweden during prosperity. In terms of value, the cyclical percentage change in exports is slightly higher than that of imports. But Sweden runs habitual import surplus on her merchandise trade; and, thus, starting from the average import and export value of 1924–6, the absolute change in the balance of trade is only an increase of the surplus of 0·36 mn. kronor, as shown in Table 41. This result would seem to suggest that the net change in the Swedish balance of merchandise trade is neutral with respect to 1 % increase or decrease in the real income both at home and abroad. But, on the average of the period under investigation, the Swedish cycle is less violent than the world; as is shown by the equation:

$$\log (\text{World real income}) = 1·14 \log (\text{Swedish real income}).$$

This fact leads to a larger percentage increase in the value of exports; and, consequently, the export surplus becomes 3·1 mn. kronor.[1] Therefore, we may conclude that the pattern of the Swedish balance of merchandise trade is to show a cyclical surplus in times of general world prosperity and a cyclical deficit during world depression. Moreover, the predominant factor in determining the pattern would seem to be the difference in the amplitude between the Swedish cycle and the world cycle.

4. *Income account as a whole.* Sweden runs net receipts on account of all other current transactions. The two most important credit items are shipping services and interest receipts; whereas, all other items show only small net receipts.

[1] The import value also increases, but slightly. This is due to the change in import prices.

The change in Swedish shipping income may be related to world money income; and the regression equation is:

$$\log \text{(Swedish shipping income)} = 1 \cdot 63 \log \text{(World income)},$$

with $R = 0 \cdot 91$.

Associated with a $1 \cdot 14\%$ increase in world real income and starting from the average value of 1924–6, the increase of shipping income in kronor is $3 \cdot 95$ mn.

For the period from 1924 to 1928, the net interest receipts of Sweden were as follows:

TABLE 42. *Net interest receipts of Sweden* (*in mn. kronor*)

Year	Amount	Year	Amount
1924	+ 6	1932	+138
1925	+ 3	1933	+ 89
1926	+ 7	1934	+ 76
1927	+19	1935	+ 99
1928	+25	1936	+ 84
1929	+30	1937	+123
1930	+20	1938	+109
1931	+10		

Broadly speaking, this item did not exhibit any marked cyclical behaviour. This was primarily because of the nature of the Swedish foreign investment. As nearly three-quarters of it consisted of foreign government bonds, it can hardly be expected that the yield was very sensitive to world economic fluctuations. Moreover, as Sweden became a regular capital-exporting country only since the middle of the 'twenties, the steady yearly increase of the net receipts from 1924 to 1929 reflected the income from an increased volume of foreign investment rather than the prosperity of the world. But undoubtedly the fall in the receipts during 1930 and 1931 was attributable to the world depression, which entailed the default of foreign interest payments to Sweden. The amount of interest receipts from 1932 onward showed a spectacular increase, the absolute amount in the 'thirties being five to six times that in the 'twenties. Strictly speaking, the figures in these two periods are not comparable, as the estimates for the latter period cover a wider field.[1] But the increase in the net receipts was also due to two other reasons.

[1] Skandinaviska Kreditaktiebolaget, Quarterly Report, October 1934.

On the one hand, as nearly two-thirds of the foreign bonds issued in the Swedish market or bought by Swedish nationals in the 'twenties were bonds in terms of the American dollar, the depreciation of krona thus leads to an increase of interest receipts in kronor. On the other hand, the increase in net receipts was also due to a decrease of interest payments by Sweden as a result of the stoppage of dividend payments on shares and debentures of the Kreuger Company. Moreover, as defaults of loans and suspension of interest payments by foreigners increased during 1933 and 1934, Swedish interest receipts fell again as compared with 1932.[1] Nevertheless, when the payments were resumed again in the later 'thirties, Swedish net receipts rose again.

However, in general, the net receipts for all other current transactions taken together tend to rise and fall with the world trade cycle. On the basis of exports, imports and shipping income, the net increase in the surplus would, on the average, be 7·01 mn. kronor, given a 1% expansion in Sweden associated with a 1·14% expansion in the world. Therefore, we may conclude that the cyclical pattern of the Swedish income account tends to show an alternate surplus and deficit with the general world prosperity and depression.

(iii) SWEDISH LONG-TERM CAPITAL EXPORTS

By the middle 'twenties, Sweden had attained the status of a regular long-term capital-exporting country.[2] Among the items in the long-term capital account, purchase and sale of foreign and home securities showed constant and consistent

---

[1] The most notable example was the suspension of the service payments of the German bonds. It has been estimated that at the end of 1933, the total default on loans amounted to 44·7%; and that during 1934 this percentage increased to two-thirds.

[2] Before World War I, Sweden was a debtor country, floating loans regularly abroad for home economic expansion. But by the beginning of the nineteen-twenties, she had become practically self-sufficient in regard to the supply of capital to her home industries; and, in the first three years of the 'twenties, there was a considerable outflow of capital. As this outflow mainly took the form of the repurchase of Swedish bonds held abroad, her foreign indebtedness was substantially reduced. Nominal value of Swedish bonds held in the foreign countries in 1914 was 1,155 mn. kr. and, by 1924, it was reduced to 415 mn. kr. (Vide Skandinaviska Kreditaktiebolaget, 'Sweden's Foreign Bond Debts', in the quarterly report of July 1931.)

changes with respect to the general world cycle, as can be seen in Table 43.

TABLE 43. *Components of Swedish long-term capital account (in mn. kronor)* *

Year	Net sale or purchase of foreign and home securities	Net movement of long-term capital
1924	+ 33	+ 18
1925	− 7	− 32
1926	− 44	+ 16
1927	− 46	+155
1928	− 65	−118
1929	− 22	− 12
1930	−387	−392
1931	+ 95	−140
1932	+104	+124
1933	+ 38	+ 55
1934	− 63	− 48
1935	+ 6	+ 22
1936	− 11	+ 23
1937	− 7	−122
1938	− 50	− 50

* Net export is indicated by a minus sign and net import by a plus sign.

It can be seen that the net purchase of foreign and home securities tends to rise during world prosperity and changes into net sale in times of depression. Or, in other words, through this channel, Sweden exports long-term capital in prosperity and imports capital during depression. The fundamental factor determining such cyclical net purchase or sale would seem to have been the less violent amplitude of the Swedish cycle relative to the world cycle.[1] For instance, during general world prosperity, Swedish capital tends to move outward seeking higher returns; and conversely. Nevertheless, in spite of world depression in 1930, there was an abnormal outflow of Swedish long-term capital, which was caused by the heavy purchase of German bonds by the Kreuger Company.

The totals for the net long-term capital movements include also the items such as government participation in foreign new issues, other long-term investments, etc. Although broadly reflecting the world cycle, the figures for the net movements show contrary changes to those for net purchase or sale of

[1] As indicated in the above, the Swedish cycle was, on the average, less violent than the world cycle.

securities in some years. These contrary changes, however, can be explained. The net inflows during 1926–7 were the results of (1) a flotation in the U.S.A. by the Swedish State, intended for investment in state commercial undertakings; (2) foreign borrowing by certain municipalities; and (3) the raising of industrial capital for expansion by the Swedish companies affiliated with the Match Trust.[1] Another contrary change occurred in the year 1931. This was due to the loan operations of the Kreuger Company, which raised two loans in the Swedish market on behalf of foreign governments, chiefly Germany.[2] The year 1936 was also an exception.

In conclusion, for the inter-war period, the Swedish long-term capital has a broad tendency to show a net export in prosperity and a net import during depression.

(iv) EQUILIBRIUM IN THE SWEDISH BALANCE OF PAYMENTS

In Fig. 21 the annual figures for the balance on income account and the net movement of long-term capital are compared. As expected, the balance on income account showed a net surplus during the prosperous 'twenties; and, moreover, the yearly increases indicated a very close correlation with world expansion. The balance was steadily increasing from 1925 onward with the exception of 1928; and, at the peak of world prosperity in 1929, it reached the level of 277 mn. kronor. The relatively small surplus in 1928 was mainly due to the fall of the value of exports caused by industrial strikes and lock-outs in the principal Swedish export industries. With the coming of the crisis in 1930, it showed a sharp decline; and, in the next year it even changed into a deficit. In 1932, mainly because the recorded value of the interest receipts showed a substantial increase, the income account had a small surplus; and, during the recovery period of the 'thirties it remained favourable.

The course of the long-term capital movement has already been explained in the last section. In spite of the fact that its cyclical movements tended to offset broadly the change in the

---

[1] Skandinaviska Kreditaktiebolaget, 'Sweden's Import and Export of Capital', Quarterly Report, January 1927.
[2] B. Thomas, *Monetary Policy and Crisis*, p. 183.

balance on income account, its yearly figures often showed large discrepancies. In Fig 22, the yearly net payments or net receipts arising out of these two accounts are shown; and the balancing items are also given.

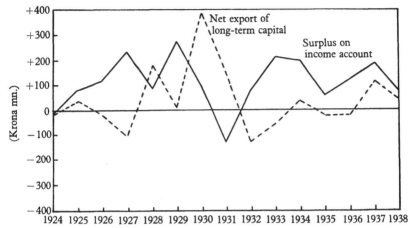

Fig. 21. Cyclical equilibrium in the Swedish balance of payments (in millions of kronor). In this diagram, the net export of capital is indicated by a positive sign

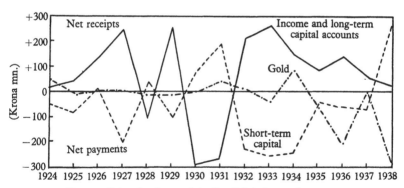

Fig. 22. Balancing items of the Swedish balance of payments
(in millions of kronor)

For the period as a whole, the curve for net receipts or payments on income and long-term capital account showed violent changes; but there were net receipts in most years. As to the balancing items, the gold movement played no part until the later 'thirties. In the 'twenties the gold movement, at a very low level, was not always in the direction which would be suggested by the curve of net receipts or payments. On the other hand, the curve for short-term capital movements had a very close inverse correlation with the curve for net receipts. Most of this 'equilibrating' short-term capital movement resulted in a net addition or reduction in the foreign exchange reserves held by the Riksbank in Sweden. For instance, when there was a net receipt in a given year, the Swedish nationals sold their foreign exchange to the Riksbank, whose stock was thus increased; and conversely. Therefore, the changes in the foreign exchange reserves, besides performing the function of balancing items, also induced corresponding changes in the internal monetary conditions in Sweden, which will be discussed in the next section.

(v) THE COURSE OF SWEDISH BALANCE OF PAYMENTS IN THE INTER-WAR PERIOD

The severe dislocation of production consequent upon World War I was gradually overcome in the middle 'twenties; and the years from 1924 to 1929 in Sweden were marked by mild economic expansion. Wholesale prices showed a downward movement; but industrial production expanded, productive efficiency increased, unemployment fell and real wages rose.[1] But this favourable situation can be seen in its true significance only in relation to her foreign trade, or her whole balance of payments. From 1924 to 1930, her industrial production increased by 23%; whereas her export quantity increased by more than 32%. Because of the high ratio of export to national income and especially because of the importance of exports to several of her main industries, such as the mining, wood, and general engineering industries,[2] this external stimulating force upon the Swedish internal economy cannot be overlooked. As a matter of fact, there were two special factors responsible for the expansion of her exports.[3] First, because Sweden had a special technical superiority in the production of telephones, separators, wires, ball-bearings, etc., the boom in Germany and the U.S.A. greatly stimulated the demand for such goods from

[1] Montgomery, op. cit. pp. 23–38.   [2] Vide supra, Table 40.
[3] Thomas, op. cit. p. 177.

Sweden. The same applied to the Swedish export of iron ore. Another favourable factor was the secular increase in the world consumption of paper and other forestry products. In brief, partly due to technical superiority in the production of certain manufactures and partly due to being the main supplier in the world market of certain 'expanding' commodities, Sweden could share fully the world economic expansion in the 'twenties.

Moreover, in her total balance of payments Sweden had net receipts from foreigners during the period 1924–9 (except 1928). The consequent increase in the foreign exchange reserves of the Riksbank led to a rise of liquidity in the Swedish money market. In contrast to the situation in the U.K. and the U.S.A., the discount rate of the Riksbank was able to be reduced, as shown in Table 44. This fact had, no doubt, a favourable and stimulating effect upon the internal expansion in Sweden during this period.

TABLE 44. *Discount rates of central banks*

Year	Riksbank (%)	Bank of England (%)	Federal Reserve Bank (%)
1924	5·50	4·00	4·14
1925	5·17	4·57	3·81
1926	4·50	5·00	3·99
1927	4·15	4·65	3·85
1928	4·01	4·50	4·42
1929	4·74	5·50	4·92
1930	3·72	3·42	3·82

Sweden was not very seriously affected by the world depression until late in 1930. The depression spread to Sweden in much the same way as in the case of the U.K. It was through the channel of a financial crisis caused by capital outflow, joined with the adverse effect of falling exports. In the second half of 1930, output and employment in her main export industries fell; and, during 1931, the slump was also felt by the industries producing mainly for home market.[1] From 1929 to 1932, the decrease in the output of the former was 34% while the latter fell only about 13%.[2]

In the autumn of 1931 Sweden had a financial crisis in her external affairs. The income account changed from a surplus of

[1] Cf. Montgomery, op. cit. p. 32. In 1929, Swedish export value was 1,813 mn. kronor; it fell to 1,550 mn. in 1930 and 946 mn. in 1931.
[2] Ibid. p. 33.

163

97 mn. kronor in the previous year to a deficit of 127 mn. kronor in 1931. This was, however, temporarily balanced by an inflow of foreign short-term capital into Sweden, resulting from the confidence crisis in various parts of the Continent. But as world depression spread and deepened, these foreign short-term funds began to withdraw; and it has been estimated that, in the three months from June to August 1931, no less than 216 mn. kronor of it was withdrawn.[1] Furthermore, the foreign loan operations of the Kreuger Company added fuel to this already smouldering situation. Two loans during the summer and autumn were raised in Sweden by this undertaking on behalf of foreign governments, and the proceeds were used to acquire foreign exchange. The foreign exchange reserves of the Riksbank had decreased during 1931 by about 240 mn. kronor;[2] and, moreover, gold holdings also decreased by export. Consequently, Sweden followed the U.K. off gold and depreciated the krona.

Whether the depreciation of the krona had any considerable favourable effect upon Swedish foreign trade is difficult to determine quantitatively. It would seem that the favourable effect, if any, was on the whole very small. In Table 45, the actual movements of Swedish imports from and exports to countries with and without depreciated currencies are compared.

TABLE 45. *Value and percentage of change of Swedish imports from and exports to certain countries (in mn. kronor)**

Countries	Exports to			Imports from		
	Value in 1929	Value in 1932	Decrease (%)	Value in 1929	Value in 1932	Decrease (%)
All countries	1,813	946	47·7	1,776	1,169	36·0
Countries on gold:						
U.S.A.	198	100	49·6	246	125	49·3
France	102	56	45·3	52	30	42·8
Netherlands	70	32	54·0	74	47	36·3
Belgium	57	26	54·4	33	26	21·2
Countries off gold:						
U.K.	450	242	46·3	308	194	37·1
Denmark	115	61	47·7	125	73	41·6
Finland	50	28	43·9	11	9	14·0

* Source: *International Trade Statistics*, 1930 and 1933.

[1] Thomas, op. cit. p. 184.
[2] League of Nations' *Central Banks*, 1933.

On *a priori* grounds, as a result of the depreciation of the krona, Swedish exports to the countries on gold should fall less than those to the countries off gold. But the table shows that the reduction in the world demand for Swedish exports was fairly uniform as between different countries. As to imports, the percentage falls were different for the countries on gold and for the countries off gold, being on the whole heavier in the case of the former. But it is difficult to draw any definite conclusions as to the effect of the depreciation of the krona; for the different percentage falls may also reflect the difference of the income demand for imports from different countries. This is obvious at least in the case of the U.S.A., whose imports into Sweden consisted of high income elasticity goods. Moreover, the three countries used to represent the countries off gold all belonged to the sterling area. The linking of the krona to the pound sterling may have increased the share of the sterling area countries' imports in the total.

Furthermore, the percentage fall in the total value of Swedish exports was even larger than that in the total value of Swedish imports. This sounds paradoxical, as the contrary phenomenon would be expected to be associated with the depreciation of a country's currency. However, it can be explained. On the one hand, it was due to the unfavourable change of the terms of trade against Sweden during the world depression; and, on the other, it was due to the relatively smaller amplitude of economic contraction in Sweden.

Therefore, the abandonment of the gold standard and the subsequent stabilisation *vis-à-vis* the pound sterling did not have the effect of an over-all increase of exports and decrease of imports, as would be expected. Nevertheless, this measure placed Sweden in a position to adopt an independent expansionary monetary policy, upon which the compensatory budgetary and public-works policies of the Swedish Government were based. It is beyond the scope of the present study to discuss the role of these compensatory policies in the Swedish recovery. But one thing seems to stand out quite clearly, viz. the actual revival of Sweden was predominantly due to the recovery of Swedish exports. A few figures may be useful to illustrate our argument.

As a matter of fact, from 1929 to 1932, public works expenditures, though counter-cyclical, increased only slightly; and it was not until 1934 that their scale became really large.[1] At that time, Swedish exports had already begun their revival. Nevertheless, such counter-cyclical public spending provides one reason why Sweden weathered the depression better than other countries.[2]

The factors responsible for the Swedish recovery may be briefly summarised. The main force came from abroad. First of all, there was the relatively earlier recovery of the sterling area countries.[3] As these countries, in the pre-Depression days, took about one-half of Swedish exports, their recovery contributed greatly towards the expansion of Swedish exports. Moreover, the increasing building activity all over the world, especially in the U.K., during the earlier recovery period, stimulated the demand for Swedish timber exports. Wood-pulp was also demanded for manufacturing paper, artificial silks, etc., which showed an enormous expansion in the 'thirties. After 1934, the world rearmament programmes favoured the Swedish exports of iron ore and other iron and steel manufactures.

Because of the importance of exports in Swedish economy, their expansion provided a direct and effective stimulus to Swedish recovery. The favourable conditions in her merchandise exports, together with increase in the net receipts of all other current transactions, resulted in a steady rise of the surplus on income account in the later 'thirties. But, on the other hand, the net export of long-term capital during 1933–8 amounted only to 120 mn. kronor. This under-lending on long-term account gave rise to an accumulation of foreign exchange and gold in the Riksbank, as shown in Table 46.

[1] The Swedish public spending, including relief works, emergency works and state enterprise, during the period 1929–35 was as follows:

	In mn. kronor
1929/30	23·1
1930/31	32·5
1931/32	66·2
1932/33	75·8
1933/34	246·9
1934/35	204·3

(The figures are taken from G. Wilson, 'Public Works Policy', in *Democratic Sweden*, edited by M. I. Cole, p. 38.)

[2] From the peak of 1929, Swedish income had fallen only about 16% in 1932.

[3] Vide supra, Table 12.

THE BALANCE OF PAYMENTS

(in millions

	1924	1925	1926	1927	1928
I. INCOME ACCOUNT					
A. *Merchandise:*					
Exports	+ 1,261	+ 1,361	+ 1,420	+ 1,617	+ 1,576
Imports	− 1,425	− 1,449	− 1,491	− 1,588	− 1,711
Balance	− 164	− 88	− 71	+ 29	− 135
B. *Other items:*					
Net freight receipts [2]	+ 142	+ 149	+ 169	+ 183	+ 183
Emigrants' remittances	+ 30	+ 33	+ 35	+ 35	+ 35
Net interest receipts	+ 6	+ 3	+ 7	+ 19	+ 25
Tourist receipts or expenditures	− 20	− 20	− 20	− 24	− 28
Balance	+ 158	+ 165	+ 191	+ 213	+ 215
Balance of income account	− 6	+ 77	+ 120	+ 242	+ 80
II. NET GOLD MOVEMENT	+ 52	− 2	+ 2	+ 1	− 11
III. CAPITAL ACCOUNT					
A. *Long-term capital movement:*					
Amortisation receipts and payments [3]	—	—	—	—	—
Purchase and sale of:					
(a) Real estate	—	—	—	—	—
(b) Domestic securities	+ 33	+ 13	+ 15	+ 70	+ 28
(c) Foreign securities	—	− 20	− 59	− 116	− 93
Other long-term investment	− 15	− 25	+ 60	+ 155	{ − 118
New capital issues					
Balance	+ 18	− 32	+ 16	+ 109	− 183
B. *Short-term capital movement:*					
Change in short-term debts	—	—	—	—	—
Change in short-term assets	− 56	− 88	+ 12	− 200	+ 38
Balance	− 56	− 88	+ 12	− 200	+ 38
Balance of capital account	− 36	− 120	+ 28	− 91	− 145
IV. RESIDUE ITEM	− 10	+ 45	− 150	− 152	+ 76

[1] Compiled from League of Nations' *Balance of Payments* of various years and Skandinaviska Kreditaktiebolaget, quarterly reports. In this table, the '—' sign indicates that the data are not available.

of kronor)

1929	1930	1931	1932	1933	1934	1935	1936	1937	1938
+1,813	+1,550	+1,135	+ 964	+1,093	+1,316	+1,312	+1,529	+2,012	+1,844
-1,776	-1,667	-1,439	-1,169	-1,108	-1,320	-1,495	-1,651	-2,137	-2,087
+ 37	- 117	- 304	- 205	- 15	- 4	- 183	- 122	- 125	- 243
+ 205	+ 189	+ 139	+ 117	+ 115	+ 121	+ 124	+ 136	+ 164	+ 190
+ 35	+ 30	+ 26	+ 35	+ 20	+ 12	+ 12	+ 14	+ 17	+ 14
+ 30	+ 20	+ 10	+ 138	+ 89	+ 76	+ 99	+ 88	+ 123	+ 109
- 30	- 25	+ 2	+ 4	+ 3	- 3	+ 9	+ 4	+ 7	+ 4
+ 240	+ 214	+ 177	+ 294	+ 227	+ 206	+ 244	+ 242	+ 311	+ 317
+ 277	+ 97	- 127	+ 89	+ 212	+ 202	+ 61	+ 120	+ 186	+ 74
- 11	- 3	+ 38	+ 7	- 43	+ 78	- 63	- 208	0	- 282
—	—	- 2	+ 25	+ 18	+ 16	+ 16	+ 16	- 115	—
—	—	—	- 2	—	—	—	—	—	—
+ 35	- 6	+ 21	+ 16	- 23	- 6	+ 38	+ 44	- 1	+ 52
- 57	- 381	+ 74	+ 88	+ 61	- 57	- 32	- 55	- 6	- 102
—	—	- 5	- 3	- 1	- 1	—	+ 18	—	—
+ 10	- 5	- 228	—	—	—	—	—	—	—
- 12	- 392	- 140	+ 124	+ 55	- 48	+ 22	+ 23	- 122	- 50
—	—	+ 3	- 53	+ 84	- 108	0	- 29	+ 48}	+ 257
- 95	+ 79	+ 187	- 174	- 333	- 138	- 45	- 30	- 116}	
- 95	+ 79	+ 190	- 227	- 249	- 246	- 45	- 59	- 68	+ 257
- 107	- 313	+ 50	- 103	- 194	- 294	- 23	- 36	- 190	+ 207
- 159	+ 219	+ 30	+ 7	+ 25	+ 14	+ 25	+ 124	+ 4	+ 1

[2] After deduction of expenditures for coal, oil, etc. in foreign ports.
[3] Amortisation payments, effected by means of repurchases of Swedish bonds from abroad are included in the item, 'Purchase and sale of domestic securities'.

TABLE 46. *Cumulative change in the net receipts on balance of payments and foreign exchange reserves in the Riksbank (in mn. kronor)*

Year	Net receipts*	Gold and foreign exchange in Riksbank†
1933	+267	+ 380
1934	+421	+ 431
1935	+504	+ 567
1936	+647	+ 784
1937	+741	+ 1,063
1938	+765	+ 997

* Vide supra, Fig. 24.
† *Central Banks*, various years. Except in 1938, the figures have been adjusted for the domestic production of gold.

It can be seen that between the end of 1932 and that of 1938, the Riksbank's holding of foreign exchanges and gold increased by nearly 1,000 mn. kronor, mainly because of insufficient long-term lending. This fact created easy monetary conditions in Sweden. As shown in Table 47, both long-term and short-term interest rates in Sweden progressively fell; and, in spite of an increase in the amount of deposits, the cash-ratio went up.[1] The increase in the liquidity in Sweden due to the state of her balance of payments helped to maintain the cheap money policy.

TABLE 47. *Internal monetary conditions in Sweden**

Year	Total deposits (mn. kr.)	Cash reserves (mn. kr.)	Cash-ratio (%)	Yields on long-term government bonds (%)	Commercial bill rate (%)
1924–9 (av.)	3,500	87	2·5	4·69	4·68
1930	3,631	89	2·4	4·18	3·72
1931	3,554	88	2·5	4·22	4·09
1932	3,556	133	3·7	4·32	4·39
1933	3,629	333	9·2	4·02	3·17
1934	3,553	287	8·1	3·47	2·50
1935	3,632	281	7·8	3·19	2·50
1936	3,833	393	10·3	3·12	2·50
1937	4,000	543	12·7	3·04	2·50
1938	4,260	538	12·6	2·34	2·50

* *Statistical Year-book*, various years.

[1] In view of exchange risks, the commercial banks generally sold the exchange acquired from their clients to the Riksbank; but their cash reserves were thereby increased.

CHAPTER X

THE AUSTRALIAN BALANCE OF PAYMENTS

(i) GENERAL REMARKS

The pattern of cyclical behaviour of the Australian balance of payments is here studied as an illustration taken from an agricultural country.

Before we proceed, several broad facts which Australia has in common with all the agricultural countries should be pointed out. The first fact is that the internal economic fluctuations of this type of country are extremely sensitive to, and are predominantly determined by, the external factors. This is because of their dependence on the world market for the sale of their annual produce. The distribution of world natural resources makes them follow the classical pattern of the international division of labour. Their home economic activity consists mainly of the production of one or a few specialised primary staples, which are used to exchange with the rest of the world for manufactured goods. Especially in those countries with a smaller density of population and, hence, a high average productivity of labour, a large part of the annual produce cannot be consumed locally and has to be disposed of in the world market. The amount they can sell is closely correlated with the level of world income; but by the very nature of the commodities it tends to remain fairly stable as between world prosperity and depression. Nevertheless, because of the high degree of dependence on world demand and because of the inelastic supply, the prices and hence the value of their total annual production are sensitive to the change in the world income and tend to have violent cyclical fluctuations. As the level of their internal investment is generally low, exports become the most important source in generating income. Therefore, the violent cyclical fluctuations in export value induce corresponding fluctuations in their national income.

Moreover, the internal economic activity in these countries is also sensitive to external forces because of the cyclical instability in the international flow of long-term capital. As a matter of fact, these countries rely upon foreign long-term capital for their internal investment or development purposes. In general, the absolute amount of foreign lending by the world creditors tends to move positively with the world cycle. In general world prosperity the increased lending by them to the agricultural countries further strengthens economic expansion in the latter; whereas the decreased lending (or, the net repatriation of long-term capital) during a slump reduces investment activity and thus aggravates the contraction.

The second fact is that the pattern of cyclical behaviour of the income account of the agricultural countries is just opposite to that of the industrial countries. That is, it tends to show an alternate deficit and surplus in relation to world prosperity and depression. In Table 48, the data for eleven important world agricultural countries are shown. The countries are Argentina, Bulgaria, Denmark, Estonia, Finland, Hungary, Latvia, Lithuania, Norway, Poland, Australia and New Zealand.

TABLE 48. *Balance of merchandise trade of eleven agricultural countries (in millions of U.S. dollars at 1929 parity)**

Year	Balance of merchandise trade
1924	− 57
1925	− 118
1926	− 149
1927	− 159
1928	− 212
1929	− 295
1930	− 106
1931	+ 192
1932	+ 244
1933	+ 233
1934	+ 169
1935	+ 179
1936	+ 183
1937	+ 83
1938	+ 59

* Compiled from *Statistical Year-book*, various years.

The cyclical pattern of the agricultural countries' balance of merchandise trade is interesting. It tends to show a deficit in prosperity and a surplus during slump and recovery. In the prosperous 'twenties, the deficit was increasing with economic expansion; and the largest deficit was in the year 1929 when the boom reached its peak. As depression came, it changed into a surplus; and in 1932 the surplus amounted to 244 mn. dollars compared with the deficit of 295 mn. dollars in 1929. During the recovery period of the 'thirties, the surplus was gradually decreasing. In the comparatively prosperous year of 1937 it was reduced to only 83 mn. dollars. The general reason for this cyclical pattern would seem to be that the effect of the relative quantity changes tends to more than offset the effect of the relative price changes. For instance, in prosperity, the terms of trade change in favour of this type of country. Therefore, the deficit in the balance of merchandise trade must be caused by a large unfavourable change in the relative quantities. This explanation is supported by the results of our calculations. As is shown in Table 4 and Table 6, the difference in the magnitude of import and export income elasticity of all the agricultural countries tends to result in a large and unfavourable change in relative quantities in prosperity.

Among all the other current transactions, interest and dividends are the largest debit item and tend to be rigid. Other items show great cyclical variations, but their absolute amounts are relatively small. Therefore, all other transactions taken as a whole constitute a net debit item during the different phases of the trade cycle.

The income account of the eleven agricultural countries for the period 1927–36 is given in Table 49. It can be seen that the balance on income account tends to show a net deficit in prosperity and a net surplus in depression.

TABLE 49. *Income account of the eleven agricultural countries (in millions of U.S. dollars at 1929 parity)**

Year	Trade and other current items	Interest and dividends	Net balance
1927	− 11	− 490	− 501
1928	− 56	− 531	− 587
1929	− 153	− 559	− 712
1930	− 10	− 472	− 482
1931	+ 321	− 420	− 99
1932	+ 341	− 318	+ 23
1933	+ 279	− 280	− 1
1934	+ 307	− 263	+ 44
1935	+ 277	− 252	+ 24
1936	+ 288	− 263	+ 25

* *Statistical Year-books*, various years.

(ii) THE PATTERN OF CYCLICAL BEHAVIOUR IN THE AUSTRALIAN INCOME ACCOUNT

1. *Exports.* In Australia, primary production is more than one-fourth of the total national income produced.[1] Consequently, she is specialised in primary exports, which constitute nearly 95 % of the value of total exports. The four main groups of foodstuff and raw material exports are, in the order of importance, wool, wheat, hides and skins, and meat. Moreover, these groups of exports not only bear a high percentage to their respective annual total production in Australia, but also, in some cases, constitute the principal source of supply in the world market, as is shown in Table 50.

TABLE 50. *Australian principal exports*

Groups of commodities	Ratio to total exports (%)	Ratio to annual production in Australia* (%)	Ratio to total world supply† (%)
Wool	40·5	83·7	41·4
Wheat and flour	19·2	69·0	15·1
Hides and skins	6·7	84·3	3·1
Meat	4·6	20·0	‡

* Based upon 1928/29 figures. *Official Year-book of Australia.*
† The ratio represents the percentage of total world trade in the commodity which is supplied by Australia. Here, 1935 figures are used because the figures for the earlier years are not available. See League of Nations' *International Trade in Raw Materials and Foodstuffs*, 1935.
‡ Not available.

Another feature may be noted in passing. Nearly one-half of Australian exports is sent to the U.K. This concentration of market would mean a greater instability for Australian exports, because they are also liable to random changes particular to the market.

With regard to the various export elasticities, we can make two *a priori* deductions from the above salient facts. First, because of the high concentration in foodstuffs and agricultural raw materials, the income elasticity of world demand will be small; and, moreover, because Australia is the principal supplier of her chief exports in the world market, the increase and decrease of the export prices would not induce corresponding

[1] Clark and Crawford, op. cit., pp. 23–4, 50 and 73.

proportionate changes in the export quantity. Secondly, as a result of the concentration of markets together with the low elasticity of supply, Australian export prices will be sensitive to changes in the world demand and will tend to change more than proportionately to world income. These expectations are confirmed by the statistical calculations.

$$\text{Log (Quantity of exports)} = 0 \cdot 2205 \log \text{(World real income)}$$
$$- 0 \cdot 6648 \log \left(\frac{\text{Australian export price}}{\text{Competitors' export price}[1]} \right),$$

with $R = 0 \cdot 92$,

$$\text{Log (Australian export price)} = 2 \cdot 0224 \log \text{(World real income)},$$
with $R = 0 \cdot 81$.

The equations reveal that in spite of the low income elasticity, the great cyclical variability in the export prices will still lead to violent changes in the value of exports. Because of the importance of the exports in the total home production and because of the dependence of a large part of home investment upon the condition of the export industries,[2] Australian national income follows, in general, the course of her exports and therefore also tends to show violent cyclical movements. In Fig. 23, the value of exports, the value of total home primary production and the national income, after their respective trends have been eliminated, are compared. The close correlation between the exports and primary production is what should be expected, as, on the average, more than 75 % of the home primary produce was sold in the world market. The broad cyclical similarity between national income and exports (or, primary production) is also great; but, in the later 'twenties, the former tended to lie consistently above the latter while the reverse was true during the depression. This discrepancy, however, is explained by the factor of public investment. During the later 'twenties, the public investment programme was heavy; but it fell to an insignificant level in the slump.[3] Nevertheless, on the whole, we

---

[1] The competitors' export prices are compiled by combining the indices of Canada, New Zealand and South Africa (in terms of pounds sterling).

[2] For instance, a part of public investment, such as the land settlement programme, and private investment in mill industries were predominantly dependent upon the prospect in export industries.

[3] Vide infra, Table 54.

may say that, in the inter-war period, the variation in exports has been the predominant factor in determining Australian income.

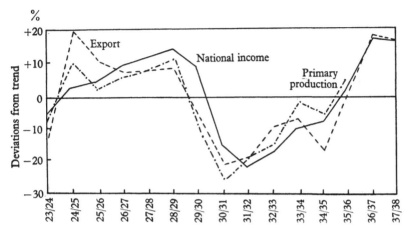

Fig. 23. Indices of the export value, total home primary production and the national income

2. *Imports.* The Australian imports consist mainly of producers' goods and other manufactures, as shown in Table 51. Therefore its income elasticity tends to be high.

TABLE 51. *Principal Australian imports*
(average of 1926/7 *and* 1927/8)

Commodity groups	Total (%)
Metal, metal manufactures and machinery	32·0
Textiles	25·8
Oils, fats and waxes	6·4
Chemicals	3·4
Rubber manufactures	3·2
Total	70·8

Log (Quantity of imports) = 2·796 log (Australian real income)

$$-0·673 \log \left(\frac{\text{Import price with tariff}}{\text{Cost of living index}} \right),$$

with $R = 0·98$.

The import prices are determined by world income. Their cyclical change is, on the average, only half as violent as that of export prices.

Log (Import price) = 1·03 log (World real income),

with $R = 0·83$.

3. *Other invisible items.* In the inter-war period Australia ran a net deficit on all other current transactions. The largest debit item was the overseas interest and dividend payments. The average value for the period amounted to more than £A30 mn. per annum, or about 5% of her annual income. Because a very large part of Australian foreign indebtedness was in the form of fixed-interest bonds in terms of the creditors' currencies, the interest payments did not show strong cyclical movements. These payments were partly offset by the net receipts from shipping and other services. The latter tended to rise in prosperity and to fall in depression; but, nevertheless, their absolute change was not large.

The cyclical fluctuations in the net payments on all other current transactions may be represented by the equation:

log (Net payments on all other current transactions)
= 0·47 log (Australian money income),

with $R = 0·69$.

4. *Balance on income account.* On the basis of the various elasticities, we can calculate the cyclical change in the balance on income account. Let us assume that the world and the Australian real income fall by 1% simultaneously. The net fall in the import quantity would be, on the average, 2·39%.[1] As to exports, the quantity would decrease by 0·2205%. But, as the fall of Australian export price was, on the average, larger than that of her competitors' price,[2] her export quantity would be increased by the effect of substitution. On the basis of the

---

[1] The regression equation of cost of living on Australian real income is:

log (Cost of living) = 0·43 log (Australian real income).

Associated with a 1% decrease in real income everywhere in the world, the change in the import quantity is

−2·7963 + 0·6732 (1·03 − 0·43)%, or −2·39%.

[2] With a 1% decrease in the world real income Australian prices fall by 2·0224%, while her competitors' prices fall by 1·32%.

stated price elasticity, the increase in export quantity due to this effect would be 0·469%. Therefore the net change in export quantity is an increase of 0·2485%. This paradoxical result is in accord with the actual facts, as the Australian trade statistics did show an increase in export quantity during the Great Depression.

Taking into account the change in the terms of trade and starting from the average value of 1925/6–1927/8, we find that, associated with a 1% contraction of world real income, the Australian balance of merchandise trade would benefit by a surplus of £A2·84 mn. But during the period under study, Australian economic fluctuations tended, on the average, to be less violent than those of the world as a whole. The relationship is given by the equation:

$$\log (\text{Australian real income}) = 0\cdot81 \log (\text{World real income}).$$

This fact would decrease the size of the surplus during a slump. The results are compared in Table 52.

TABLE 52. *Cyclical pattern of the Australian income account*

	1% decrease in real income in Australia and in the world (£A mn.)	1% decrease in the world real income associated with a 0·81% decrease in Australian income (£A mn.)
Imports	+5·31	+4·04
Exports	−2·47	−2·47
Other current transactions	+0·19	+0·15
Net balance on income account	+3·03	+1·72

The cyclical pattern of the Australian income account is just opposite to that of the typical industrial countries. During cyclical fluctuations, the effect of the change in the terms of trade is more than offset by that in the relative quantities. Consequently, Australia tends to show an alternate deficit and surplus in relation to the general world prosperity and depression.

(iii) FACTORS INFLUENCING THE IMPORT OF LONG-TERM CAPITAL

During this period, the long-term capital movements showed a large inflow in the prosperous 'twenties, changed into a net export in the slump, and resumed their traditional direction with the recovery in the 'thirties. Can we find any explanation for this?

There are no available data covering all kinds of long-term capital inflow in the 'twenties. For the period 1920–8, Wood has made the following estimates:[1]

TABLE 53. *New money raised abroad* (£A mn.)

Raised by	Amount
Government	210
Municipalities	16
Business	26
Private	14
Total	266

The largest amount of overseas borrowing in the 'twenties was incurred by public bodies. This growth of overseas indebtedness reflected the tremendous expansion of loan expenditure of the Australian government on land settlement projects and on other public works.[2] Internal public debts were also growing, but their absolute amount was much less than the overseas borrowing because the loan expenditure could not be raised at home on such favourable terms as prevailed in the London market.[3]

The private and business borrowing were a relatively small part of the total; but the fundamental factor in determining the demand was the expansion of manufacturing industries in Australia. As a matter of fact, since 1915, Australian industries, such as motor vehicles, electrical and wireless equipment, textiles, etc., had been engaging in raising capital abroad.[4] The tariff amendments after 1921 gave further protection to these industries and thus stimulated their expansion. The inflow of foreign long-term capital for this purpose went on at an accelerated rate; and, during the period from 1922/3 to 1928/9, Australian industrial production increased by more than 30%.

The Australian demand for foreign long-term capital during the 'twenties was no doubt determined by her internal economic

[1] G. Wood, *Borrowing and Business in Australia*, p. 211.
[2] During that time the Australian Government adopted these policies in order to encourage immigration. W. R. Maclaurin, *Economic Planning in Australia, 1929–36*, pp. 20–5.
[3] E. R. Walker, *Australia in the World Depression*, p. 25.
[4] Wood, op. cit. p. 208.

expansion. Nevertheless, the heavy inflow was also facilitated by the favourable conditions abroad. At that time, Australia was pictured to the overseas investor as a land of plenty with opportunities comparable to those in the U.S.A. The U.K. and the U.S.A., with a favourable balance on income account, were anxious to buy Australian bonds.[1] In the case of the U.K., Australia's ease in raising new money in London was also due to the British desire to encourage emigration.[2] As a result British long-term investment in Australia at the end of 1930 reached 13·3% of her total overseas investment, which was only below those in India and Canada.[3]

The year 1927/8 marked the climax of the inflow of foreign long-term capital, during which the borrowing by Australian public bodies alone amounted to £A54·3 mn. In the next year, the public borrowing fell to an insignificant level of £A2·1 mn., and the total net inflow of this year was only £A8·3 mn. This was the combined result of unfavourable internal and external changes. Externally, there was the general stringency in the principal world capital markets. The Wall Street boom had substantially reduced the American long-term capital exports, which fell to one-third of the 1928 level. The decrease in the favourable balances of the British and French income accounts reduced their abilities to lend abroad. At the same time Australian internal development was also very discouraging. As has been pointed out, Australia in the 'twenties was regarded as a very attractive field for foreign investment; and this sentiment had encouraged a large capital inflow. But as early as 1927 the sentiment had changed; and foreign investors began to suspect that the loans had been used extravagantly.[4] The fall of the export prices of wool and wheat and the growth of unemployment at home reacted adversely upon foreign investors. As the depression in Australia deepened, they began to withdraw their capital. Moreover, as Australian public investment showed a very strong cyclical rise and fall,[5] the public bodies did not try to raise any new money abroad during the depression. As a result, the long-term capital account showed a net export.

[1] Maclaurin, loc. cit.   [2] Walker, op. cit. p. 26.
[3] Royal Institute of International Affairs, *Problems of International Investment*, p. 142.
[4] Walker, op. cit. pp. 105–14.   [5] Vide infra, Table 54.

During the recovery of the 'thirties, the foreign long-term capital resumed its inflow again. But the amount was very small, being only about one-tenth of the level of 1927/8. As the government bonds were being retired the inflow was mainly in the form of direct investment.

In brief, the fundamental factor determining Australian long-term borrowing during the inter-war period was the fluctuation of economic activity at home. Moreover, the boom or slump in Australia in turn encouraged or discouraged foreign investors in lending to her.

(iv) EQUILIBRIUM IN THE AUSTRALIAN BALANCE OF PAYMENTS

The foregoing discussion has shown that, in relation to the general world prosperity and depression, the Australian income account runs an alternate deficit and surplus; and that Australia tends to increase her long-term borrowing abroad when business is on the upswing, and to decrease it in the converse case. Thus, there is a natural tendency towards cyclical equilibrium in the Australian balance of payments. The actual movements in the income account and in the long-term capital account are shown in Fig. 24. It can be seen that this broad offsetting tendency exists. Nevertheless, there were discrepancies; and the discrepancy in the earlier year of the Great Depression, i.e. 1929/30 was very great.

The curve for annual net payments or net receipts arising out of current and long-term capital transactions is shown in Fig. 25, in which the short-term capital and gold movements are also given. The inverse correlation between the curve for net payments and that for the short-term capital movements is very high; and, moreover, the gold movement, though showing smaller changes, is in the same direction as the short-term capital movement. In other words, in the case of Australia, both the short-term capital and the gold are the balancing items for her balance of payments. Since there was no short-term money market to attract 'equilibrating' international funds the short-term capital used for the purpose of balancing net receipts or payments was, in fact, the banking funds of Australian trading banks held in London. The general practice of the banks

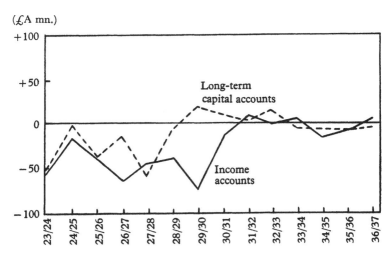

Fig. 24. Comparison of Australian income and long-term capital account (in millions of £A). [In this diagram, import of capital is indicated by − and export by +]

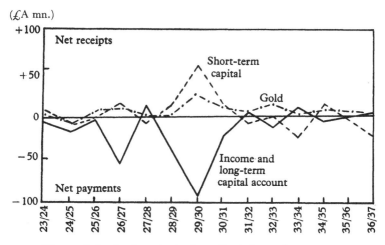

Fig. 25. Balancing items in the Australian balance of payments (in millions of £A)

12-2

was to accumulate foreign exchange in London when there were net receipts; and these reserves were relied upon to meet the demand for foreign exchange arising out of net payments.[1] In this manner the changes in the London reserves provided an automatic adjustment to her balance of payments and wide fluctuations in her exchange rate could be avoided. Nevertheless, the extent of this operation is limited and it cannot sustain long and large net payments. The actual events during 1929/30–1930/31 provide a good illustration. Although recession in the Australian export industries came as early as 1928 because of the fall in the prices of her principal exports, yet the home income level was maintained by public investment. During the year 1929/30, foreign long-term capital began to withdraw from Australia as a result of the general rush for liquidity; and the world depression had decreased the Australian export value to only 70% of the 1928/29 level. On the other hand, imports fell but little. The consequent net payments in her balance of payments, according to the recorded value, reached the level of £A91 mn. The foreign funds of Australian banks declined by about £A59 mn., in addition to a net export of gold of £A25 mn. As a result, Australia was forced to abandon the practice of the gold standard by prohibiting gold exports; and the currency depreciated. In the next year, in spite of the heavy fall in imports, the continuance of long-term capital withdrawal and the decline in exports still resulted in a necessity for net payments. The foreign funds further decreased and gold was exported. With the U.K., Australia virtually suspended the gold standard; and the average exchange rate for the year was 29% of its old gold parity.

[1] When payments are due to Australia, as, for instance, for goods exported (or for loans raised abroad), the exporter draws a bill on the overseas importer for the value of the goods. He generally discounts his bill of exchange with a trading bank in Australia. The bank credits his account with the amount of the payments made. It then collects the amount from the overseas importer and adds that amount to its exchange funds held in London. The liabilities of the bank in Australia increase; but, as the balance in London is regarded as the secondary reserve, the bank does not normally transfer it to Australia. The converse is true when payments are made by Australia. Therefore, the yearly net payments or receipts due to current and long-term capital transactions will be reflected in a net decrease or increase of the balances in London.

(v) THE INFLUENCE OF EXTERNAL FACTORS UPON THE AUSTRALIAN HOME ECONOMY

The changes in Australian home economic activity are very sensitive to, and are predominantly determined by, those in the outside world, the link being through the trading relations; and the cyclical pattern in the Australian balance of payments gives a convenient summary.

The years preceding the depression were years of rising industrial activity and national income in Australia. This expansion, however, had to a large extent been based upon external factors. The first important external factor was the high export prices associated with the world prosperity. During these years, the terms of trade were becoming progressively favourable to Australia, and her export quantity was also rising. Many export producers enjoyed increasing incomes; and, through the multiplier effect, the whole economy was prosperous. Secondly, the prosperity was also due to heavy public investment, but this investment was made possible because of inflow of foreign long-term capital. As has been shown above, throughout this period, there was a steady inflow of long-term capital, amounting on the average to more than £A30 mn. a year.

But the seeds of the ensuing depression were also sown during this expansion stimulated by the external forces.

First, the prosperity at home had increased the activity in the manufacturing industries; and a deliberate protective tariff policy was imposed. Consequently, prices were maintained artificially high in Australia. Moreover, social legislation and wage policy increased labour cost.[1] The unsheltered export industries, though sharing the prosperity due to the increasing world demand, had already felt the growing pressure of high costs; and their vulnerable position became clear as soon as the world depression came.

Secondly, encouraged by the ease of obtaining overseas loans, the Australian government embarked upon extensive public works and other development schemes. Much of this public

---

[1] During the 'twenties, the general level of wages was rising, partly because of the adjustment of the basic wages by the Arbitration Court, and partly because of the automatic adjustment of wages to rising home prices on the basis of the cost-of-living index. Vide Walker, op. cit. pp. 119–22 and 130–1.

expenditure was later found to be 'unproductive'; or, in other words, it turned out to be incapable of producing financial returns sufficient to cover the interest payments.[1] Moreover, in the pursuit of such policy, the government had indulged in some uneconomic expansion. For instance, the government appeared often to have offered higher prices for raw materials than the prevailing market prices, thus causing some uneconomic expansion of plants.[2] The development policy also stimulated both intensive and extensive agricultural and pastoral expansion. Wheat acreage and wool production greatly increased.[3] From 1922/3 to 1928/9, the former rose from 9·8 mn. to 14·9 mn. acres; and the latter from 727 mn. to 968 mn. pounds. Other export commodities showed the same tendency. The increased production was able to be exported as long as the world demand was maintained. But in the depression, declining demand together with increased supply caused a sharp fall in the export prices.

Thirdly, the heavy import of capital increased the relative importance in the Australian balance of payments of a rigid debit item, i.e. the overseas interest payments. By 1928/9, they had risen to £A35 mn., which, compared with the value of exports of £A138 mn. in the same year, was certainly formidable. But the transfer problem was not too difficult with the continued inflow of foreign capital into Australia. Nevertheless, this difficulty came to a head when the inflow of capital stopped in the world depression.

The depression was spread to Australia through the abrupt fall of the prices of her main exports, i.e. wool and wheat. The fall of wool prices was mainly due to the growth of supply over the boom years. In addition to careful breeding and pastoral improvement which increased the weight of the average fleece, high export prices had greatly encouraged the increase in sheep flocks.[4] At the same time, the production in other producing countries had also increased.[5] Unfortunately, consumers' demand for woollen manufactures was expanding less than for the products of other manufacturing industries;[6] and, conse-

---

[1] Maclaurin, op. cit. pp. 20–1. [2] Ibid. pp. 30–1.
[3] Ibid. [4] Walker, op. cit. pp. 85–7.
[5] League of Nations' *Memorandum of Production and Trade*, p. 15.
[6] Vide supra, Table 10.

quently, the world demand for raw wool did not keep pace with the increased output. For instance, taking 1925 as base, the increases in the activity of the woollen industries of the principal countries in 1928 were: the U.S.A., 102; France, 110; Sweden, 108; the U.K. 108 and Germany 114.[1] In contrast, the total world raw wool production had increased by about 15% during the same period. Given the increasing level of world output, the inelasticity of supply and the less rapid expansion of consumers' demand, the decline of the price was inevitable. This long-term trend was accentuated by the cyclical fall in world demand. As the activity in the principal manufacturing countries began to shrink in 1928, its effect was immediately reflected in an abrupt fall of Australian wool prices.

The same thing applied to the case of wheat. In spite of the downward trend of wheat prices, the total world production had increased by about 22% from 1922 to 1928,[2] because of the expansion of acreage in new countries and also the increased yield per acre all over the world. In the case of Australia, her rate of expansion was even ahead of that of the world. For the same period, production increased by about 45%.[3] However, during this period, wheat prices were being maintained by the increase in stocks.[4] The year 1928 yielded a bumper harvest, which started the sharp fall in wheat prices; and moreover, with the world depression, the rate of fall was further accentuated.

The price elasticity of world demand being low, the fall in the Australian export prices led to a reduction of export value. During the year 1928/9, the Australian value of exports began to fall. In the next year, as her quantity of exports was also decreasing because of the world depression, the value of exports fell 35% from the 1927/8 level. Such a heavy fall in her exports precipitated the crisis in Australia; and, moreover, the economic contraction was further accentuated by the withdrawal of foreign long-term capital.

The above discussion has brought to light at least two facts which are common to all the agricultural countries during

---

[1] German figures refer to worsted spinning only. All these figures are taken from the League of Nations' *Memorandum of Production and Trade*.

[2] Imperial Economic Committee, *The Wheat Situation*, 1931, pp. 90, 101 and 103.

[3] Ibid. [4] Ibid.

world depression. First, the exports of the agricultural countries are generally concentrated in the commodities, the world demand for which expands less rapidly than for other commodities entering into international trade. The world prosperity, by maintaining the quantity of exports of these countries, conceals this fundamental difficulty. Indeed, boom conditions stimulate the increase of price, which in turn encourages increased production in these countries. Nevertheless, prices can still be maintained during prosperity because of an accumulation in stocks. But the fall in prices is bound to be abrupt and violent as soon as the world demand begins to shrink and the accumulated stocks are released. The price-elasticity of world demand being low, the fall in prices leads to direct decrease in the value of exports, which, through the operation of the multiplier, causes a violent shrinkage in the national income.

Second, the cessation of foreign lending by the world creditors to these countries will lead directly to a further reduction of their internal economic activity, as a large part of their investment is built upon the inflow of foreign long-term capital. However, it has often been said that the effect of a decrease or cessation of long-term capital import during the depression is to lead to an unfavourable change in the terms of trade of the agricultural countries. Moreover, it has been proved that in the early 'twenties a correlation between capital movements and the terms of trade exists in the case of New Zealand, India and Argentina.[1] But this phenomenon does not necessarily mean any cause-and-effect relationship between them. On the contrary, both of them are fundamentally determined by the world cycle, as has been shown above. During the depression, agricultural prices tend to fall faster than industrial prices; and, therefore, the terms of trade become unfavourable to the agricultural countries. At the same time, the depression decreases their borrowing and discourages lending by creditors to them. However, after the depression has started capital movements may cause further unfavourable changes in the terms of trade because of the transfer of interest payments. That is to say, during the depression, the payments of the rigid interest items will make it necessary for these countries to push

[1] F. Hilgerdt, 'Foreign Trade and the Short Business Cycle', in *Economic Essays in Honour of Gustav Cassel*, pp. 273–92.

THE AUSTRALIAN BALANCE OF PAYMENTS

on to the world market more exports, thus accentuating the decrease of prices.

The Australian depression was the result of external forces. Judged by the fall in national income, the downswing in Australia during 1929/30–1932/3 was less severe than in the U.S.A., Canada, and Chile. But the unemployment figure showed a situation as severe as any. In the year 1932/3, unemployment was at the level of 29%. This paradox was due to the fact that, in spite of a rising income during 1926/7–1928/9, unemployment also grew. Even in the year of world boom, i.e. in 1929, the trade union unemployment figure was already 11·1%. As to the balance of payments, the balance of trade turned from its habitual deficit into a surplus during 1930/1–1932/3. The total balance on income account for the three years as a whole showed net payments of only £A5 mn., compared with about £A45 mn. in the average pre-Depression years. But the surplus on trade account does not mean that the Australian situation was less serious than that in the other countries whose balance of trade was running on an increasing deficit or had changed from a surplus into a deficit. This is because the Australian surplus was achieved at a low level of exports and national income. Moreover, the Australian position was certainly not easy, as the foreign long-term capital continued to withdraw.

Recovery set in relatively early in Australia and was well maintained. Just as the depression in Australia was mainly the result of external forces, so it was external forces which were responsible for her recovery in the 'thirties.

TABLE 54. *Public investment and total gross home investment in Australia (£A mn.)*

Year	Public investment*	Total gross home investment†
1928–29	40·1	167·0
1929–30	29·5	136·0
1930–31	14·1	103·0
1931–32	9·2	80·0
1932–33	10·3	64·0
1933–34	14·8	81·0
1934–35	19·7	109·0

* Maclaurin, op. cit. p. 180.
† Including budgetary deficit. Clark and Crawford, op. cit. p. 63.

185

Both public investment and total gross home investment in Australia followed a strong cyclical pattern, as shown in Table 54. In fact, the rise of home investment was stimulated by the favourable external changes after 1934.

As can be seen from Fig. 23, the curve for national income and the curve for export nearly coincide after 1934. This may give support to our argument that the Australian recovery was originated by external factors. In addition to the general increase of Australian export quantity consequent upon the world recovery, there were two other factors which were of special assistance to the Australian recovery. The first was the phenomenal rise in the Australian export prices of wool, which took place early in 1933, as shown in Table 55. The reason for the rise was the absence of large world stocks of wool together with a short clip during 1933.[1]

TABLE 55. *Average export prices of greasy wool (pence per pound in Australian currency)* *

Year	Price
1924–29 (average)	19·3
1929–30	11·3
1930–31	9·2
1931–32	9·0
1932–33	9·1
1933–34	16·3
1934–35	10·0
1935–36	14·0
1936–37	16·5

* *Official Year-book of Australia*, various years. From 1934/5 onward, the figures are average market price per pound in Australia. Comparison of the figures of the earlier years shows that the average market prices were generally lower than the export prices.

Secondly, the stimulus to the Australian internal economy also came from an increase in the production of gold for export in response to the rise of the world price. In 1930 Australia produced about 470 thousand fine ounces of gold; in 1934 the production had increased to about 890 thousand fine ounces, almost all of which was exported.[2]

[1] Royal Institute of International Affairs, *Problems of International Investment*, pp. 292–3.
[2] *Official Year-book*, 1930 and 1934.

THE BALANCE OF PAYMENTS

(in millions of

	1923/4	1924/5	1925/6	1926/7
I. INCOME ACCOUNT				
A. *Merchandise trade:*				
Exports	+ 116·7	+ 161·1	+ 144·4	+ 133·4
Imports	− 140·6	− 146·6	− 151·3	− 164·2
Balance	− 23·9	+ 14·5	− 6·9	− 30·8
B. *Other items:*				
Interest and dividends incomes				
Shipping incomes	− 28·5	− 29·5	− 32·0	− 33·2
Other services [2]				
Balance	− 28·5	− 29·5	− 32·0	·· 33·2
Balance of income account	− 52·4	− 15·0	− 38·9	− 64·0
II. NET GOLD MOVEMENT	+ 2·8	− 9·6	+ 3·8	+ 10·8
III. CAPITAL ACCOUNT				
A. *Long-term capital movement:*				
Changes in Government debt overseas [3]	+ 48·1	+ 0·1	+ 37·5	+ 11·8
Private direct investment [4]	—	—	—	—
Changes in sinking fund investment overseas	—	—	—	·—
Changes in debt in Australia	—	—	—·	—
Changes in other Australian assets overseas	—	—	—	—
Balance	+ 48·1	+ 0·1	+ 37·5	+ 11·8
B. *Short-term capital movement:*				
Changes in assets at home [5]	—	—	—	—
Changes in assets overseas [6]	+ 7·2	− 10·5	0	+ 16·2
Balance	+ 7·2	− 10·5	0	+ 16·2
Balance of capital account	+ 55·3	− 10·4	+ 37·5	+ 28·0
IV. RESIDUE ITEM	− 5·7	+ 35·0	− 2·4	+ 25·2

[1] This table is compiled from League of Nations' *Balance of Payments* of various years. In this table the sign '—' indicates that the data are not available.

[2] It includes: (i) insurance, (ii) tourist expenditures, (iii) government payments, (iv) receipts from export of non-monetary gold and (v) other sundry items.

[3] It includes: (i) long-term securities of commonwealth, State and local bodies, (ii) other public debt held abroad, and (iii) Commonwealth investment abroad.

OF AUSTRALIA, 1923/4–1936/7 [1]

Australian pounds)

	1927/8	1928/9	1929/30	1930/1	1931/2	1932/3	1933/4	1934/5	1935/6	1936/7
	+140·4	+138·1	+96·2	+77·8	+77·6	+80·0	+92·4	+83·8	+100·5	+119·9
	−147·0	−147·4	−136·6	−63·0	−46·1	−58·8	−61·3	−74·7	−86·4	−93·0
	−6·6	−9·3	−40·4	+14·8	+31·5	+21·2	+31·1	+9·1	+14·1	+26·9
		−34·9	−36·2	−34·5	−28·6	−29·3	−29·6	−29·1	−29·4	−29·8
	−35·0 {	+6·3	+7·4	+5·1	+4·5	+4·8	+4·4	+5·2	+5·5	+5·7
		−0·6	−2·9	+0·7	+1·5	+1·1	+0·8	+1·2	+2·8	+3·9
	−35·0	−29·2	−31·7	−28·7	−22·6	−23·4	−24·4	−22·7	−21·2	−20·2
	−41·6	−38·5	−72·1	−13·9	+8·9	−2·2	+6·7	−13·6	−7·1	+6·7
	+1·8	+0·8	+24·7	+9·8	+5·3	+12·3	+1·0	+0·5	+1·3	+0·3
	+54·3	+2·1	−3·5	−1·5	−2·6	+0·3	−2·8	−1·9	−2·1	−1·0
	—	—	—	—	—	—	+2·2	+5·3	+3·8	+3·8
	—	+7·8	—	−0·3	+0·1	−2·0	+2·2	−1·0	+1·1	−0·1
	—	−0·3	−0·9	−0·2	+1·2	+3·9	—	+0·6	+0·2	+0·6
	—	−1·3	−14·5	−8·8	−3·5	−16·5	+1·3	+3·5	+2·5	—
	+54·3	+8·3	−18·9	−10·8	−4·8	−14·3	+2·9	+6·5	+5·5	+3·3
	—	—	+1·8	+4·9	+0·4	−1·3	+0·5	−4·3	−1·4	−2·3
	−7·5	+11·8	+56·8	+8·7	−9·3	+0·3	−23·6	+17·4	−5·5	−24·6
	−7·5	+11·8	+58·6	+13·6	−8·9	−1·0	−23·1	+13·1	−6·9	−26·9
	+46·8	+20·1	+39·7	+2·8	−13·7	−15·3	−20·2	+19·6	−1·4	−23·6
	−7·0	+17·6	+7·7	+1·3	−0·5	+5·2	+12·5	−6·5	+7·1	+16·6

[4] It includes: (i) undistributed profits reinvested in Australia, and (ii) other investments.
[5] It includes: (i) bank balance in Australia by overseas banks, and (ii) changes in trade money held temporarily in Australia on overseas account.
[6] It includes: (i) short-term securities, bank advances, etc. of governments, and (ii) short balances held in London by Australian banks. The figures for 1923/4–1927/8 are taken from A. Wilson, *Capital Imports and the Terms of Trade*, p. 36.

CHAPTER XI

THE CHILEAN BALANCE OF PAYMENTS

(i) GENERAL REMARKS

Chile is here chosen as a typical mining country. In mining countries, a very high percentage of total home production is concentrated in one or a few mining industries. As they are, in general, economically less-developed countries, the products of these industries are little demanded at home, and, therefore, are mainly exported for the use of world heavy industries. Consequently, the internal economy of these countries is sensitive and vulnerable to world cyclical fluctuations. Moreover, since activity in the world heavy industries tends to fluctuate much more violently than the general economic activity, the amplitude of cyclical fluctuations in these countries is generally greater than that of the world as a whole.

What pattern of cyclical behaviour does the balance of payments of this type of country exhibit? As to the merchandise trade, the exports are mainly demanded by heavy industries; and, therefore, its income elasticity tends to be high. For the imports, which consist mainly of capital goods and other manufactures, the home demand also tends to be elastic with respect to income change. *A priori*, these two elasticities may not be much different. Thus, with an equal magnitude of economic change both at home and abroad, the change in the relative quantities tends to be small. But by the nature of the imports and exports, the cyclical change in the terms of trade is bound to be great. For instance, during a period of world prosperity, as the change in the relative prices in favour of this type of country leads to a larger percentage change of the value of exports, there tends to be an export surplus. But the more violent amplitude of fluctuation at home will tend to cancel a part of this surplus. Therefore, in general, we may expect that the pattern of cyclical behaviour in the merchandise trade of this type of mining country is a surplus in times of prosperity and a deficit during a slump.

187

The actual facts support this argument. The most important mining countries and their main exports are given in Table 56.[1]

TABLE 56. *The composition of the exports of the main mining and extractive-industry countries*

Countries	Main exports	Total (%)
Bolivia	Tin and other minerals	95
Venezuela	Petroleum	90
Chile	Nitrates of soda and copper	85
Mexico	Gold, silver and petroleum	80
Malaya	Tin and rubber	65
Iran	Petroleum	60
Peru	Petroleum and ores	55
Ecuador	Petroleum and ores	50

The cyclical change in the balance of trade of these countries is shown in Table 57.

TABLE 57. *The cyclical change in the balance of trade of eight mining countries (in millions of U.S. dollars, at the 1929 parity)* *

Year	Balance of trade
1924	+326
1925	+366
1926	+406
1927	+356
1928	+392
1929	+415
1930	+174
1931	+179
1932	+161
1933	+186
1934	+275
1935	+263
1936	+277
1937	+355
1938	+216

* Compiled from *International Trade Statistics* of various years.

The changes in the total trade balance of the mining countries closely reflect the world trade cycle. Since these countries habitually run an export surplus on the balance of trade, the size of the surplus rises in prosperity and falls during depression.

[1] Although the content of mining products in her exports is high, yet South Africa would seem, on balance, to be a mixed economy of mining and agriculture. Therefore, we exclude her.

In the 'twenties, the largest surplus occurred in 1929; and, in the 'thirties, it was in 1937. These two years were the peaks of the booms in the two periods. Moreover, the amplitude of variations was very great. In the depression, the balance was less than half of its boom level.

Being debtors, these countries incur net interest and dividends payments each year. There are no available estimates for these payments. However, their fluctuations may be expected to be smaller than those of trade. Therefore, the cyclical changes in the balance on income account are predominantly determined by the changes in the balance of merchandise trade. If a country belonging to this type has a habitual deficit on income account, then the very large fall in the favourable balance of trade in depression will necessarily increase the amount of deficit. If, on the other hand, a country has a habitual surplus on income account, a sharp fall in the trade balance may turn it into a deficit during depression.

(ii) THE CYCLICAL PATTERN OF THE CHILEAN BALANCE OF TRADE

In the years just before the Depression, the ratio of the value of exports to Chilean national income was roughly from 30–35%. This showed that a very large proportion of her home production was engaged in making exports. Moreover, the degree of specialisation in her exports was very high. More than four-fifths of her exports consisted of only two commodities, i.e. nitrates of soda and copper. In other words, Chile was not only greatly dependent upon the world markets, but this dependence was concentrated upon two mining raw materials for world heavy industries.

Of her imports, more than 70% were manufactured goods; and she also imported foodstuffs amounting to 15% of her total imports. Among the manufactured imports, machinery and textiles bulked large.

During cyclical fluctuations, the variations in the import and the export quantity are respectively determined by Chilean and by world income. By the nature of the imports and exports, the two income elasticities tend to be high. This is confirmed by statistical calculations.

$$\text{Log (Quantity of imports)}$$
$$= 3 \cdot 25 \text{ log (Index of industrial production)}$$
$$- 0 \cdot 32 \text{ log} \left(\frac{\text{Import price}}{\text{Cost of living}}\right),$$

with $R = 0 \cdot 87$.[1]

$$\text{Log (Quantity of exports)} = 3 \cdot 39 \text{ log (World real income)}$$
$$- 0 \cdot 17 \text{ log} \left(\frac{\text{Export price}}{\text{World export price}}\right),[2]$$

with $R = 0 \cdot 92$.[3]

The Chilean import and export prices are correlated closely with world real income and the cyclical change in the terms of trade is large, as is shown by the following equations:

$$\text{log (Chilean import price)} = 1 \cdot 5 \text{ log (World real income)},$$

with $R = 0 \cdot 84$.

$$\text{log (Chilean export price)} = 2 \cdot 85 \text{ log (World real income)},$$

with $R = 0 \cdot 81$.

From these four equations, we can see that, because the cyclical change in the relative quantities is small, the balance of trade is predominantly determined by the cyclical change in the terms of trade. However, because Chilean home production is specialised in heavy industries' raw materials, her internal economic activity tends, on the average, to fluctuate more violently than the general world economic activity. The relationship between the Chilean and the world activity for the period under study is represented by the equation:

$$\text{log (Chilean industrial production)}$$
$$= 1 \cdot 234 \text{ log (World real income)}.$$

This fact tends to lead to a larger cyclical rise or fall of import quantity relative to export quantity.

---

[1] 1928–38 (trend eliminated). No real income index is available for the period under study.

[2] World export prices have been converted from gold to pesos.

[3] 1924–38 (trend eliminated).

On the basis of these equations, we can derive the cyclical pattern of the Chilean balance of trade.[1]

TABLE 58. *The cyclical pattern of the Chilean balance of trade (in mn. pesos)*[2]

	Both Chilean and world economic activity increased by 1%	1% increase in world activity associated with 1·234% increase in Chilean
Imports	− 51·9	− 61·8
Exports	+112·9	+112·9
Net increase in favourable balance	+ 61·0	+ 51·1

The cyclical pattern of the Chilean balance of trade is that it tends to have a surplus in times of world prosperity and a deficit during world depression.[3] The more violent economic fluctuations at home cancel a part of this cyclical surplus or deficit; but the fundamental pattern is not changed. Moreover, the magnitude of the change in the trade balance is very great. Given a 1% increase in economic activity everywhere in the world, the balance would increase by 61·1 mn. pesos, which is equal to 8% of the balance in the peak year of 1928.[4]

(iii) THE CHILEAN BALANCE OF PAYMENTS IN THE 'TWENTIES

Chile in the later 'twenties shared fully the general economic prosperity prevailing in the world. Expanding world demand resulted in an increase in her exports and also stimulated the

---

[1] Two more equations required for the calculation of Table 59 are:

$$\log (\text{Cost of living}) = 0.76 \log (\text{Chilean industrial production}),$$

and

$$\log (\text{World prices in pesos}) = 2.15 \log (\text{World real income}).$$

[2] The calculations are based upon the average values of 1925–6.

[3] As the Chilean balance of trade shows a habitual surplus, this is equivalent to saying that the amount of the surplus would tend to increase in prosperity and to decrease in the slump.

[4] The actual net balance of Chilean merchandise trade in 1926–38 is as follows (in mn. pesos).

1926	+ 199·5	1933	+149·1
1927	+605·4	1934	+245·9
1928	+768·5	1935	+169·4
1929	+706·4	1936	+202·1
1930	− 54·1	1937	+504·5
1931	+133·7	1938	+172·3
1932	+ 68·2		

export prices. Export value increased steadily from 1926 to 1929; and the value in 1929 amounted to about 160% of that in 1924. Consequently, home business conditions were on the upswing, which was reflected in an increase of 30% in general industrial production from 1927 to 1929.[1] Imports increased too; but the net export surplus steadily increased during this period. In the peak year of 1928, it reached the amount of 769 mn. pesos.[2]

Nevertheless, in spite of this general prosperity, there was a fundamental weakness in the Chilean balance of payments, which made the Chilean internal economy especially vulnerable to the world depression. The weakness was due to over-specialisation in exports and over-borrowing.

First, as has been shown above, more than four-fifths of Chilean exports was concentrated in only two mining products, i.e. nitrates and copper. The danger of over-specialisation was further increased because both the quantity and prices were very sensitive to the world economic fluctuations. However, so long as the world was in a prosperous condition, this danger was concealed. But there was no doubt that any great shrinkage in the world demand, as in the case of the Great Depression, would bring a drastic fall in both quantity and prices, and, hence, a catastrophic effect upon the internal economy of Chile. Moreover, there was another development unfavourable to Chile in the 'twenties. During and since World War I, the production of synthetic nitrates had increased all over the world; but, at the same time, Chile's own productive capacity had also increased as a result of the inflow of American capital and of the application of new technique.[3] As a whole, world productive capacity in the 'twenties approached four million tons per year; whereas consumption, even in 1928–30, did not exceed two million tons.[4] All these difficulties confronting the Chilean economy came to a head with the onset of the Great Depression.

Secondly, in common with other Latin-American countries, Chile in the 'twenties took the advantage of the offers of American issuing houses to borrow huge amounts of money on terms

[1] This index is not available for the earlier years.
[2] In 1929, while exports were still rising, the relatively larger increase in imports had reduced the export surplus to 706 mn. pesos.
[3] C. Lewis, *America's Stake in International Investments*, pp. 259–62.
[4] Ibid.

which overlooked the unstable character of her internal economy. The amount of money raised in New York on long-term alone during 1926–30 reached 1,495 mn. pesos.[1] In addition, Chile also borrowed from other countries. The amount raised from the U.K. alone was perhaps one-third of what she borrowed from the U.S.[2] A large amount of foreign borrowing from 1926 onward was used for the purpose of meeting Chilean budgetary deficits[3] and for other non-productive purposes. It has been estimated that, in 1930, the percentage of external public indebtedness to the total foreign capital employed in Chile was as high as 32%.[4]

The over-borrowing in the 'twenties increased the rigid interest payments in the Chilean balance of payments; and, at the same time, these borrowings had not been used to produce revenue to meet the service payments. However, so long as the foreign capital continued to flow in, Chile could live beyond her means and her interest payments could be met. The cessation of the inflow of foreign long-term capital and the sharp decline in the export surplus as a result of world depression threw the Chilean economy into a desperate position.

[1] Aggregate new dollar loans raised by Chile in New York for the period 1926–30 were as follows (in mn. pesos converted at the annual average rate of pesos to U.S. dollars):

1926	437·1
1927	146·8
1928	441·2
1929	321·2
1930	149·0
Total	1,495·3

(Vide Lewis, op. cit. p. 624.)

There were also direct investments from the U.S.A. For instance, investments in industrial minerals excluding oil increased by U.S. $51·2 mn. from 1924 to 1929. (Lewis, op. cit. p. 584). The increase in American investment in Chilean public utilities was, during the same period, U.S. $65·7 mn. (Ibid.)

[2] League of Nations' *Balance of Payments*, 1934, p. 114.

[3] In 1913 export taxes on nitrates and their by-products contributed more than 90% of total Chilean government ordinary revenue. The fall in the exports after World War I decreased this revenue and, hence, budgetary deficits steadily increased in the 'twenties. (Vide Ellsworth, *Chile: An Economy in Transition*, p. 10.)

[4] Royal Institute of International Affairs, *Problems of International Investment*, p. 225.

(iv) THE WORLD DEPRESSION AND THE CHILEAN
BALANCE OF PAYMENTS

The world depression was directly transmitted to Chilean economy through the reduction in her exports. The severity of the impact of world depression may be gauged from the figures given in Table 59.

TABLE 59. *The fall of Chilean exports*

Year	Quantity of exports	Prices of exports	Value of exports
1929	100	100	100
1930	66·2	87·4	57·9
1931	58·3	61·7	36·0
1932	30·0	41·1	12·3

The world economic contraction led to a drastic fall both in the quantity and in the prices; and, consequently, the value of exports in 1932 was only one-eighth of that in 1929.[1] The decline was heavier than in any other country in the world. With regard to the percentage decline in the value of both exports and imports between 1929 and 1932, Chile headed thirty-nine countries which represented about 90% of the total value of world trade.[2]

The decline in exports was immediately reflected in the index of mineral production, which, on the base 1929, was 70·3 in 1930, 48·1 in 1931, and 26·2 in 1932. The nitrate production, which in 1924–5 had been valued at about £23·5 mn. (gold), was worth less than £2 mn. (gold) in 1932–3.[3] Nevertheless, the adverse external influences were at first confined to the mining industries. In fact, the index of general industrial production in Chile remained practically unchanged in 1930. Because of this, the value of imports fell much less than that of exports, thus resulting in a deficit in the balance of trade. The depressing effect of falling exports together with the import surplus was generally felt in 1931, during which the index of

[1] As to copper exports, apart from declining demand and the collapse of export prices, there were two other factors, which hit Chile especially hard. First, the imposition by the U.S.A. of an import duty of four cents per pound on copper was equivalent to the closing of her market to Chilean exports. Secondly the rise of the Southern Rhodesian copper industry gave very keen competition to Chilean copper. (Vide H. V. Hudson, *Slump and Recovery*, p. 343.)

[2] League of Nations' *World Economic Survey*, 1932–3, p. 214.

[3] Hudson, op. cit. p. 341.

THE CHILEAN BALANCE OF PAYMENTS

general industrial production declined about 25% compared with 1929.

Chile's difficulties in the balance of payments were not confined to this. She still had the rigid interest payments to meet. Foreign borrowing was impossible at that time. Besides increasing the difficulty of transfers, the cessation of the inflow of foreign capital meant a further contraction of economic activity in Chile, a large part of which was, in the past, dependent upon foreign capital.

There are no comprehensive and complete estimates for the Chilean balance of payments for the period under study. But

TABLE 60. *The Chilean balance of payments, 1929–32*
(in mn. pesos)

	1929	1930	1931	1932
Total net payments:				
Imports adjusted[1]	− 1,374·3	− 1,222·5	− 599·4	− 176·6
Exports adjusted[2]	+ 1,236·0	+ 915·4	+ 591·1	+ 190·1
Balance	− 138·3	− 307·1	− 8·3	+ 13·5
Interest, government obligations	− 199·3	− 245·2	− 120·3	—
Interest, other obligations	− 92·5	− 87·2	− 78·8	—
Interest and dividends, private investment	− 136·0	− 102·0	− 51·0	—
Balance	− 427·8	− 434·4	− 250·1	—
Total net payments	− 566·1	− 741·5	− 258·4	+ 13·5
Balanced by:				
Export of gold[3]	+ 0·7	+ 1·7	+ 0·1	+ 8·7
Loss of Central Bank reserve	+ 89·7	+ 106·9	+ 130·8	—
Government bond issue	+ 202·2	+ 280·8	—	—
Other government loans[4]	+ 75·9	+ 243·2	+ 54·0	+ 22·4
Other loans[5]	+ 165·0	+ 158·0	—	—
Total	+ 533·5	+ 790·6	+ 184·9	+ 31·1
Interest payments in default:				
Government	—	—	− 105·8	− 255·9
Others	—	—	− 123·7	− 80·6

[1] The value of imports has been adjusted to exclude the imports into Chile by the principal foreign copper, nitrate and iron producers out of the proceeds of the sale of their products abroad.

[2] The minerals are partly produced by foreign capital; and, therefore, only cost of production plus taxes remains in Chile. The figures in the table include only the value arising out of such foreign operations and the value of other Chilean produce.

[3] From League of Nations' *International Trade Statistics*.

[4] Net amount of foreign banking advances.

[5] Net loans and banking advances under the heading of External Guaranteed Debt of the State.

the estimates made by Ellsworth for 1929–32 may give some idea of the changes in the depression. After re-arrangement, they are reproduced in Table 60.[1]

The service items may have been underestimated. According to another estimate, the net interest and dividends payments in the period from January to June 1930 alone amounted to 447·1 mn. pesos.[2] In addition, there were net payments on account of other current transactions, which amounted to 66 mn. pesos in the same period.[3] But, in any case, the net interest payments bulked large and, as a whole, lacked flexibility. The transfer difficulty was especially great during world depression, because, on the one hand, the trade balance was deteriorating, and, on the other, foreign capital ceased to flow in or even tended to flow out. In 1929 and 1930, as foreign capital still moved inward, the interest payments by Chile could be maintained in spite of unfavourable conditions in trade account. As the inflow of capital was reduced to an insignificant scale in the next two years, Chile could only default her interest payments.

In brief, the cyclical change of the balance of payments in depression had at least three adverse effects upon the Chilean internal economy. First, the abrupt fall in the value of exports directly and immediately reduced the level of internal activity. Second, the cessation of capital inflow accentuated the downward swing, as a part of Chilean productive activity was dependent upon foreign capital. Third, the rigid debt service item gave rise to transfer difficulties.

(v) THE RECOVERY

The depression in Chile was very severe indeed. All economic indices indicated this. The decline in government expenditure was from 1,190 mn. pesos in 1929 to 1,132 mn. in 1930; and, in 1932, it was only 704 mn.[4] The loss of Central Bank reserves put a great strain upon the home money market; and, consequently, the discount rate was raised from 6% to 7% in August 1930 and to 9% in May 1931. Commercial bank reserves

---

[1] Ellsworth, op. cit. p. 10.
[2] League of Nations' *Balance of Payments*, 1932, p. 65.
[3] Ibid.   [4] Ellsworth, op. cit. p. 13.

declined too. They fell from an average of 175 mn. pesos in 1929 to 107 mn. pesos in June 1931. The total volume of internal credit (consisting of bank notes and deposits) decreased rapidly from the average level of 1,040 mn. pesos in the fourth quarter of 1929 to the very low level of only 660 mn. pesos in the third quarter of 1931. During the same period, agricultural production and building activity shrank rapidly, the latter in 1932 being only about one-half of its 1929 level.

However, the Chilean economy registered an early recovery in the course of 1933; and, since then, the recovery was steady and uninterrupted. One of the reasons responsible for the early recovery was the State policy towards building activity in 1933.[1] Indeed, the building industries were the most prosperous during the 'thirties. But the external factors were very important in restoring and maintaining the level of activity in her principal export industries. The world recovery and, in the later 'thirties, the rearmament programme in the world stimulated the demand for principal Chilean exports. The index of quantity in 1937 rose to three times the lowest level in 1932 and was only 6% below the peak year of 1929. Moreover, in addition to the tendency to a cyclical rise, the prices of her principal exports, i.e. copper and nitrates, were further maintained by two international agreements. As to nitrates, the Paris Agreement of 1934 provided for a sliding scale of prices fixing the price relation between synthetic and Chilean natural nitrates, and, in addition, gave Chile a fixed share in certain European markets.[2] As regards copper, the International Restriction Agreement in 1935, though not an attempt at price-fixing, limited the world output to ensure stability of markets and prices, which was also beneficial to Chile.[3]

The measures of exchange depreciation and control, besides being able to restrict the quantity of imports, had the effect of giving protection to the Chilean home manufacturing industries, which, in turn, stimulated the level of internal economic activity. In many fields of manufacturing industries, especially the consumers' goods industries, Chilean home production

---

[1] Ellsworth, op. cit. pp. 27–30. A tax remission law was passed in 1933. According to this law, buildings placed under construction before the end of 1935 were entitled to a remission of taxes for a period of ten years.

[2] Hudson, op. cit. p. 250.   [3] Ibid. pp. 245–9.

gradually replaced the imports and was able to meet the minimum demands of the home market.[1] The amount of new capital raised by the manufacturing industries rose from 149 mn. pesos in 1933 to 397 mn. pesos in 1934; and, since then, increased considerably each year.[2]

As compared with the pre-depression situation, the position of the Chilean balance of payments was also much improved because of the increased diversity of her exports. As shown by Table 61, the tendency to diversification is clear, though the absolute amounts are relatively small. Nevertheless, the relative importance of nitrates and copper in total exports decreased.

TABLE 61. *Diversification of Chilean exports*
(quantity in thousand metric tons)

	1928		1936	
	Quantity	Value in total (%)	Quantity	Value in total (%)
Grains	116·0	2·4	145·4	3·0
Beans, peas and lentils	58·0	2·1	76·4	4·9
Wool	12·0	2·7	12·8	4·6
Fruits	—	—	20·2	1·6
Hides and skins	6·4	1·3	7·5	2·7
Nitrates	2,833·2	47·6	1,403·0	28·2
Copper	335·9	31·6	246·0	38·0

[1] Ellsworth, op. cit. p. 31.   [2] Ellsworth, loc. cit.

CHAPTER XII

THE CANADIAN BALANCE OF PAYMENTS

The Canadian economy is a mixed one. In contrast to the highly industrialised or purely agricultural countries, her exports are more diversified, consisting of foodstuffs, agricultural and mining raw materials and, to a lesser extent, manufactured products. Although a large proportion of her exports consists of foodstuffs, she is also an important world supplier of certain raw materials. Next to Sweden, she is the world's largest exporter of forestry produce. The world industries also depend upon her for non-ferrous metals, furs and skins, etc. Since manufacturing industries in Canada are more developed relative to other agricultural countries, she exports manufactured goods, especially agricultural machinery.

In common with other agricultural countries, Canada is extremely dependent upon export trade. Partly because the land is less densely populated and partly because home manufacturing industries are still in the early stage of development, a large proportion of her specialised products has to be sold abroad. Consequently, her home production and national income are very sensitive to the fluctuation of the world demand.

(i) THE PATTERN OF CYCLICAL FLUCTUATIONS IN THE CANADIAN INCOME ACCOUNT

1. *Exports*

More than four-fifths of Canadian exports consists of eight groups of commodities, as shown in Table 62.

The relatively high percentage of raw materials would lead us to expect that the income elasticity of the world demand for Canadian exports would be higher than that for the exports of purely agricultural countries. Because she is a principal supplier of certain exports in the world market, the effect of price

TABLE 62. *Composition of Canadian exports (average 1928–9)*

Commodities	Total exports (%)	Total home production exported (%)
Grain and flour	39·5	56·7
Wood and paper products	20·8	45·1
Non-ferrous metals	6·7	40·2
Machinery and vehicles	6·1	—
Cattle, meat and fish	5·3	—
Furs and skins	3·5	— (Not important)
Butter and cheese	2·5	—
Gold and silver	1·8	—

changes upon quantities exported would be small. These ideas are confirmed by our statistical calculations.

$$\log \text{(Quantity of exports)} = 1{\cdot}5179 \log \text{(World real income)}$$
$$- 0{\cdot}3492 \log \left(\frac{\text{Canadian export prices}}{\text{Competitors' prices}^1} \right),$$

with $R = 0{\cdot}91$.

Furthermore, because of her dependence upon the world market, Canadian export prices are predominantly determined by world income, as shown by the equation,

$$\log \text{(Canadian export prices)} = 2{\cdot}041 \log \text{(World real income)},$$

with $R = 0{\cdot}97$.

With regard to the cyclical fluctuations in export quantity and prices, Canada occupies a position in between the agricultural and the mining countries. The cyclical changes in both quantity and prices are elastic to world income; but their amplitudes are smaller than those for mining countries and greater than those for agricultural countries. Thus, during different phases of the world trade cycle, the Canadian value of exports tends to be very unstable. As exports bear, on the average, a high ratio of about one-third to the total production of goods in Canada, the great variability of her internal economic activity is due to external influences.

2. *Imports*

Though rapidly industrialised during the period under study, Canada has not attained the stage of self-sufficiency in manu-

---

[1] For the period under study, the index of competitors' prices changes 1·0719 % with a 1 % increase or decrease of world income.

facturing production. Consequently, she still depends upon the outside world for manufactured goods. The most important groups of imports are, in order of importance, textile manufactures, machinery (including farm implements and electrical goods and apparatus), iron and steel manufactures, petroleum and coal and automobiles.[1] The cyclical fluctuations in the quantity of imports are closely correlated with Canadian income and relative prices, as shown in the equation:

$$\log (\text{Quantity of imports}) = 1 \cdot 7506 \log (\text{Canadian real income})$$
$$- 1 \cdot 3364 \log \left(\frac{\text{Import prices with tariff}}{\text{Cost of living index}^2} \right),$$

with $R = 0 \cdot 98$.

The change in import prices is given by the equation

$$\log (\text{Import prices}) = 1 \cdot 03 \log (\text{World real income}),$$

with $R = 0 \cdot 87$.

A comparison of the various elasticities for exports and imports reveals some interesting results. As given by the equations, the income elasticity for imports is slightly larger than that for exports; but its price elasticity is also larger. Therefore, given an equal cyclical fluctuation in Canada and in the world, the net change in the relative quantities will not tend to be large. But the effect of the change in the terms of trade will be great in determining the cyclical change in the balance of trade. On the average, the export prices tend to fluctuate twice as violently as the import prices. Consequently, Canada has a favourable change in her balance of trade in times of world prosperity and a converse change during depression.

3. Other current transactions

Canada incurs net payments on all other current transactions. The debit items are interest and dividend payments, freight and shipping payments and sundry payments; while the credit items are tourist receipts and exports of non-monetary gold. Except for the gold exports, all other transactions are influenced by cyclical fluctuations.

---

[1] This was roughly the situation in the 'twenties. In the 'thirties, owing to industrialisation, the import of machinery was much reduced; but these were still important groups of imports.

[2] $\log (\text{Cost of living index}) = 5 \cdot 354 \log (\text{Canadian real income}).$

(a) *Net interest and dividends payments.* The annual gross and net figures are given in Table 63.

TABLE 63. *Canadian interest and dividends payments (in mn. dollars)*

Year	Gross payments	Gross receipts	Net payments
1926	240	32	−208
1927	257	41	−216
1928	275	46	−229
1929	322	61	−261
1930	348	59	−289
1931	330	48	−282
1932	302	37	−265
1933	264	38	−226
1934	268	57	−211
1935	270	64	−206
1936	311	75	−236
1937	302	76	−226
1938	307	66	−241

Broadly speaking, Canadian borrowing and lending during the inter-war period had the general effect of increasing both Canadian assets and liabilities abroad in the 'twenties, and, after the Depression, of reducing Canadian liabilities and increasing Canadian assets abroad.[1] This involved changes in the composition of Canadian foreign assets and liabilities, which in turn influenced the long-term trends of gross service payments, and receipts. During the boom in the 'twenties and the early years of the Depression, Canadian public bodies borrowed heavily, mainly in the form of fixed-interest bonds, bringing with them rigid service payments. Hence we see that, in spite of economic contraction in the years 1930–2, the gross service payments tended to rise. In the subsequent three years, because of the decline of the earnings of foreign direct investments in Canada, the gross payments fell.[2] With the rise of these earnings consequent upon Canadian recovery, the gross payments rose again in the later 'thirties. As a whole, the gross payments showed a slightly upward trend.

The Canadian investment abroad was mainly in the form of direct investments;[3] therefore, Canadian gross service receipts

[1] Dominion Bureau of Statistics, *The Balance of Canadian International Payments*, ch. 15.

[2] During the 'twenties, the proportion of dividends payments was, on the average, about two-fifths of total gross payments.

[3] The Canadian direct investment abroad had grown from $855 mn. in 1926 to $1,031 mn. in 1937.

showed marked cyclical fluctuations, as is shown in Table 63. Moreover, as a result of the increased investment in the 'thirties, the gross receipts had a clear upward trend.

From Table 63, it can be seen that, because the absolute changes in the gross receipts are relatively small, the yearly changes in Canadian net payments followed those of gross payments. The net payments were correlated, though not closely, with the Canadian money income, as shown by the equation:

$$\log \text{(Net interest and dividends payments)}$$
$$= 0.31 \log \text{(Canadian money income)},$$

with $R = 0.64$.[1]

(b) *Net shipping and freight payments.* These payments are determined by the change in the value of Canadian trade, which is closely correlated with Canadian income. The equation is

$$\log \text{(Shipping payments)}$$
$$= 1.196 \log \text{(Canadian money income)},$$

with $R = 0.84$.[1]

(c) *Net tourist receipts.* This item varies very closely with the level of world money income, as can be seen from the equation:

$$\log \text{(Net tourist receipts)}$$
$$= 1.20 \log \text{(World money income in Canadian dollars)},$$

with $R = 0.91$.[2]

(d) *Sundry payments.* This includes such items as immigrants' remittances, advertising transactions, royalties, government receipts and payments, etc. No single one of these items is large, although the aggregate is substantial. In spite of their heterogeneous nature, the aggregate tends to show a cyclical variability, rising in prosperity and falling during slump.

4. *The cyclical fluctuations of the balance on income account.*

Based upon the elasticities given above, we may calculate the change in the balance on income account associated with a 1% increase or decrease in Canadian and world real income. As can be seen from Table 64, its pattern of cyclical fluctuations is that

---

[1] The variables are reduced to link relatives.
[2] Link relatives.

it tends to show a surplus in times of prosperity and a deficit during slump.

TABLE 64. *The pattern of cyclical behaviour of the Canadian income account**

	(1) 1 % increase in real economic activity both in Canada and in the world ($ mn.)	(2) 1 % increase in world's economic activity associated with 1·57 % increase in Canada's activity ($ mn.)
Exports	+44·10	+44·10
Imports	−20·73	−36·58
Interest payments	− 0·85	− 1·50
Shipping payments	− 0·27	− 0·50
Tourist receipts	+ 1·17	+ 1·17
Net increase in surplus on income account	+23·42	+ 6·69

* Other equations employed in the calculation of this table are:
  log (Canadian money income) = 1·397 log (Canadian real income),
  log (World money income)   = 1·50 log (World real income).
The calculations are based upon the average values of 1926–8.

Moreover, during the period under study, the economic fluctuations in Canada tend, on the average, to be more violent than those of the world as a whole. Further calculation shows that the Canadian real income rises or falls 1·57 times more than the world real income. This more violent economic fluctuation in Canada is only partly due to the type of her internal economy. Being a mixed economy producing mining and other raw materials for world industries, as well as agricultural products, the cyclical swing of her productive activity should naturally be greater than that of the world, which comprises many agricultural countries. But, as a matter of fact, the more violent cyclical fluctuations in Canada are mainly due to the preponderance of American influence. Broadly speaking, Canadian income fluctuations are quite similar to the pattern set by the U.S.A. This is because 45–50% of Canada's current receipts come from the U.S.A. either in payments for her exports or as the expenditure of American tourists. As the receipts from the U.S.A. have followed the course of her national income, therefore Canadian income is directly linked with American income, which, as has been shown in Chapter VIII, fluctuates much more violently than the world average. As shown in Table 64, the more violent fluctuations in Canada tend to reduce the magnitude of the surplus on income account during prosperity, but they do not change the fundamental pattern.

Two conclusions may be drawn from the results of these calculations. First, the Canadian pattern, which tends to show an alternate surplus and deficit in relation to world prosperity and depression, is similar to that of mining or industrial countries. Secondly, among the constituent items of the income

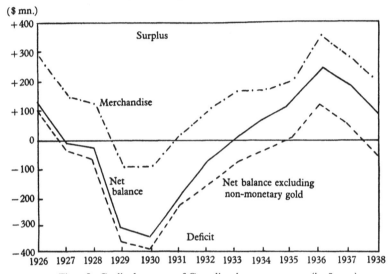

Fig. 26. Cyclical pattern of Canadian income account (in $ mn.)

account, the exports and imports have the greatest cyclical variability. As shown by the figures in column (2), given a 1% increase in world real income coupled with a 1·57% increase in Canadian income, the values of exports and imports will increase, on the average, by 3·5 and 3·3% respectively. The net payments arising out of the other current transactions tend to increase in prosperity; but their absolute change is not great. Because of this, the net changes in the balance on income account are predominantly determined by those in the merchandise trade.

In Fig. 26, the actual movements of the balance of merchandise trade, the net balance on income account and the net balance on income account excluding gold, are compared. They are generally in conformity with the results of our calculations.

The exceptions to our generalisations are the years 1927 and 1928, during which, in spite of world prosperity, the Canadian income account showed a small deficit. This, however, can be explained. During these two years, the Canadian net payments on account of all other current transactions increased, but the deficit was mainly caused by the sharp decline in the surplus from merchandise trade. While exports were increasing from 1926 to 1928, the deterioration in the balance of trade was due to the relatively larger increase in imports. There was a development boom in Canada; and consequently net home investment was especially heavy.[1] As Canada's manufacturing industries were still young in those days, this huge capital formation at home directly caused an increased demand for imported capital goods, especially from the U.S.A.[2]

(ii) THE CANADIAN LONG-TERM CAPITAL MOVEMENT

During the period under investigation, the Canadian long-term capital account reveals a net import of capital only in three years, i.e. 1929–31. But the long-term capital exported before the Depression and that after are different in nature. Before the Depression, Canada borrowed heavily abroad for home development purposes; but, on the other hand, world prosperity induced a large outflow of Canadian long-term capital, used for buying outstanding foreign securities for higher returns. On balance, there was a net outflow during these years. In the 'thirties, the outflow was mainly in the form of increased Canadian *direct* investment abroad and a net retirement of Canadian securities held abroad.

When the annual figures of the net import or export of long-term capital are examined, their yearly movements tend to have

---

[1] Cf. *Public Expenditure and Capital Formation*, p. 91, table 37. In it, the items such as 'total new construction and resource development', 'flow of new producers' goods', etc., showed very heavy increases during these years.

[2] This is not reflected in the figures given in column (2) of Table 64. The figures there are calculated on the basis of the *average* relationship between the fluctuations in the Canadian real income and those in the world. But during these two years, the rise of Canadian income relatively to that of the world was much larger than indicated by this average relationship.

a positive correlation with the world cycle. In general, the net export of long-term capital increases in times of prosperity; and, during depression, it decreases or changes into a net import. Thus, on *a priori* grounds, we may expect that the world cycle is the fundamental factor which determines Canadian long-term capital movements. In the following, we attempt to find factual evidence for this argument by analysing the movements of broad groups of Canadian long-term capital.

I. *Net Canadian issues raised abroad and the retirement of Canadian securities held abroad.*

The net import or export of Canadian long-term capital through this channel is given in Table 65.

TABLE 65. *Net retirement of Canadian foreign loans (in mn. dollar)* *

Year	New issues†	Retirement	Net movement
1927	+ 300·6	− 160·0	+ 140·6
1928	+ 207·3	− 200·0	+ 7·3
1929	+ 296·6	− 150·0	+ 146·6
1930	+ 400·3	− 110·0	+ 290·3
1931	+ 199·9	− 202·0	− 2·1
1932	+ 103·7	− 104·7	− 1·0
1933	+ 133·9	− 165·9	− 32·0
1934	+ 111·0	− 169·0	− 58·0
1935	+ 117·0	− 271·4	− 154·4
1936	+ 106·1	− 270·0	− 163·9
1937	+ 89·5	− 177·9	− 88·4
1938	+ 88·6	− 150·5	− 61·9

* Import of capital is indicated by a plus sign; and export by a minus sign.
† Excluding commissions.

Let us discusss the new issues first. Before World War I, Canada borrowed mainly in London; but, since that war, Canadian issues were sold mainly in New York.[1] Such new issues were unusually heavy in the period from 1927 to 1931, the annual amount never falling below $200 mn. and reaching a peak of $400 mn. in 1930. However, since 1931, the volume of Canadian securities issued abroad was on a much lower level, only about one-third of the amount in the boom period. The abrupt fall of this kind of Canadian borrowing was due to two reasons. First, it was the consequence of the falling-off of

[1] Except 1933–4, when new issues in London were greater.

lending by the U.S.A., which was further accentuated by the Canadian Government's restriction upon the issue of new securities in the U.S.A. Secondly, the abundance of internal funds seeking for investment as a result of a cheap money policy made a large amount of foreign borrowing less urgent in Canada.

The distribution of the new issues among different classes of Canadian borrowers is given in Table 66.

TABLE 66. *Distribution of new borrowing abroad (in mn. dollars)* *

Year	Public bodies	Railways	Industrial corporations	Total†
1927	109·6	87·6	121·4	318·6
1928	62·0	31·8	129·6	223·4
1929	112·8	110·2	89·8	312·8
1930	250·7	90·9	77·7	419·3
1931	142·4	56·8	5·7	204·9
1932	103·7	—	1·0	104·7
1933	133·6	—	2·3	135·9
1934	107·6	3·6	3·6	114·8
1935	120·2	—	0·8	121·0
1936	79·0	—	31·1	110·1
1937	88·3	4·0	0·8	93·1

* *The Canadian Balance of International Payments*, p. 139.
† Including commissions.

The demand for foreign capital through this channel is predominantly determined by the level of internal economic activity, which, because of the importance of exports, is closely connected with the world cycle. As can be seen from the table, the cyclical changes of railway and industrial borrowing are very obvious. Borrowing by Canadian public bodies showed a heavy increase during the development boom, roughly from the middle 'twenties to 1930; but their borrowing in the 'thirties was mainly confined to re-financing and thus did not show marked cyclical changes.

Broadly speaking, the retirement of Canadian securities held abroad also tended to increase in prosperity and to decrease during depression, as shown in Table 65. With regard to the method of retirement, two groups of Canadian securities may be distinguished. In some cases, the retirement is contractual, e.g. sinking fund operations, maturities, etc.; whereas, in other cases, securities may be called in for redemption. As to the former method, the issues falling due each year are a matter of chance resulting from the dates of original sale of the securities;

but the retirement by the latter method is entirely dependent upon economic conditions. Since Canadian issues are in terms of the creditors' currencies, there is less likelihood of securities being called for redemption when the Canadian dollar is at a discount; for, under such circumstances, the money cost of repayment is increased. But the Canadian dollar was usually at a discount when exports were falling and the home economy was in an unfavourable condition. This fact would decrease Canada's ability to call for redemption. The converse is true in the case of world prosperity. As shown in Table 65 the total amount of retirement was, on the average, higher in the boom period of the 'twenties and in the later 'thirties than in the depression.[1]

As to the net movements, the large retirement in the 'twenties was more than cancelled by the new issues for home development purposes. During the depression years 1931 and 1932, the net movements were practically nil. In the later 'thirties, with the recovery of Canadian exports and an abundance of home funds at a very low rate of interest, retirement was heavy while new borrowing was low. Retirement first began noticeably to exceed new borrowing in 1933; and the net retirement was exceptionally large in 1935-6 as a result of the steady recovery of Canadian exports. For the period 1933-8, the total retirement amounted to $1,205 mn., whereas the new issues were only $646 mn. The difference of $559 mn. was the decrease of Canadian foreign indebtedness.

2. *Net purchase of outstanding foreign and home securities*

The fundamental force determining the net purchase of outstanding securities is the relative amplitude of economic fluctuations at home and abroad. When expansion in the world is greater than at home, home long-term capital would tend to flow out in quest of higher returns; and, in the converse case, home capital would be repatriated by the sale of outstanding foreign securities. In the case of Canada, because the foreign securities bought and sold are of American origin and

[1] In *The Canadian Balance of International Payments*, the proportion of issues classified by the method of redemption is not given. But the fact that the retirement in 1936 and 1937 by the method of calling for redemption amounted to about one-third of the total retirements may suggest that the amount of Canadian securities issued with this option was large. (Cf. tables 20 and 21, pp. 200-1.)

the economic fluctuations in the U.S.A. are more violent than in Canada, the movement of long-term capital through this channel shows a very marked cyclical behaviour. During the prosperous 'twenties, large quantities of American securities were bought by Canadians because of relatively higher yields in the U.S.A. Such transactions were especially heavy in 1928 and the first half of 1929.[1] As depression came, the outflow was reduced to one-tenth of its former level. Since 1933, except for 1937, in addition to the repatriation of capital by selling American securities, foreigners bought Canadian bonds and stocks because economic conditions were relatively more stable in Canada.[2]

3. Net direct investment

After World War I, there was a migration of British and American capital into Canadian industry to establish branch plants. This was the result of a variety of motives, such as the search for cheaper sources of raw materials for parent companies, the desire to avoid high tariffs, etc.[3] On the other hand, Canadian enterprise also established branches in foreign countries, especially in the U.S.A. The number of Canadian enterprises which had branches in foreign countries was relatively small, but their branches were usually quite large units, mainly in public utilities.

By its nature, this kind of capital movement tends to fluctuate positively with the level of economic activity. Because of the prosperity of the 'twenties, there was an inflow of capital, especially from the U.S.A. seeking direct investment.[4] During and since the depression, there was a withdrawal of foreign capital from Canada, and the net movement was therefore outward.[5] However, in the 'thirties, this outward movement was

[1] Of course, some American securities were bought for reasons other than higher returns. For instance, they were bought for the purpose of diversifying investment portfolios of Canadian banks; and Canadian insurance companies also bought American securities mainly as reserves against business in the U.S.A.

[2] *The Canadian Balance of International Payments*, pp. 131–2.

[3] H. Marshall, F. A. Southard and K. W. Taylor, *Canadian-American Industry: A Study in International Investment*, passim.

[4] In 1931, there were roughly 1,200 separate branch units in Canada, and over two-thirds were American controlled. The total direct foreign investment in Canada at that time was estimated at more than two milliard dollars.

[5] In 1930 the import of foreign capital for direct investment was actually higher than the previous year. This is, however, due to the rise in tariffs which induced the establishment of more branch units in Canada.

also partly accounted for by the increased Canadian direct investment abroad.

4. *The long-term capital account as a whole*

The above discussion has shown that the behaviours of the different groups of long-term capital are not the same. One group may dominate the net movement in one year, others in another. Moreover, there is a shift in the composition of the net movement. Before the depression, the net export of long-term capital was mainly in the form of the buying of outstanding foreign securities; whereas, in the 'thirties, it was through the channel of the retirement of Canadian securities held abroad. Nevertheless, the fundamental force influencing these net movements was an external one, i.e. the world trade cycle. In the former period, the predominant force was, no doubt, the unprecedented economic expansion in the U.S.A. In the 'thirties, the economic uncertainty in the world and the unsteady recovery in the U.S.A. discouraged Canadian long-term capital from investment in foreign securities. Instead, the favourable exchange position consequent upon the recovery of Canadian exports induced increased optional retirement of Canadian securities held abroad.

For the period as a whole, Canada, as a capital-exporting country, tends to increase her foreign lending during world prosperity and to decrease or even to change it into net borrowing in times of world depression.

(iii) EQUILIBRIUM IN THE CANADIAN BALANCE OF PAYMENTS

We have found that, in the inter-war period, the Canadian income and long-term capital accounts tend to show offsetting cyclical changes. In general, the surplus on income account in prosperity is matched by net foreign lending and the deficit during slump is met by net repatriation of Canadian long-term capital from abroad. Moreover, this broad cyclical equilibrium is brought about because both accounts are fundamentally determined by external economic fluctuations.

The actual annual figures for the balance on income account and for the net movement of Canadian long-term capital are compared in Fig. 27. Two observations may be made. First, the approximation of these totals, though not exact, is close. Secondly, both totals show very great cyclical variability. This fact is, *inter alia*, the result of Canada's close economic connections with the U.S.A., whose internal economic fluctuations are unstable and great.

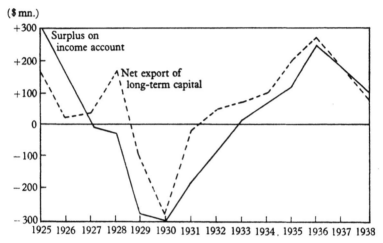

Fig. 27. The cyclical equilibrium between Canada's income account and her capital account (in $ mn.)

(iv) THE BALANCE OF PAYMENTS AND THE EXCHANGE RATE

In a particular year, the net payments or net receipts arising out of current and long-term capital transactions have to be balanced. In other words, such discrepancies will entail changes in international cash reserves and/or balancing short-term capital movements. In Fig. 28 the net receipts curve is compared with the gold curve and the short-term capital movements. As can be seen from the diagram, the balancing flow of gold is important only in 1928–9 and in 1931. In other years, either it does not change in the direction which offsets the net receipts curve, or, if it does, its magnitude is insignificant. Moreover, with the suspension of the gold standard in September 1931, monetary gold movements have not been permitted except by licence; and therefore we find that the gold curve in the 'thirties lies near the zero line.

Throughout the whole period except 1934, the curve of short-term capital does show a close inverse relationship with the curve of net receipts. Since Canada has no short-term money market at home to attract any equilibrating international funds, the short-term capital which she has relied upon for adjustment is in fact the foreign assets of Canadian chartered banks abroad. These assets consist of two parts: call loans in New York and the net balance due from foreign banks. Normally, the changes in these assets reflect the general state of the balance of payments and automatically provide balancing items to it. For instance, as Canadian exporters acquire credits from the sale of their products abroad, they transfer these to their own accounts in banks in Canada as deposits; and the banks receive the foreign exchange. As a rule, this foreign exchange is not at once transferred into Canada, as it is not required for internal cash reserve purposes.[1] If, at the same time, Canadian nationals export long-term capital to an equal amount, the foreign assets of the Canadian chartered banks abroad remain unchanged. However, if, in a given year, there are net payments or net receipts, these foreign assets will fall or rise accordingly. It is therefore in this manner that Canada, without a short money market to attract international funds, can get the necessary and automatic adjustment to her balance of payments.

This practice of accumulating foreign currency reserves in a surplus year and releasing them in times of deficit was able, in the past, to maintain the Canadian exchange rates fairly stable.[2] But there is a limit. The exchange rates cannot be kept stable if the magnitude of cyclical fluctuations is large and the deficit

---

[1] Before the establishment of the Bank of Canada in 1935, there was no legal requirement as to the cash reserve behind either bank deposits or bank-notes in Canada. The Canadian chartered banks are allowed to issue notes to the amount of their paid-up capital without any special collateral. The only regulation is that 40% of whatever cash reserves the banks see fit to hold shall be in Dominion notes. Furthermore, the Finance Acts of 1914 and 1923 have allowed the Dominion Government to issue notes to the chartered banks on the security of a wide range of collateral. (Vide P. Willis, *Foreign Banking System*, pp. 583–91.)

[2] Because of the nature of Canadian exports, the seasonal fluctuations in the Canadian balance of payments are great. The automatic changes in the chartered banks' foreign assets have also been able to prevent very wide seasonal fluctuations in the Canadian exchange rate.

continues for a number of years. This is what actually happened in Canada during the Great Depression. As indicated by the data, Canada had a very favourable balance of trade in the early 'twenties, and at the same time the net export of Canadian long-term capital was on a small scale.[1] The resulting net receipts caused an increase in the foreign assets of the chartered banks from $174·8 mn. in 1923 to $336·4 mn. in 1926.[2] The huge net payments in 1928–9 caused a decline in these assets to the

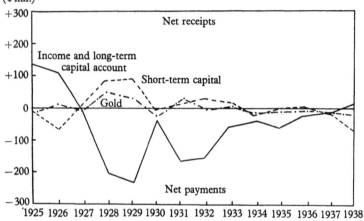

Fig. 28. Balancing items of Canadian balance of payments (in $ mn.)

amount of $190 mn., together with a net outflow of gold of $77·7 mn. Thanks to the accumulation in the earlier years, this drain did not lead to an immediate depreciation of the dollar. In 1930 the increased deficit on income account was balanced by an increased net import of long-term capital;[3] consequently, the dollar exchange rate, though weak, was able to be maintained.

The external panic of 1931 was transferred to the Canadian dollar, but not immediately through trade items. The deficit on income account showed a decrease from $337 mn. in the pre-

---

[1] From 1923 to 1926 the Canadian balance of trade (including gold and net balance on freight account) had a total surplus amounting to $1,055 mn. The net export of long-term capital (net of interest payments) for the same period was $435 mn. (Vide *Report of the Royal Commission on Banking and Currency in Canada*, table 21.)   [2] *Report of the Royal Commission*, loc. cit.

[3] In fact, the foreign assets of the chartered banks showed an increase of $0·4 mn., and there was net import of gold of $36 mn. This may suggest that the net inflow of long-term capital into Canada was actually larger than the recorded amount.

vious year to $174 mn. The panic came in through security movements. The selling of Canadian securities was due to two reasons. First, foreign holders sold them back to Canada partly because they felt that events in the U.K. had weakened the economic and financial position of the Dominion and partly because of the desire for liquidity. Secondly, Canadian holders sold in New York too; and, instead, they bought foreign securities payable in foreign currencies. For the year, the net import of long-term capital was only $8 mn. compared with $316 mn. in 1930. The overall net payment caused a further decline of the foreign assets of the chartered banks. Gold movement also showed a net outflow. Consequently, the Canadian dollar had to depreciate. The average for the year of rate to the U.S. dollar was 4% below par. Continued net payments in 1932-3 resulted in further depreciations against the U.S. dollar. At the end of 1933 the depreciation was 12%.

In brief, as Canada can derive little assistance from the 'equilibrating' shifts of international short-term funds, the adjustment of her balance of payments is dependent upon her own resources of gold reserves and foreign assets. Any cyclical change, which causes a heavy drain of these resources, will also lead to depreciation of her currency. In other words, the world cycle brings instability not only to her internal economic activity but also the external value of her currency.

(v) THE BALANCE OF PAYMENTS AND CANADIAN HOME ECONOMIC ACTIVITY

As has been shown above, the external cyclical fluctuations are extremely important in determining the internal economic activity of Canada. First, this is because Canada obtains about one-third of her national income directly from exports; and, moreover, because both the prices and quantity of her exports are highly sensitive to the trade cycle. Secondly, certain groups of Canadian industries, such as the manufacture of farm implements, grain-processing, etc., are more dependent upon the conditions of exports than on home economic activity.[1] Therefore, in the period under study, the direct and predominant stimulus to Canadian income comes from abroad.

[1] Vide supra, Table 23.

The prices of Canadian exports became weak at the end of 1928. Thanks to the world boom in the early part of 1929, the quantity of Canadian exports was fairly well maintained, although the total value of exports showed a decline compared with the previous year. However, national income continued to rise because of heavy home investment for development. In 1930, as the development began to recede, the pressure of falling Canadian exports was gradually felt. As the world depression deepened, so did the decline in Canadian economic activity. As can be seen from Table 67, the impact of world depression upon Canada was very severe indeed. Between 1929 and 1932, the average total export prices fell by 40%.[1] Though the export quantity fell less, the decline in total export value amounted to nearly 50%. The depression in exports directly and seriously affected the agricultural income, the amplitude of fluctuations of which was almost exactly equal to that for exports. The fall in national income was less than the agricultural income in the earlier years of depression because of the less rapid fall in net home investment; but, towards the end of the period, with the decline in net home investment, the depression of exports made itself felt in Canada by an all-round fall in economic activity.

The world depression started the economic contraction in Canada; and it was the world recovery which brought revival to Canada. During the depression period, public investment in Canada not only lacked any counter-cyclical tendency; on the contrary, it tended to intensify the shrinkage of Canada's internal economic activity consequent upon the world depression. Direct government outlays on public investment rose sharply in the prosperous 'twenties: between 1926 and 1929, they increased by about 100%; while from 1930 to 1933, they decreased by 68%.[2] Economic revival in Canada began in 1934 with the

---

[1] The export prices of agricultural products fell by more than two-thirds.
[2] The actual amount of public investment is as follows:

	$ mn.
1926	154
1929	313
1930	339
1933	108
1937	246

(*Public Expenditure and Capital Formation*, table 1 a, p. 31.)

The only important counter-depression measure was the enactment of the

recovery of Canadian exports. As compared with 1933, income rose by about 15% and exports by 24%.[1] In addition to the world recovery, three special factors were favourable to Canadian exports. First, the increased world activity in building industries stimulated both the export quantity and the prices of Canadian timber. Secondly, the rising gold prices in the world market induced an increased output and export of non-monetary gold from Canada. Furthermore, in the later years, the world rearmament programme increased the demand for Canadian minerals. Thus in the later 'thirties the increased Canadian exports brought a steady recovery of Canadian economic activity.

TABLE 67. *Depression in Canada (base:* 1929)

Year	Export prices	Export value*	Agricultural income	National income	Net home investment	Wholesale prices
1929	100	100	100	100	100	100
1930	84	76	76	84	88	91
1931	66	54	52	68	56	75
1932	60	47	47	53	27	70
1933	60	51	49	51	12	70

* Including non-monetary gold.

(vi) THE MONETARY FACTOR IN THE ADJUSTMENT OF THE CANADIAN BALANCE OF PAYMENTS

The foregoing discussion has shown that the broad cyclical equilibrium in the Canadian balance of payments is the result of world economic fluctuations. Therefore, we should expect that the monetary factor plays no important part in the equilibrating process; and furthermore that it would itself reflect the changes in the state of general balance of payments. Let us see if the data bear out our expectations.

There was no Central Bank in Canada before 1935. Had the monetary factor played a part in the equilibrating process, it would have operated through the channel of the chartered banks' internal credit policy with regard to their foreign reserves. In other words, the chartered banks should have

Federal Unemployment Relief Act in 1930. But the scale of relief was small. During the seven years 1930–6, only $665 mn. was spent, an average of $95mn. per annum, or less than 2% of the 1929 national income.

[1] Including non-monetary gold.

increased or decreased their loans in accordance with the increase of their foreign assets. Table 68 gives the actual banking statistics for this period.

As can be seen from the table, the total demand liabilities showed a marked cyclical variation, rising in prosperity and falling in depression. The cash reserves also rose and fell in about the same relative proportion, so that the cash-ratios (i.e. the percentage of cash reserves to total demand liabilities) remained nearly constant. What are the reasons for such constancy?

TABLE 68. *Cash reserves of Canadian chartered banks (mn. dollars)*

Year	Total demand liabilities in Canada*	Cash reserves in Canada†		Foreign reserves‡	
		Amount	Total liabilities (%)	Amount	Total liabilities (%)
1926	2,277·2	197	8·6	336	14·8
1927	2,415·1	194	8·0	300	12·5
1928	2,610·6	205	7·9	216	8·5
1929	2,696·8	212	7·9	134	5·0
1930	2,516·6	197	7·8	130	5·2
1931	2,422·8	182	7·5	127	5·2
1932	2,256·6	186	8·2	83	3·7
1933	2,236·8	195	8·7	127	5·8
1934	2,274·6	203	8·9	137	6·0
1935	2,426·8	216	8·9	132	5·4
1936	2,614·9	225	8·6	144	5·5
1937	2,775·5	240	9·1	91	3·3
1938	2,823·7	252	8·9	170	6·1

* Including notes in circulation, demand deposits, time deposits and deposits of Dominion and Provincial Governments.

† Cash reserves prior to March 1935 include gold, coin and Dominion notes held by the chartered banks in Canada; and, also, deposits in the Central Gold Reserves not earmarked. Since that date, they include also notes and deposits with the Bank of Canada. The Act of 1935 requires the chartered banks to carry reserves in these forms amounting to at least 5 % of their total deposit liabilities in Canada. (*Canada Year-book*, 1938, p. 915.)

‡ This is the sum of call loans elsewhere than in Canada and net balances due from banks outside Canada. The figures for 1926–32 have been taken from *Report of Royal Commission* (op. cit.); for 1933–8, they are compiled from League of Nations, *Commercial Banking*.

During the period under study, the predominant factor responsible for the change in the total demand liabilities, or the volume of internal credit was the variation in bank loans. Since the interest rate charged by the banks on loans was very rigid, remaining at 3% from the early 'twenties until May 1933, the demand for bank loans was predominantly determined by economic conditions.[1] In Canada, loans were generally granted

[1] *Report of Royal Commission*, op. cit. pp. 27–9.

THE BALANCE OF PAYMENTS

(in millions

	1924	1925	1926	1927	1928
I. INCOME ACCOUNT					
A. *Merchandise:*					
Exports	+ 1,060·1	+ 1,271·4	+ 1,272	+ 1,215	+ 1,341
Imports	− 793·1	− 875·7	− 973	− 1,057	− 1,209
Balance	+ 267·0	+ 395·7	+ 299	+ 158	+ 132
B. *Other items:*					
Net exports of non-monetary gold	—	—	+ 30	+ 32	+ 40
Net tourist receipts	+ 88·0	+ 112·6	+ 53	+ 63	+ 79
Net interest and dividends incomes	− 213·9	− 207·1	− 208	− 216	− 229
Net freight and shipping incomes	+ 7·7	+ 6·8	− 9	− 12	− 20
Net total of all other current transactions	− 22·5	− 13·1	− 38	− 35	− 34
Balance	− 140·7	− 100·8	− 172	− 168	− 164
Net balance of income account	+ 126·3	+ 294·9	+ 127	− 10	− 32
II. NET MONETARY GOLD MOVEMENT	− 20·4	− 10·3	+ 1·0	− 7·2	+ 48·5
III. CAPITAL ACCOUNT					
A. *Long-term capital:*					
Net new issue of Canadian securities abroad [2]				+ 300·6	+ 207·3
Retirements of Canadian securities owned abroad [2]		− 218·7	− 191·2	− 160·0	− 200·0
Net purchase of outstanding foreign and domestic securities [2]				− 184·0	− 188·0
Net direct investment [2]		+ 52·0	+ 177·1	+ 27·6	+ 18·1
Government receipts (including reparations) [2]		—	—	+ 10·5	+ 6·0
Insurance transactions, N.O.P. [2]		—	—	− 15·0	− 12·0
Balance		− 166·7	− 14·1	− 20·3	− 168·6
B. *Short-term capital:*					
Change in estimated net assets of Canadian banks abroad [2]		− 92·0[3]	− 58·2[3]	+ 16·1	+ 86·6
Balance		− 92·0	− 58·2	+ 16·1	+ 86·6
Net balance of capital account		− 258·7	− 72·3	− 4·2	− 82·0
IV. RESIDUE ITEM	− 105·9	− 25·9	− 55·7	+ 21·4	+ 65·5

[1] Figures for 1924 and 1925 are taken from League of Nations' *Balance of Payments*; and figures for the rest of the period from *Public Expenditure and Capital Formation.*
[2] Not available.
[3] Report of Royal Commission, op. cit.
[4] Besides the first three items, the capital outflow (including short-term capital) is estimated

OF CANADA, 1924-1938 [1]

of dollars)

1929	1930	1931	1932	1933	1934	1935	1936	1937	1938
+1,178	+880	+601	+495	+530	+648	+732	+954	+1,041	+844
-1,272	-973	-580	-398	-366	-484	-526	-612	-776	-649
-94	-93	+21	+97	+164	+164	+206	+342	+265	+195
+37	+39	+57	+70	+82	+114	+119	+132	+145	+161
+90	+88	+82	+65	+45	+56	+53	+67	+79	+63
-261	-289	-282	-265	-226	-211	-206	-236	-226	-241
-38	-33	-25	-28	-22	-27	-14	-17	-25	-10
-45	-49	-27	+35	-45	-28	-33	-44	-58	-68
-217	-244	-195	-193	-166	-96	-81	-98	-85	-95
-311	-337	-174	-96	-2	+68	+125	+244	+180	+100
+36·4	-35·7	+32·2	+2·9	+6·0	-4·3	-2·1	-0·6	0	-4·5
+296·6	+400·3	+199·9	+103·7	+133·9	+111·0	+117·0	+106·1	+89·5	+88·6
-150·0	-110·0	-202·0	-104·7	-165·9	-169·0	-271·4	-270·0	-177·9	-150·5
-105·0	-13·0	-24·0	-16·0	+51·0	-8·9	+51·0	+7·8	-4·8	+28·9
+15·0	+22·9	-1·2	-31·1	-74·3	-50·8	-52·2	-74·2	-82·6	
+4·5	+6·5	+1·3	—	—	—	—	—	—	-42·0[4]
+19·0	+9·0	+34·0	-1·0	-1·0	+3·0	-18·0	-26·0	10·0	
+80·1	+315·7	+8·0	-49·1	-56·3	-96·9	-173·6	-256·3	-185·8	-75·0
+87·8	-0·4	+27·7	+37·7	+23·9	-18·9	+0·1	+2·6	-13·0	-60·0[5]
+87·8	-0·4	+27·7	+37·7	+23·9	-18·9	+0·1	+2·6	-13·0	-60·0
+167·9	+315·3	+35·7	-11·4	-32·4	-115·8	-173·5	-253·7	-198·8	-135·0
+106·7	+57·4	+106·1	+104·5	+28·4	+52·1	+50·6	+10·3	-18·8	-39·5

at $102 mn. (*Canada Year-Book* 1939). The figure $42 mn. is arrived at by deducting the outflow of short-term capital of $60 mn. (See the next footnote.)

[5] This figure is compiled from League of Nations' *Commercial Banks.* It includes such items as balances due to foreign banks, balances due from foreign banks, short foreign loans, and discounts.

in the following form: farmers sold their cereal to the grain dealers, who in turn borrowed from the banks on the basis of warehouse receipts for the cereal in store. When exports were rising, grain dealers bought increasing amounts of cereal and therefore demanded more loans from the banks; and conversely. As the banks' total demand liabilities were rising, they could maintain their cash-ratio constant by increasing their holdings of Dominion notes by applying to the Dominion government on the security of a wide range of collateral.[1]

Thus, the fluctuations of the demand for bank loans and the consequent change in total demand liabilities were generally beyond the control of the banks; and, moreover, it was the practice of Canadian banks that no deserving request for a credit accommodation should be refused.[2] As the demand for loans was closely connected with the external forces, the fluctuations in the internal volume of credit reflected directly the state of the general balance of payments, instead of being an active factor in causing changes in it.

Partly because of the nature of the demand for loans and partly because of the possibilities of getting the Dominion notes as reserves, there did not exist any apparent connection between the variations in internal credit and foreign reserves. As shown in Table 68, the foreign reserve ratios showed sharp cyclical changes. As these foreign reserves could earn income, the banks tended to let them accumulate in surplus years; and, consequently, the ratio of foreign reserves to total demand liabilities rose, e.g. in 1926–7. During the depression, when the drain was heavy, the banks let the ratio fall.

In brief, monetary changes in Canada were passive and did not play any causal influence in the adjustment of the Canadian balance of payments in the period under study.

[1] Willis, loc. cit.
[2] J. Viner, *The Canadian Balance of International Indebtedness*, pp. 175–7.

CONCLUSION

From the foregoing results we reach the following conclusions.

(1) The trade cycle is a world-wide phenomenon and the occurrence of its different phases tends to show an international synchronisation. The critical element in the international spread of prosperity and depression is the highly cyclical behaviour of international spending on commodities and services and of international decisions to invest. The balance of payments of a country is compounded of a mixture of these cyclical fluctuations. Its dynamic equilibrium in a given phase of the trade cycle is reached when the fluctuation in the balance on income account is matched by an equal and opposite fluctuation in the balance on long-term capital account.

(2) In an open system, the national incomes of different countries are closely linked together by the operation of the foreign-trade multiplier. A country cannot insulate itself from the external influence of the world trade cycle, as world prosperity and depression directly affect the value of its exports, which is of the same importance as home investment in generating income. The impact of this external influence upon a home economy cannot be judged from its share in world trade; nor can it be judged from the stage of its economic development. It has been found that the crucial element is the percentage of exports to national income; and that highly industrialised countries are as liable to external influence as primary producing countries if this percentage is high.

(3) The rise or fall in home income generally exerts an immediate influence towards expansion or contraction abroad, because of the consequent change in the demand for imports. Its influence upon the world economy is dependent upon the country's share in world trade. The larger the share, the more important its influence. The international trade cycle starts and tends to be world-wide, when prosperity or depression occurs in one or a group of countries relatively large in the world economy.

(4) The general features of cyclical fluctuations in world income are registered and expressed in the variation of world trade in goods and services and of the volume of international long-term lending and borrowing. Both of them tend to expand in times of general world prosperity and to contract during depression and recession. But owing to the difference in their economic constitution, individual countries tend to react differently to this world-wide movement. Our empirical studies have shown that, in addition to the general cyclical rise and fall of trade and of long-term capital flow, there are shifts in the distribution among different countries during different phases of the world trade cycle. In other words, there are different patterns of cyclical behaviour for the balance of payments of different countries.

(5) The constituent items of the balance of payments tend to show different cyclical sensitivity; and the predominant factors in determining the cyclical patterns differ from country to country. But in spite of these facts, we have been able to derive some general conclusions by classifying countries into different types on the basis of the predominant features of their trade structures. In our empirical studies, five types of country have been distinguished. With regard to the cyclical patterns of their income accounts, industrial and mining types generally tend to show an alternate surplus and deficit in relation to general world prosperity and depression; whereas the agricultural type tends to have the opposite pattern.

(6) When the cyclical fluctuations in the balance on long-term capital account of different types of country are taken into consideration, we find that these fluctuations generally tend to offset those in the balance on income account. The tendency towards offsetting fluctuations is a normal phenomenon; and the explanation lies in the determining force of the general world cycle.

(7) The balance of payments of a country is temporarily out of equilibrium when the cyclical fluctuations of these two fail to offset each other completely. International short-term capital movements and changes in international cash reserves act as the

balancing items in closing this gap; and when acting in this way their movements are passive. But our empirical studies have further shown that the operations of these two are not equally important in the different countries. Wherever there exists no home short money market as in the less-developed countries, the change in international cash reserves is mainly relied upon for balancing purposes. Nevertheless, if the deficits to be balanced are large and sustained for a number of years, the reserves will be exhausted and exchange rates cannot be maintained.

INDEX

Average propensity to import, *see* Propensity to import

Balance of payments:
classical theory of equilibrium, 1–3
cyclical equilibrium of different types of country, 18, 131–2, 149–50, 160–2, 178–80, 191, 211–12, 221
dynamic equilibrium, 7
equation, 5–6
Balance of trade, *see* Income account

Capital account, *see* Long-term capital movement *and* Short-term capital movement
Clark, C., 25n., 42n., 185n.

Degree of specialisation, 30–4
Division of labour, 3, 27

Elasticity of demand for exports:
income-, international comparison, 50; of three most important industrialised countries, 54–8
price-, international comparison, 50
Elasticity of demand for imports:
income-, definition of, 35; international comparison, 42; method of calculation, 35n., 40; of different groups of commodities, 45–7, 112–13; of individual commodities, 114–16; of representative countries belonging to different types, 121, 148, 155, 173, 190, 201
price-, international comparison, 42
Elasticity of substitution:
price-, between homogeneous commodities in a given market, 73–5; between homogeneous commodities in the world market, 71–3; between imports and home substitutes, 75–6; between similar groups of commodities in the world market, 69–71; definition of, 68; method of calculation, 69
Elasticity of supply of primary produce, 13, 125

Exchange depreciation, effect of, 61–2, 164–5
Exchange depreciation and balance of payments, 180, 215
Exchange depreciation and critical value of import and export price elasticity, 76–8
Export, as determinant of national income, 7–9, 20, Chap. v, 172–3

Foreign exchange reserve, 22, 178–80, 213–14, 218
Foreign lending, 3; and home economic activity, 19–21, 127–31

Gold movement and abnormal short-term capital movements, 163
Gold movement and mechanism of adjustment, 138–42, 161, 180, 214
Gregory, T., 133n., 139n.

Harrod, R. F., 8n., 13, 135n.

Imports, time-lag in demand for, 102
Imports and national income, *see* Propensity to import
Income account:
cyclical patterns of different types of country, 124, 149, 152, 156, 169–70, 175, 188–9, 191, 204
factors determining the cyclical pattern, 9–18
Interest rate, *see* Long-term capital movement *and* Short-term capital movement
Investment and national income, 84–93
Investment and trade cycle, 177, 185–6, 208, 216, 217

Kaldor, N., 23, 135n.
Keynes, J. M., 105n., 134n.

Long-term capital movement:
cyclical pattern of borrowing countries, 19–20, 175–8, 192–3
cyclical pattern of lending countries, 20–1, 126–31, 158–60, 211
effect on interest rates, 23

For EU product safety concerns, contact us at Calle de José Abascal, 56–1°,
28003 Madrid, Spain or eugpsr@cambridge.org.

www.ingramcontent.com/pod-product-compliance
Ingram Content Group UK Ltd.
Pitfield, Milton Keynes, MK11 3LW, UK
UKHW042209180425
457623UK00011B/118